IS A REWARDING DESTINATION FOR THE HOLIDAY VISITOR
Ten good reasons for choosing Nairn

1) Quality cuisine & accommodation
2) Award-winning beaches
3) Fine land and marine wildlife habitat
4) Award-winning events
5) Two 18-hole championship golf courses
6) Award-winning daily entertainments
7) Leisure harbour
8) Heritage, museums and visitor attractions
9) Good sports centre, recreational facilities & watersports
10) Historical landmarks

**For further information see a Nairn Leisure Guide or contact
Tourism & Entertainments Office, Nairn District Council,
The Court House, High Street, Nairn IV12 4AU.
Tel: (01667) 456144. Fax: (01667) 452056.**

**Our beach has attained the standards necessary to
receive this award of distinction**

MAPS

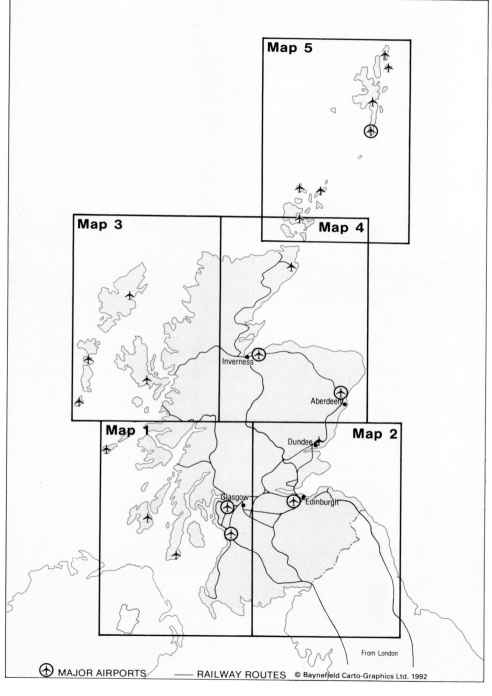

Map 5

Map 3

Map 4

Inverness

Aberdeen

Map 1

Dundee

Map 2

Glasgow

Edinburgh

From London

⊕ MAJOR AIRPORTS — RAILWAY ROUTES © Baynefield Carto-Graphics Ltd. 1992

MAP 1

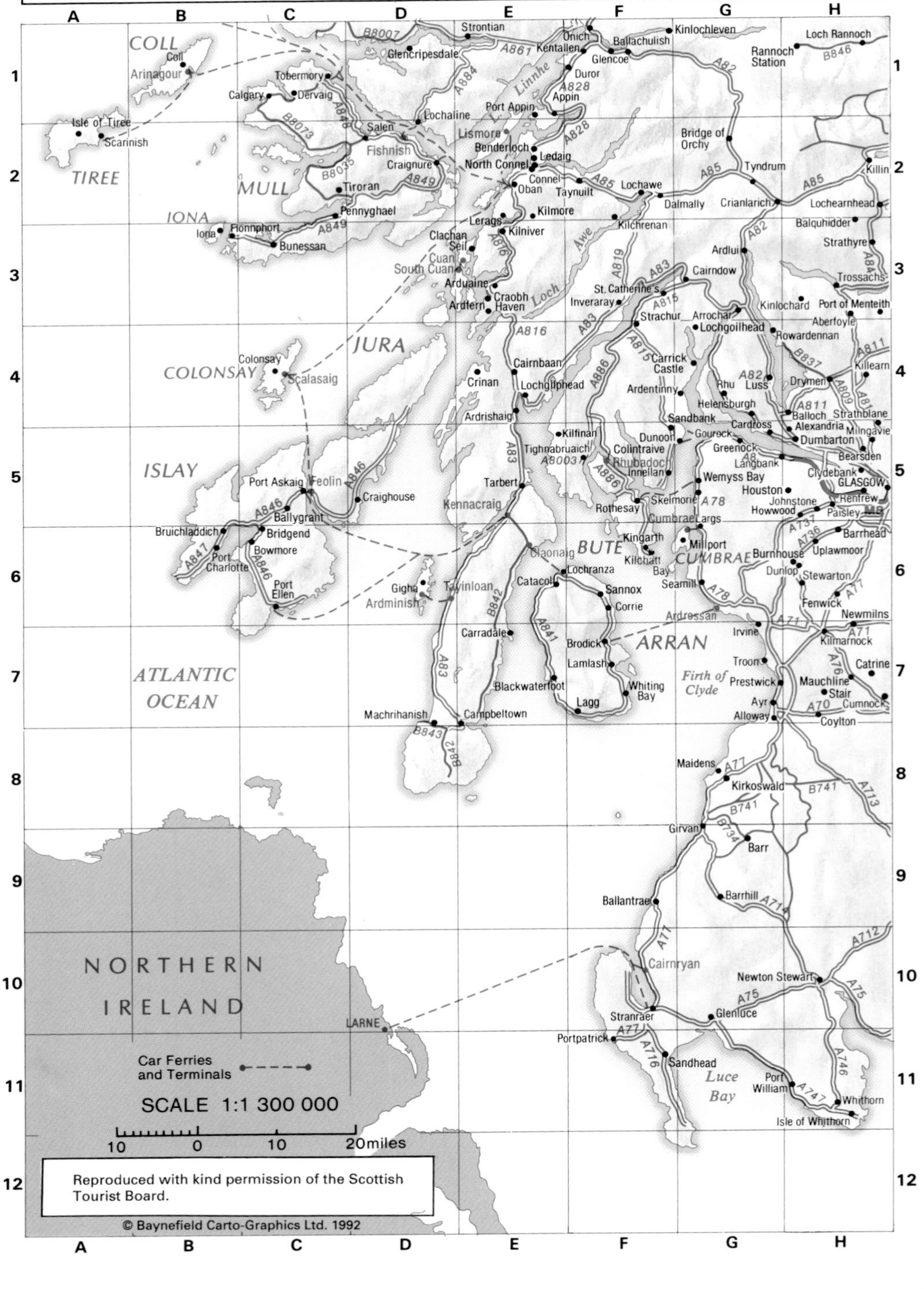

COLL
Arinagour
Coll

Isle of Tiree
Scarinish

TIREE

IONA
Iona
Fionnphort
Bunessan

MULL
Tobermory
Calgary
Dervaig
Salen
Fishnish
Craignure
Tiroran
Pennyghael

Strontian
Glencripesdale
Glencoe
Onich
Kentallen
Ballachulish
Kinlochleven
Loch Rannoch
Rannoch Station

Lochaline
Port Appin
Appin
Duror
Bridge of Orchy
Killin

Lismore
Benderloch
Ledaig
North Connel
Connel
Oban
Taynuilt
Lochawe
Tyndrum
Crianlarich
Killin
Lochearnhead
Balquhidder
Strathyre

Kilmore
Kilninver
Lerags
Clachan Seil
South Cuan
Cuan
Kilchrenan
Dalmally
Trossachs
Port of Menteith
Aberfoyle

Arduaine
Ardfern
Craobh Haven
St. Catherine's
Inveraray
Cairndow
Ardlui
Kinlochard
Rowardennan

COLONSAY
Colonsay
Scalasaig

JURA

Crinan
Cairnbaan
Lochgilphead
Ardrishaig
Strachur
Carrick Castle
Ardentinny
Rhu
Luss
Drymen
Killearn
Strathblane
Milngavie

ISLAY

Port Askaig
Feolin
Ballygrant
Bridgend
Bowmore
Bruichladdich
Port Charlotte
Port Ellen

Craighouse
Tarbert
Kennacraig

Helensburgh
Sandbank
Dunoon
Colintraive
Rhubadoch
Innellan
Gourock
Greenock
Cardross
Balloch
Alexandria
Dumbarton
Bearsden
Clydebank
GLASGOW
Renfrew
Paisley
Johnstone
Houston
Howwood
Barrhead
Uplawmoor

Kilfinan
Tighnabruaich
Skelmorlie
Wemyss Bay
Rothesay
Cumbrae
Largs

BUTE
Kingarth
Kilchattan Bay
Millport
CUMBRAE
Seamill
Ardrossan
Burnhouse
Dunlop
Stewarton
Fenwick
Newmilns

Giaonaig
Tarvinloan
Catacol
Lochranza
Sannox
Corrie
Irvine
Troon
Prestwick
Kilmarnock
Mauchline
Catrine

Gigha
Ardminish
Brodick
Lamlash
ARRAN
Firth of Clyde
Ayr
Stair
Cumnock

Carradale

Blackwaterfoot
Whiting Bay
Lagg
Alloway
Coylton

Machrihanish
Campbeltown

ATLANTIC OCEAN

Maidens
Kirkoswald
Barr
Girvan

Ballantrae
Barrhill

NORTHERN IRELAND

Cairnryan
Newton Stewart
Glenluce
Stranraer
Portpatrick
Sandhead
Luce Bay
Port William
Whithorn
Isle of Whithorn

LARNE

Car Ferries and Terminals

SCALE 1:1 300 000

10 0 10 20miles

MAP 2

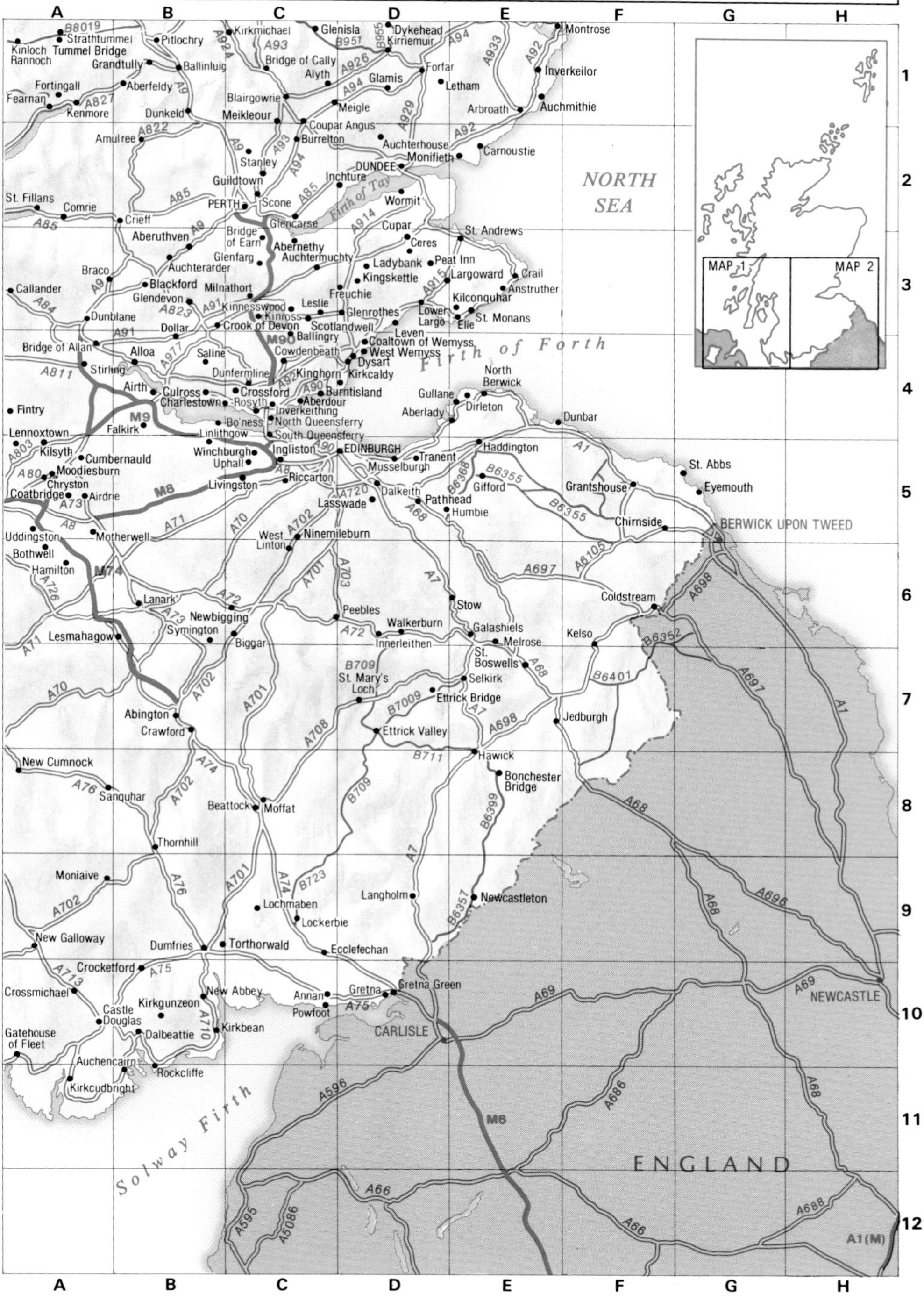

MAP 1   MAP 2

NORTH SEA

Firth of Forth

Firth of Tay

Solway Firth

ENGLAND

BERWICK UPON TWEED

NEWCASTLE

CARLISLE

EDINBURGH

DUNDEE

PERTH

Kinloch Rannoch · Strathtummel · Tummel Bridge · Kirkmichael · Glenisla · Dykehead · Kirriemuir · Montrose
Fortingall · Pitlochry · Grandtully · Bridge of Cally · Alyth · Forfar · Inverkeilor
Fearnan · Aberfeldy · Ballinluig · Glamis · Letham · Auchmithie
Kenmore · Dunkeld · Blairgowrie · Meigle · Arbroath
A827 · Meikleour · Coupar Angus · Auchterhouse · Monifieth · Carnoustie
Amulree · Stanley · Burrelton · Inchture
St. Fillans · Comrie · Guildtown · Scone · Wormit
Crieff · Bridge of Earn · Glencarse · Cupar · St. Andrews
Braco · Aberuthven · Glenfarg · Abernethy · Ceres · Peat Inn
Callander · Auchterarder · Auchtermuchty · Ladybank · Largoward · Crail
Dunblane · Blackford · Milnathort · Kingskettle · Anstruther
Glendevon · Kinnesswood · Leslie · Freuchie · Kilconquhar
Bridge of Allan · Dollar · Kinross · Glenrothes · Lower Largo · Elie · St. Monans
Stirling · Saline · Crook of Devon · Ballingry · Leven
Alloa · Dunfermline · Cowdenbeath · Coaltown of Wemyss · West Wemyss
Airth · Culross · Crossford · Kinghorn · Kirkcaldy · Dysart
Charlestown · Rosyth · Aberdour · Burntisland · Gullane · North Berwick
Falkirk · Bo'ness · Inverkeithing · North Queensferry · Aberlady · Dirleton · Dunbar
Fintry · Linlithgow · South Queensferry
Lennoxtown · Winchburgh · Uphall · Ingliston · Tranent · Haddington · St. Abbs
Kilsyth · Livingston · Musselburgh · Gifford · Grantshouse · Eyemouth
Cumbernauld · Riccarton · Dalkeith · Pathhead · Humbie · Chirnside
Moodiesburn · Lasswade · Ninemileburn · Coldstream
Chryston · Airdrie · West Linton · Peebles · Stow
Coatbridge · Motherwell · Walkerburn · Galashiels · Kelso
Uddingston · Lanark · Newbigging · Innerleithen · Melrose
Bothwell · Symington · Biggar · St. Boswells · Jedburgh
Hamilton · Lesmahagow · St. Mary's Loch · Selkirk · Hawick
New Cumnock · Abington · Crawford · Ettrick Bridge · Ettrick Valley · Bonchester Bridge
Sanquhar · Beattock · Moffat · Langholm · Newcastleton
Thornhill · Lochmaben · Lockerbie · Ecclefechan
Moniaive · Dumfries · Torthorwald
New Galloway · Crocketford · New Abbey · Annan · Gretna · Gretna Green
Crossmichael · Castle Douglas · Kirkgunzeon · Powfoot
Gatehouse of Fleet · Dalbeattie · Kirkbean
Auchencairn · Rockcliffe · Kirkcudbright

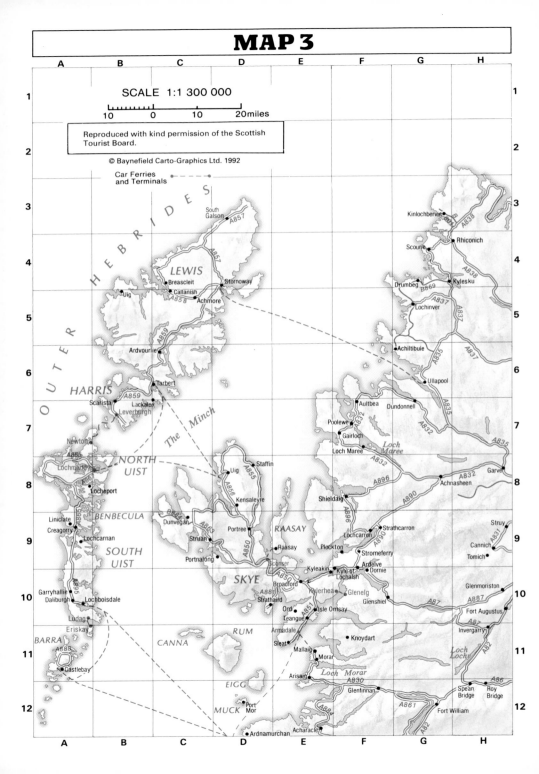

CONTENTS

Cover Photograph courtesy of Lex Vauxhall.

Pastime Publications Ltd gratefully acknowledge the assistance of The Scottish Tourist Board, Area Tourist Boards, Historic Buildings and Monuments and others in compiling this guide.

First published by The Scottish Tourist Board 1970.

UK & Worldwide Distribution by AA Publishing Ltd.

Typesetting by Servis Filmsetting Ltd.
Printed and bound by Offset Print Veneta

ADVERTISERS' INDEX

DISPLAY ADVERTISEMENTS

ALSO SEE COLOUR ADVERTS

CLASSIFIED ADVERTISEMENTS

HOTELS

ABERDEENSHIRE
Aberdeen	31
Peterhead	31

ANGUS
Dundee	31

ARGYLL
Ardfern	31
Carradale	31
Dunoon	31

AYRSHIRE
Ayr	32
Girvan	32

DUMFRIESSHIRE
Dumfries	32
Langholm	32

DUNBARTONSHIRE
Helensburgh	32

FIFE
Aberdour	32
Anstruther	32
Dunfermline	32
Markinch	32
St Andrews	33

INVERNESS-SHIRE
Arisaig	33
Fort Augustus	33
Fort William	33
Inverness	33
Newtonmore	33

KIRKCUDBRIGHTSHIRE
Castle Douglas	33
Dalbeattie	33

LANARKSHIRE
Glasgow	34

LOTHIAN
Edinburgh	34

PERTHSHIRE
Dunkeld	34
Perth	34
Pitlochry	34

ROSS-SHIRE
Kyle of Lochalsh	35
Tain	35

SELKIRKSHIRE
Ettrickbridge	35

SUTHERLAND
Lochinver	35

GUEST HOUSES

ANGUS
Kirriemuir   36

ARGYLL
Oban   36

AYRSHIRE
Ayr   36
Dalmellington   36
Kilmarnock   36
New Cumnock   36
Troon   36

CAITHNESS
Thurso   36

FIFE
St Andrews   36

INVERNESS-SHIRE
Fort William   37
Kincraig   37
North Kessock   37
Onich   37

LANARKSHIRE
Glasgow   37

LOTHIAN
Edinburgh   37
North Berwick   38

NAIRNSHIRE
Nairn   38

PERTHSHIRE
Perth   38

ROSS-SHIRE
Invergordon   38
Stromeferry   38

ROXBURGHSHIRE
Kelso   38

STIRLINGSHIRE
Stirling   38

SCOTTISH ISLANDS
Arran   38
Skye   38

A B E R D E E N S H I R E

A N G U S

A R G Y L L

Please mention this Pastime Publications guide

Please turn to page 40 to find Places of Interest

Please mention this Pastime Publications guide

21

L
A
N
A
R
K
S
H
I
R
E

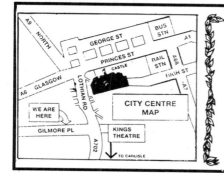
L
O
T
H
I
A
N

THE PALACE OF HOLYROODHOUSE

"HOLYROOD IS A HOUSE OF MANY MEMORIES. WARS HAVE BEEN PLOTTED, DANCING HAS LASTED DEEP INTO THE NIGHT, MURDER HAS BEEN DONE IN IT'S CHAMBERS...NOW, ALL THESE THINGS OF CLAY ARE MINGLED WITH THE DUST...BUT THE STONE PALACE HAS OUTLIVED THESE CHANGES."

Robert Louis Stevenson. Edinburgh, Picturesque Notes. 1878

THE QUEEN'S OFFICIAL RESIDENCE IN SCOTLAND IS OPEN TO THE PUBLIC THROUGHOUT THE YEAR EXCEPT IN LATE JUNE DURING THE ROYAL VISIT TO SCOTLAND AND OCCASIONALLY AT OTHER TIMES. FOR FURTHER INFORMATION CALL: 0131 556 1096. TICKET OFFICE OPEN 1ST APRIL-31ST OCTOBER, MON–SAT 09.30-17.15; SUN 09.30-16.30. 1ST NOVEMBER-31ST MARCH, MON–SUN 09.30-15.45.

LOTHIAN

SEE COLOUR ROAD MAPS ON PAGES 5-10

MORAYSHIRE

PERTHSHIRE

PERTHSHIRE

RENFREWSHIRE

Loch Assynt, Sutherland – Photo: Scottish Tourist Board

	Type of accommodation	Number of rooms	Room facilities	Packed Lunches	Season dates	Price p.p. B/B or B.B.E.M.	Special features

HOTELS

ABERDEENSHIRE
Aberdeen

	Type of accommodation	Number of rooms	Room facilities	Packed Lunches	Season dates	Price p.p. B/B or B.B.E.M.	Special features
Stephen Taylor (Mr.), Water Wheel Inn, 203 North Deeside Road, Bieldside, Aberdeen. Tel: (011224) 861659.	Inn 4 Crowns	25	Ensuite fac. Col. TV. H/Dryer. Phone. Trouser press. Tea/coffee.	Yes	All year	On Appl.	Luxury hotel only 10 mins. from city centre, airport or train station.
J. Byers (Mr.), The Brentwood Hotel, 101 Crown Street, Aberdeen. Tel: (01224) 595440.	Hotel 4 Crowns Commended	65	All ensuite. Col. TV. Tea/coffee. No smoking rooms avail.	Yes	All year	B & B if sharing: Mon-Thurs £35.00p.p. Fri, Sat & Sun £20.00p.p.	City centre location with private car park. Special weekend breaks.
Peterhead Andrew Davis (Mr.), Waterside Inn, Fraserburgh Road, Peterhead AB42 7BN. Tel: (01779) 471121.	Hotel 5 Crowns Commended	110	All Ensuite. Tea/coffee Fac. Inhouse movie system.	Yes	All year	D.B.&B.: £38 (sharing)	Swimming pool and leisure club. Excellent cuisine, award winning chefs. Outstanding friendliness.
ANGUS **Dundee** Reservations, Stakis Dundee (Earl Gray Hotel), Earl Gray Place, Dundee. Tel: (01382) 200072.	Hotel 5 Crowns Commended	104	All rooms ensuite. Tea/coffee. Telephone. C.H. TV.	Ask	All year	B.B.E.M. from: £88 (single) £115 (twin)	Overlooking Tay River. 5 mins walking distance from town. Ample parking. Leisure club with pool.
ARGYLL **Ardfern** D. Garland (Mrs.), Galley of Lorne Inn, Ardfern, by Lochgilphead PA31 8QN. Tel: (01852) 500 284.	Hotel 2 Crowns Commended	9	All W.H.B. Heating. TV. Tea/coffee tray. 2 ensuite.	N/A	Jan-Dec	B.&B. £22-£35	Traditional Highland inn. Excellent food. Log fires. Loch-side setting.
Carradale M. Cook (Mrs.), Ashbank Hotel, Carradale PA28 6RY. Tel: (01583) 431650.	Hotel 3 Crowns Commended	6	Most en suite. All with WHB. Tea/coffee.	Yes	All year	B.&B. from £19.	Area of outstanding beauty. Convenient for ferries to the Isles.
Dunoon M. Greig (Mr.), Royal Marine Hotel, Hunter's Quay, Dunoon PA23 8HJ. Tel: (01369) 5810.	Hotel 3 Crowns Commended	35	Ensuite TV. Phone	Ask	All year	From £30 D.B.B.	Warm welcome. Good food. Friendly staff. Great prices. Beautiful area.
J. Thomas (Mr.), The Ardtully Hotel, 297 Marine Parade, Hunter's Quay, Dunoon PA23 8HN. Tel: (01369) 702478.	Hotel 3 Crown Commended	10	C.T.V./Video. Mini bar/fridge. Tea/coffee fac. Ensuite.	Yes	Jan-Dec	B.&B.: £20-£25	Outstanding views of the Clyde Estuary and surrounding hills.

Please mention this Pastime Publications guide

	Type of accommodation	Number of rooms	Room facilities	Packed Lunches	Season dates	Price p.p. B/B or B.B.E.M.	Special features
AYRSHIRE **Ayr** Colin Craig (Mr.), Kingsley Hotel, 10 Alloway Place, Ayr KA7 2AA. Tel: (01292) 262853.	Hotel 1 Crown Approved	6	C.H. TV. Tea/coffee. W/H basin	Yes	All year	B.&B.: Single from £17.50 double/twin from £16.00	Warm welcome. Excellent cooking. Centrally situated with wonderful panoramic views. Reasonably priced accommodation.
Girvan D. Taylor (Mr. & Mrs.), Southfield Hotel, The Avenue, Girvan KA26 9DS. Tel: (01465) 4222.	Hotel Pending 3 Crowns	7	All ensuite. TV. Radio. Hairdryer. Tea/coffee	Yes	All year	B.&B. from £25. B.B.E.M. from £35.	5 miles from Turnberry Golf Course. Fully Licensed. Bar meals/A la carte.
DUMFRIESSHIRE **Dumfries** H.M. McFeat (Mr.), Carrutherstown Hotel, Carrutherstown, Dumfries. Tel: (01387) 84 268.	Hotel	8	H.&C. C.H. Tea/coffee fac. Satellite TV. Radio alarms.	Yes	All year	B.&B. £15.	Situated on A75 (Euroroute) between Gretna and Dumfries.
Langholm Hart Manor Hotel, Eskdalemuir, by Langholm. Tel: (013873) 73217.	Hotel 3 Crowns Commended	7	5 ensuite	Yes	All year	B.&B.: £25. B.B.E.M.: £40.	Clay pigeon shooting. Salmon/trout fishing call (013873) 70203. Hill walking, birdwatching, quad bike trekking.
DUNBARTONSHIRE **Helensburgh** Stephen Nixon (Mr.), Ross Lea Hall Hotel, Ferry Road, Rhu, Helensburgh G84 8NF. Tel: (01436) 820684.	Hotel 4 Crowns Commended	39	Tea/coffee. C.T.V. C.H. D.D. telephone. All ensuite.	Yes	All year	On Application	Beautiful country house, enroute to West Coast, Highlands and Islands.
FIFE **Aberdour** The Woodside Hotel, High Street, Aberdour KY3 0SW. Tel: (01383) 860328.	Hotel	21	All ensuite. C.T.V. Telephone. Trouser press.	£4.50	All year	On Application	Listed building in pretty village offers free golf! Bicycle loan. Sauna. Convenient for Edinburgh.
Anstruther E.D. MacFarlane (Mr.), The Spindrift, Pittenweem Road, Anstruther KY10 3DT. Tel: (01333) 310573.	Pte. Hotel 3 Crowns High Comm	8	Ensuite. Col. TV. Hospitality tray.	Ask	All year	B.&B. from: £24.50. B.B.E.M. from: £32.	Friendly relaxed atmosphere in an immaculately maintained Victorian house.
Dunfermline M. McVicars (Mr.), Pitfirrane Arms Hotel, Main Street, Crossford KY12 8NJ. Tel: (01383) 736132.	Hotel 4 Crowns	38	All ensuite	Yes	All year	On Application	Family run hotel, old world atmosphere. 10 golf courses within 10 miles.
Markinch Balbirnie House Hotel, Balbirnie Park, Markinch. Tel: (01592) 610066.	Country House 5 Crowns Deluxe	30	En suite. Trouser press. Hair dryer. Tea/coffee fac.	Yes	All year	B & B from £65.00 (sharing)	Grade A listed Georgian mansion set in 400 acre parkland.

	Type of accommodation	Number of rooms	Room facilities	Packed Lunches	Season dates	Price p.p. B/B or B.B.E.M.	Special features
St. Andrews							
V. & F. MacKenzie (Mr. & Mrs.), Yorkston Hotel, 68/70 Argyle Street, St. Andrews KY16 9BU. Tel: (01334) 472019.	Hotel 2 Crowns	10	6 ensuite. TV all rooms. Tea/coffee fac.	No	—	B.&B. from: £22.	Table licence, no bar. Convenient for town centre.
INVERNESS-SHIRE							
Arisaig							
Malcolm E. Ross (Mr.), Arisaig Hotel, Arisaig PH39 4NH. Tel: (016875) 210. Fax: (016875) 310.	Hotel	15	6 ensuite rooms. Tea/coffee. Elec. blanket. D.D. phone.	Yes	All year (except Xmas & New Year)	On Appl.	Warm, family atmosphere. Beautiful surrounding area.
Fort Augustus							
L. O'Neill (Mrs.), Inchnacardoch Lodge Hotel, Fort Augustus PH32 4BL. Tel: (01320) 366258.	Hotel 3 Crowns Commended	12	Ensuite TV. Phone. Tea/coffee.	Yes	Mar-Nov	B. & B.: £22.50-£35.00. D.B.&B.: £45.50-£53.50	Cosy bar. Lounge with log fires and magnificent views of Loch Ness.
Fort William							
Laurence Young (Mr.), The Lodge on the Loch, Creag Dhu, Onich, Fort William PH33 6RY. Tel: (0185 582) 1237. Fax: (0185 582) 1463.	Hotel 4 Crowns Highly Comm.	18	Ensuite. Phone. radio. H/dryer. Col. TV Tea/coffee	Yes	Feb - Oct	D.B. & B.: £56-£68.50	Excellent cuisine. Carefully refurbished bedrooms. Elegant cocktail bar. Log fires.
Inverness							
W.G. MacLellan (Mrs.), Winmar House Hotel, 78 Kenneth Street, Inverness IV3 5QG. Tel: (01463) 239328.	Hotel 2 Crowns Commended	8	Some ensuite. Shaver points. Tea/coffee H.&C. TV.	Yes	All year	B. & B. from: £17 (single)	Excellent base for touring the Highlands.
Angus Fyfe (Mr.), Clan MacDuff Hotel, Fort William PH33 6RW. Tel: (01397) 702341.	Hotel 3 Crowns Commended	30	All ensuite Colour TV Tea/coffee	Yes	1 Apr-31 Oct	B. & B. from £18 D.B. & B. from £27.50	Quiet location. Excellent centre for touring. Spring/ Autumn special offers.
Newtonmore							
Helen Coyle (Mrs.), Balavil Sport Hotel, Main Street, Newtonmore PH20 1DL. Tel: (01540) 673 220.	Hotel 3 Crowns Commended	50	Ensuite. C.T.V. C.H. Tea/coffee	Yes	All year	On Application	Indoor swimming pool and sauna. Entertainment programme. Golf, bowling, fishing and tennis.
KIRKCUDBRIGHTSHIRE							
Castle Douglas							
D. Fulton (Mr.), The Imperial Hotel, 35 King Street, Castle Douglas DG7 1AA. Tel: (01556) 502086.	Hotel 4 Crowns Commended	12	CTV. Phone. Radio. H/dryer. Tea/coffee. Bath or shower.	Yes	All year	B.&B. from £25. B.B.E.M. from £31.50.	Old coaching inn, centrally situated. Good Scottish home cooking. A warm welcome awaits you.
Dalbeattie							
J.M. Thompson (Mrs.), Clonyard House Hotel, Colvend, Dalbeattie Tel: (01556) 630372.	Hotel 4 Crowns Commended	15	All ensuite	Yes	All year	B. & B. double: £27.50. B. & B. single: £35.00	Ground floor rooms with private patios. Restaurant and bar meals.

Please mention this Pastime Publications guide

	Type of accommodation	Number of rooms	Room facilities	Packed Lunches	Season dates	Price p.p. B/B or B.B.E.M.	Special features
LANARKSHIRE **Glasgow** Andrew Bonner (Mr.), The Kelvin Park Lorne Hotel, 923 Sauchiehall Street, Glasgow G3 7TE. Tel: 0141-334 4891	Hotel 4 Crowns Commended	98	All ensuite. C.T.V. Video channel. Tea/coffee fac. Trouser press. Hairdryer.	Yes	All year	B. & B. from: £20. Dinner Supper £12.	West End location close to art galleries. Underground car park.
Jury's Pond Hotel, Great Western Road, Glasgow. Tel: 0141-334 8161.	Hotel 4 Crowns Commended	133	Ensuite Tea/coffee C.T.V. Phone. Radio.	Yes	Jan-Dec	B.&B. sharing £39.20.	Superb leisure centre: 2 swimming pools, sauna, jacuzzi. 2 bars, restaurant and conference facilities.
LOTHIAN **Edinburgh** A. Thomson (Mrs.), Navaar House Hotel, 12 Mayfield Gardens, Edinburgh EH9 2BZ. Tel: 0131-667 2828.	Hotel 3 Crowns Commended	6	Twin, double, family. Col. TV. ensuite, tea/coffee.	Yes	All year	£25.00-£30.00	Large comfortable rooms. Good food. Jazz - Tues. evenings. 2 bars - real ales.
J. McBride (Mr.), The Nova Hotel, 5 Bruntsfield Crescent, Edinburgh. Tel: 0131-447 6437 Fax: 0131-452 8126.	Hotel 2 Crowns Commended	10	All facilities	No	All year	B. & B. £25	Great Victorian bar. Upmarket bedrooms.
M.T. Borland (Mr.), Rothesay Hotel, 8 Rothesay Place, Edinburgh EH3 7SL. Tel: 0131-225 4125. Fax: 0131-220 4350.	Hotel 3 Crowns Commended	36	Ensuite, Col TV, phone, tea/coffee.	Ask	All year	B. & B. from £25.00	Central. Restaurant. Bar. Convenient shopping, theatres. Children welcome.
J.C. Veitch (Mr.), Dunstane House Hotel, 4 West Coates, Edinburgh EH12 5JQ. Tel: 0131-337 6169.	Hotel 2 Crown Commended	15	4 ensuite. 11 private shower & Washbasin.	No	All year	B.&B. from £25-£36.	Historic Victorian mansion 5 minutes from town centre. Private parking.
Bruntsfield Hotel, 69 Bruntsfield Place, Edinburgh EH10 4HH. Tel: 0131-229 1393.	Hotel 4 Crowns Commended	50	Ensuite. Sat. TV. Radio. Phone. T/press. Tea/coffee.	Ask	All year	D.B.&B. from £45.	Ample free car parking; 1 mile from city centre; children welcome.
PERTHSHIRE **Dunkeld** Bill Ormerwood (Mr.), Merryburn Hotel, Station Road, Birnam PH8 ODS. Tel/Fax: (01350) 727216.	Hotel Listed Approved	8	TV. CH. Radio alarms Tea/coffee/ snacks Some en-suite	Yes	All year	B & B £21 DB & B £34	Ideal base for touring. We can arrange many interesting activities.
Perth White Horse Inn, 5 North William Street, Perth. Tel: (01738) 28479.	Hotel	15	Ensuite TV Coffee/tea	Yes	All year	B. & B.: £28 single room. B.B.E.M.: £38 single room.	
Pitlochry Moira F. Bartrop (Mrs.), Tigh-na-Cloich Hotel, Larchwood Road, Pitlochry PH16 5AS. Tel: (01796) 472216.	Hotel 3 Crowns Commended	12	All double/twins with ensuite fac. 2 single rooms	From £3.50	Mar-end Oct.	B. & B. from £18 D.B. & B. from £28	Whole hotel is 'no smoking'. Good home cooked food.

	Type of accommodation	Number of rooms	Room facilities	Packed Lunches	Season dates	Price p.p. B/B or B.B.E.M.	Special features
ROSS-SHIRE **Kyle of Lochalsh** Jacqueline Gillick (Miss), The Castle Inn, Dornie, Kyle of Lochalsh IV40 8DT. Tel: (0159 985) 205. Fax: (0159 985) 429.	Hotel 3 Crowns Commended	12	7 ensuite, 5 basic. C.H. TV. Phone. Tea/coffee.	Yes	All year	B. & B.: £20.50-£29.50	Situated 5 mins walk from Eilean Donan Castle overlooking Skye.
Tain John Wynne (Mr.), Morangie House Hotel, Morangie Road, Tain IV19 1PY. Tel: (01862) 892281.	Hotel 4 Crown Commended	26	All ensuite Tea/coffee TV. C.H. Phone. Radio.	Yes	All year	B.&B. from £35.00	Fine Victorian mansion famous for its wonderful Scottish food. All luxuriously appointed.
SELKIRKSHIRE **Ettrickbridge** V. Meister (Mrs.), Ettrickshaws Hotel, Ettrickbridge, Selkirk TD7 5HW. Tel: (01750) 52229.	Hotel 4 Crown Commended	6	All ensuite Elec. Blankets C.H. Phone Hair dryers Tea/coffee	Yes	All year	B.&B.: £30-£35. D.B.&B.: £46-£51.	Spectacular scenery, peace and quiet. Bar and restaurant open to non- residents.
SUTHERLAND **Lochinver** W. Hutchison, The Culag Hotel, Lochinver IV27 4LF. Tel: (015714) 270.	Hotel	38	20 pte. bathroom 18 W.H.B.	Yes	All year	B. & B. from £15.00	We can cater for large groups from £20 D. B. & B.

Passing place near Achnasheen

Please mention this Pastime Publications guide

GUEST HOUSES

	Type of accommodation	Number of rooms	Room facilities	Packed Lunches	Season dates	Price p.p. B/B or B.B.E.M.	Special features
ANGUS **Kirriemuir** Maureen Marchant (Mrs.), The Welton of Kingoldrum, Kirriemuir DD8 5HY. Tel: (01575) 574743.	Farm House 3 Crowns Commended	3	Radio/alarm Coffee/tea making 1 ensuite & C.T.V. 1 private. 1 H.&C.	Yes	All year	B.&B. from £15. D.B.&B. from £24	Panoramic views. Excellent base for touring, hill walking and skiing. Also available - Self Catering Accommodation - S.T.B. 3/4/5 Crown Commended.
ARGYLL **Oban** C. MacDonald (Mrs.), Bracker, Polvinister Road, Oban PA34 5TN. Tel: (01631) 64302.	Guest House 2 Crowns Commended	3	All ensuite. Tea/coffee. TV. CH.	No	Mar-Oct	B.&B.: £15-£17 p.p.	Beautiful, quiet residential area within walking distance of town. Parking available.
AYRSHIRE **Ayr** Julia K. Clark (Mrs.), Eglinton Guest House, 23 Eglinton Terrace, Ayr KA7 1JJ. Tel: (01292) 264623.	Guest House 1 Crown Commended	6	2 ensuite. C.T.V. C.H. Tea/coffee making	Yes	All year	B.&B. from £14	Ideally situated for beach, harbour, town centre, tennis, swimming and golfing.
Dalmellington Anne Taveren (Mrs.), Benbain, Cumnock Road, Dalmellington KA6 7PS. Tel: (01292) 550556.	House Commended	3	All on ground level - no stairs.	Yes	All year	B.&B. £15. D.B.&B. £24.	House is 2 miles from village off B741. 1,000 feet up on Beach Craig.
Kilmarnock L. E. Howie (Mrs.), Muirhouse Farm, Symington, Kilmarnock. Tel: (01563) 830218.	F'House 1 Crown Commended	2	1 double 1 twin	Yes	All year	B.&B. from £16	Traditional farmhouse. Centrally heated. TV lounge. Golf, sports, beaches nearby.
New Cumnock Marjorie Caldwell (Mrs.), Low Polquheys Farm, New Cumnock KA18 4NX. Tel: (01290) 338307.	Farm	2	Tea/coffee, biscuits. TV. CH. 1 family, 1 twin	Ask	Apr-end Oct	B.&B. £12. B.B.E.M. £18-£20	Working farm near main road. Central heating, television and tea/coffee facilities.
Troon M. Tweedie (Mrs.), The Cherries, 50 Ottoline Drive, Troon KA10 7AW. Tel: (01292) 313312.	Guest House 2 Crowns Commended	3	1 ensuite. 2 H. & C. Col. TV. Tea/coffee.	No	All year	From £16.00	Quiet location on golf course near beaches and restaurants. Private parking.
CAITHNESS **Thurso** J.D. Falconer (Mrs.), Murray House, 1 Campbell Street, Thurso, Caithness. Tel: (01847) 895759.	House 2 Crowns High Comm	4	No smoking. 1 ensuite 2 shower rooms. Tea/coffee. C.H. C.T.V. W.H.B.	Ask	All year	B.&B. from £15-£20	Warm, friendly atmosphere. Private parking. Two miles from Scrabster to Orkney ferry.
FIFE **St. Andrews** J. Mansell (Mr. & Mrs.), Edenside House, Edenside, St. Andrews KY16 9SQ. Tel: (01338) 838108.	Guest House 3 Crowns Commended	9	All ensuite. Tea/coffee CTV. CH.	No	Mar-Oct	B.&.B. £20-£25	Non-smoking converted farmhouse on bird sanctuary. Parking. Ideal for golfers and discerning guests.

	Type of accommodation	Number of rooms	Room facilities	Packed Lunches	Season dates	Price p.p. B/B or B.B.E.M.	Special features
Valerie K. Mayner (Mrs.), The Larches, 7 River Terrace, Guardbridge, by St. Andrews. Tel: (01334) 838008.	Guest House 1 Crown Commended	3	H.&C. W.H.B. T.V. C.H. Tea/coffee	Yes	All year	B.&B. from £16	Residents lounge. Every convenience and home comfort. Wonderful welcome and wonderful food.

INVERNESS-SHIRE
Fort William

	Type of accommodation	Number of rooms	Room facilities	Packed Lunches	Season dates	Price p.p. B/B or B.B.E.M.	Special features
J. Campbell (Mrs.), The Grange, Grange Road, Fort William PH33 6JF. Tel: (01397) 705516.	House 2 Crowns Deluxe	3	2 ensuite fac. 1 private fac.	No	Mar-Nov	B. & B. from £26.00	Refurbished Victorian house with loch views and fine hospitality.
C. MacLeod (Mrs.), "Clintwood", 23 Hillview Drive, Corpach, Fort William PH33 7LS. Tel: (01397) 772 680.	Guest House 2 Crowns High Comm	3	Shower/bath, WC, W/h basin, ensuite. C.TV. H/dryer. Teamaking fac.	No	Apr-Oct	B.&B. £19	Modern villa with high standard of accommodation - 2 double/ 1 twin. Warm welcome awaits you.

Kincraig

	Type of accommodation	Number of rooms	Room facilities	Packed Lunches	Season dates	Price p.p. B/B or B.B.E.M.	Special features
Laurel Neck (Mrs.), Grampian View, Kincraig, by Kingussie PH21 1NA. Tel: (01504) 651383.	Guest House 2 Crowns Commended	5	Ensuite. Tea/coffee.	Yes	Jan-Dec	B. & B. £17.00	Elegant Victorian house. Centrally situated for touring many local amenities.

North Kessock

	Type of accommodation	Number of rooms	Room facilities	Packed Lunches	Season dates	Price p.p. B/B or B.B.E.M.	Special features
C.M. Fraser (Mrs.), Chrystal's Farmhouse, Tore-Mains Farm, Tore, nr. North Kessock IV6 7SA. Tel: (01463) 811337.	F'House	4	1 twin, 2 double 1 single W.H.B. in 2 rooms	No	Jan-Nov	B.&B. from £15.	A traditional sandstone farmhouse 100 years old. Very homely and peaceful. Breathtaking scenery. Good food and log fires.

Onich

	Type of accommodation	Number of rooms	Room facilities	Packed Lunches	Season dates	Price p.p. B/B or B.B.E.M.	Special features
Ronald Young (Mr.), Camus House Lochside Lodge, Onich, by Fort William. Tel: (01855) 821200.	Guest House 3 Crowns Commended	7	Ensuite. Teasmaids. Elec. blankets.	Yes	Jan-Nov	B.&B. £17-£27.	

LANARKSHIRE
Glasgow

	Type of accommodation	Number of rooms	Room facilities	Packed Lunches	Season dates	Price p.p. B/B or B.B.E.M.	Special features
Moira Ireland (Mrs.), Blairmains Farm, Harthill ML7 5TJ. Tel: (01501) 751278.	Guest House Pending	8	W.H.B. Phone. Tea/coffee.	Yes	All year	B. & B. from £14.50 B.B.E.M. from £19.50	Centrally located adjacent to motorway - ideal touring base.

LOTHIAN
Edinburgh

	Type of accommodation	Number of rooms	Room facilities	Packed Lunches	Season dates	Price p.p. B/B or B.B.E.M.	Special features
Cathy Kelly (Mrs.), Highland Park Guest House, 16 Kilmaurs Terrace, Edinburgh EH16 5DR. Tel: 0131-667 9204.	Guest House 1 Crown Commended	5	WH.B. C.H. Col. T.V. Tea/coffee tray	No	Jan-Dec	B. & B. from £13-£20	Quiet location. Near city centre. Unrestricted street parking.
Brenda Simpson (Mrs.), Daisy Park Guest House, 41 Abercorn Terrace, Edinburgh. Tel: 0131-669 2503. Fax: 0131-669 0189.	Guest House. 2 Crowns Commended	6	3 ensuite.	No	Jan-Dec	B. & B. from £17-£25	20 mins. by bus to city centre. Easy access to A1 - near the beach.
June Dorrian, Claymore Guest House, 68 Pilrig Street, Edinburgh. Tel: 0131-554 2500	Guest House 2 Crown Commended	6	3 ensuite 1 pte. bathroom 2 basic WHB	No	Jan-Dec	B.&B. From £16-£23	Warm, friendly centrally situated family run guest house. Excellent value.

	Type of accommodation	Number of rooms	Room facilities	Packed Lunches	Season dates	Price p.p. B/B or B.B.E.M.	Special features
North Berwick Kate Patrick (Mrs.), "Cosyden", 16 Marly Green, North Berwick EH39 4QX. Tel: (01620) 893069/894052	House 2 Crowns Commended	1	Pte. double bedroom. Bathroom. Sittingroom.	No	All year	B. & B. £18	Private accommodation. Attractive peaceful surroundings. Beautiful beaches. Edinburgh 30 mins.
NAIRNSHIRE **Nairn** Pamela Hudson (Mrs.), Durham House, 4 Academy Street, Nairn IV12 4RJ. Tel: (01667) 452345.	House 2 Crowns Commended	3	TV.C.H. Tea/coffee Hairdryer. 1 ensuite.	Yes	All year	B.&B. from £15. B.B.E.M. from £23.	High standard of accommodation and food. Spacious car park.
PERTHSHIRE **Perth** Elizabeth D. Hosie (Mrs.), Tigh Mhorag Guest House, 69 Dunkeld Road, Perth PH1 5RP. Tel: (01738) 622902.	Guest House 3 Crowns Commended	6	2 double-ensuite 1 twin-ensuite 1 family 2 singles	No	All year	B.&B. £16-£18. D.B.&B. £22.50	An ensuite twin room is situated on the ground floor.
ROSS-SHIRE **Invergordon** J.C. Brown, Craigaron Guest House, 17 Saltburn, Invergordon IV18 0JX. Tel: (01349) 853640.	Guest house 2 Crowns Commended	4	2 ensuite. 1 public shower C.H. C.T.V. Tea/coffee fac.	No	4 Jan-21 Dec.	B.&B. from: £14.50-£23.	Seafront. Comfortable rooms. Good cooking. 5 mins drive town centre.
Stromeferry Pat Davey (Mrs.), Soluis mu Thuath, Braeintra, Achmore, Stromeferry. Tel: (0159 987) 219.	Guest House 2 Crowns Commeded	4	Ensuite. C.H. T.V. Tea/coffee	No	Feb-Nov	B.&B.: £15-£18	Quiet location in lovely countryside. Owner built with wheelchair access.
ROXBURGHSHIRE **Kelso** I. & M. Forrester (Mr.& Mrs.), Homebank House, Birgham, Coldstream TD12 4ND. Tel: (01890) 830285.	Guest House 2 Crowns Commended	2 double & twin	C.T.V. Tea/coffee 2 bath/shower	Yes	All year	B.&B. £17.50. E.M. £12.50. .	Beautiful country house by the Tweed. Hirsel Golf Course nearby.
STIRLINGSHIRE **Stirling** Agnes Thomson (Mrs.), Tiroran, 45 Douglas Terrace, Stirling FK7 9LW. Tel: (01786) 464655.	House Highly Commended	2	Tea/coffee C.H. H/dryers.	No	Apr -Oct.	B. &B. £14.50-£15.	Homely welcome in this modern house situated in residential area.
ISLE OF ARRAN **Brodick** Mairi M. Thompson (Mrs.), Carrick Lodge, Brodick KA27 8BH. Tel: (01770) 302550.	Guest House 2 Crowns Commended	6	Ensuite shower/bath. TV. CH. Tea/coffee. Hairdryer.	Ask	Feb-Oct.	B.&B. £16-£20 Dinner £10.50	Sandstone house in own grounds with panoramic views. Ample parking.
ISLE OF SKYE **Broadford** M.A.B. MacGregor (Mrs.), Langdale House, Waterloo, Breakish IV42 8QE. Tel: (01471) 8221376.	House 3 Crowns Commended	3	H. & C. & C.H. Tea/coffee. Sky TV. Ensuite.	No	All year	B. & B. £16, ensuite £18.	Dinner, licensed, vegetarian and ceoliac food also available. Superb panoramic views.

EDITORIAL CONTENT

In the following Places of Interest section you will find natural wonders, from ancient mountains and forests, to lochs, country parks and estates; wildlife and rare breeds, both native and foreign. There are castles, great houses, cottages, industrial sites and beautiful and historic gardens to visit. Boat trips and steam trains offer a leisurely view of the scenery; heritage centres recall Scots famous in all kinds of fields. Museums display exhibits from Scotland and the rest of the world: some concentrate on special subjects, others offer a fascinating glimpse into local history and personalities. Art galleries feature permanent exhibitions of international stature, from Old Masters to Scottish colourists, while others have changing exhibitions by contemporary artists, sculptors and craftsmen. Scotland can be seen at work in distilleries, potteries and crystal works, wood turneries, jewellery studios, tanneries and many other places, large and small; and at play in parks, swimming pools, leisure centres, ice rinks and theatres.

The information is divided into the following geographical sections:-
Borders, Edinburgh, Lothian, Fife, Perth, Angus, Aberdeen, North East, The Northern Highlands, Western & Central Highlands, Central & South West Scotland, Glasgow and Scotland's Islands.

Within these sections the places of interest are listed alphabetically.

Abbreviations:
The abbreviations used in the entries are listed below, together with the head offices of the organisations concerned.

HS
Historic Scotland in the care of the Secretary of State for Scotland and maintained on his behalf by the Scottish Development Department, Historic Scotland, 20 Brandon Street, Edinburgh EH3 5RA. Tel: 0131-244 3101.

FE
Forest Enterprise, 231 Corstorphine Road, Edinburgh EH12 7AT. Tel: 0131-334 0303.

NTS
The National Trust for Scotland, 5 Charlotte Square, Edinburgh EH2 4DU. Tel: 0131-226 5922.

RSPB
The Royal Society for the Protection of Birds, 17 Regent Terrace, Edinburgh EH7 5BN. Tel: 0131-556 5624.

SWT
Scottish Wildlife Trust, 16 Cramond Glebe Road, Edinburgh EH4 6NS. Tel: 0131-312 7765.

OPENING STANDARD
This refers to the hours during which HS locations are open to the public:
April to September: Mon-Sat 09.30-18.00, Sun 14.00-18.00.
October to March: Mon-Sat 09.30-16.00, Sun 14.00-16.00.

DISTANCES
The distances indicated in the location of entries are approximate and are normally the shortest by road, except in a few remote places where they are "as the crow flies".

READERS ARE ADVISED TO CHECK ADMISSION TIMES AND OTHER DATA

PLACES OF INTEREST

BORDERS

Abbey St. Bathans Trout Farm
Turn off A1 at Grantshouse (A6112 to Duns), take 1st or 2nd unclassified road to right. Signposted Abbey St. Bathans thereafter. Easter-Sept, Apr, May, Sept: Open weekends and bank holidays, 13.00-17.00. June, July, Aug: Open daily, 13.00-17.00. Entrance charge (includes feed for fish). Parking available. Gift shop, restaurant. Tel: (0136 14) 203.
Trout farm and shop selling fresh and smoked trout, and other products. Gallery with display of work by Scottish craftsmen and artists. Pictish Broch. Site of Cistercian Priory. Riverside walks through oak woodlands up to moorland.

Abbotsford House
A7, 2.5m SSE of Galashiels. Late Mar-end Oct. Mon-Sat 10.00-17.00, Sun 14.00-17.00. Tel: (01896) 2043.
Sir Walter Scott's romantic mansion built 1817-1822. Much as in his day, it contains the many remarkable historical relics he collected, armouries, the library with some 9,000 volumes and his study. He died here in 1832. Free car park, with private entrance for disabled drivers. Teashop and gift shop.

Peter Anderson of Scotland Cashmere Woollen Mill and Museum
Nether Mill, Huddersfield Street, Galashiels. Jan-Dec, exc Xmas and New Year. Shop and museum: Mon-Sat 09.00-17.00, Sun (Jun-Sep only) 12.00-17.00. Tours: Mon-Fri (exc Fri pm), 10.30, 11.30, 13.30, 14.30. Entrance charge. Parking available. Mill shop. Tel: (01896) 2091.
From small beginnings into a weaving shop at the back of a church. Peter Anderson has expanded over a century to the present mill complex where the whole process of tweed manufacture - except for carding and spinning - is carried out. In a 40-minute tour visitors can see all aspects of production from spun yarn to the finished article. The museum shows the involvement of Galashiels in the woollen trade, using photographs, traditional artefacts and machinery. Refurbished Leffell water turbine wheel is harnessed to run a weaving loom within the museum.

Johnie Armstrong of Gilnockie Memorial
Carlanrig, Teviothead. Take the A7 S from Hawick for 9m then turn right on to unclassified road. Memorial is 100yds on left next to churchyard. All year. Free access. Parking available.
A stone marker marks the mass grave of Laird of Gilnockie and his men hanged without trial by King James V of Scotland, 1530. Information plaque. Wheelchair access via nearby field gate.

Ayton Castle
At Ayton, by Eyemouth, on A1, 7m N of Berwick. May-Sept, Sun 14.00-17.00, or by appointment. Entrance charge. Parking available. Tel: (018907) 81212.
Scottish Baronial style castle built in 1846 in red sandstone. Now fully lived in as a family home.

Bedrule Church
Bedrule, nr. Denholm, off A698, Bedrule/Chesters Road. Tel: (01450) 87518.
Bedrule Church, with its remarkable stained glass and armorial bearings and picturesque location high above the river, is the focus of the area from which 'fighting Turnbulls' came, numbers amongst them William Turnbull, born 1400, Bishop of Glasgow and founder of Glasgow University (1451). Although nothing remains of Bedrule Castle, the mound of Fulton Tower still dominates this reach of the Rule.

Biggar Gasworks Museum
Gasworks Road, near the War Memorial, Biggar. Daily, May-Sept. Limited car parking. Working exhibits and live steam on special occasions. Free. For details phone. (National Museums of Scotland). Tel: 0131-225 7534.
Biggar Gasworks was built in 1839 and closed in 1973 on the arrival of natural gas. It is now the only surviving coal gasworks in Scotland. The buildings, plant and associated displays give a concise picture of the coal-gas industry. Working machinery and gas lights, guided tours, display of gas appliances, video show. Limited car parking.

Biggar Kirk
Kirkstyle, Biggar. Daily till dusk. Sunday services 11.00, also 09.30 on last Sun of month. Refreshments at Gillespie Centre, 72 High Street, Biggar. (Church of Scotland). Tel: (01899) 20227.
Collegiate Church built in 1545 (on site of earlier building) by Malcolm, Lord Fleming of Biggar, uncle of Mary, Queen of Scots.

Biggar Puppet Theatre
On the B7016 E of Biggar. All year, Mon-Sat 10.00-17.00; closed Wed; Sun 14.00-17.00. Entrance charge. Parking available. Tearoom.

Licensed. Tel: (01899) 20631 (Box Office); (01899) 20521 (Administration).
Complete Victorian theatre in miniature seating 100. Attractive grounds with tearoom, shop, games, picnic area and car park. Licensed. Disabled visitors welcome but prior notice required. Induction loop.

Bowhill
Off A708, 3m W of Selkirk. Grounds and playground open 28 Apr-28 Aug (not Fri). House open 1-31 Jul. Daily (incl Fri) 12.00-17.00, Sun 14.00-18.00. (House 13.00-16.30). Dates subject to slight alteration each year. Please telephone for precise information. Tel: (01750) 20732.
For many generations Bowhill has been the Border home of the Scotts of Buccleuch. Inside the house, begun in 1812, there is an outstanding collection of pictures, including works of Van Dyck, Reynolds, Gainsborough, Canaletto, Guardi, Claude Lorraine, Raeburn, etc. Also porcelain and furniture, much of which was made in the famous workshop of Andre Boulle in Paris. In the grounds are an adventure woodland play area, a riding centre, garden, nature trails, tearoom and gift shop.

Broughton Gallery
On the A701 just N of Broughton Village. End Mar-mid Oct, mid Nov-mid Dec daily 10.30-18.00 (incl Sun); closed Wed. Free. Parking available. Tel: (018994) 234.
An imposing building designed by Basil Spence in 1938 in the style of a 16th-century Scottish fortified tower house. Contains continuous exhibitions of paintings and crafts by living British artists for sale. The walled garden contains dovecote and knot garden with fine views of the Tweeddale Hills. Nearby in Broughton Village at the corner of Biggar road is a garden which contains no less than 14,000 bedding plants.

John Buchan Centre
S end of Broughton, 6m E of Biggar. Easter-Sept, daily 14.00-17.00. Entrance charge. Parking available. (Biggar Museum Trust). Tel: (01899) 21050.
The Centre tells the story of John Buchan, 1st Lord Tweedsmuir, author of "The 39 Steps" and also lawyer, politician, soldier, historian and Governor-General of Canada. Broughton village was his mother's birthplace, and a much-loved holiday home.

Clapperton Daylight Photographic Studio
Scott's Place, E of Selkirk town centre on right near Police Station. Apr-Oct, Sat and Sun
14.00-16.30; other times by arrangement. Tel: (01750) 20523.
One of the oldest original daylight photographic studios in existence, still in family hands. With changing displays of photographs dating back to the 1860s.

Jim Clark Memorial Trophy Room
44 Newtown Street, Duns. Easter-end Oct, Mon-Sat 10.00-13.00, 14.00-17.00, Sun 14.00-17.00. Parking available. Tel: (01361) 82600, ext 36/37.
A memorial to the late Jim Clark, twice world motor racing champion, with a large number of his trophies.

The Cornice Museum of Ornamental Plasterwork
Innerleithen Road, Peebles. Entrance opposite Park Hotel main entrance. Apr-Oct, Mon-Fri 14.00-16.00, Sat 10.30-12.30 or by arrangement. Entrance charge. Tel: (01721) 20212.
Re-creation of a plasterer's casting shop illustrating methods of creating ornamental plasterwork. Car park nearby.

Coulter Motte
Off A72, 2m N of Coulter, 1.5m SW of Biggar (A702). Open all reasonable times. Free. (HS). Tel: 0131-244 3101.
Early medieval castle mound, originally moated and probably surrounded by a palisade enclosing a timber tower.

Craigcleuch Castle Collection
2m NW of Langholm on B709. Easter, May-Sept, daily 10.00-17.00, or by arrangement. Gift shop. Woodland Walks. Parking available. Tel: (013873) 80137.
Baronial Scottish stone mansion exhibiting the Craigcleuch collection, hundreds of superb selected curiosities. Fine rare tribal ethnographic carvings, sculptures, masks, painting on silk. Prehistoric American Indian carved stone animals and birds. Exquisite red coral carving. Chinese Jade animals, Japanese Ivories. Unspoiled panoramic views overlooking "Gates of Eden", woodlands.

Crumstane Farm Park
On A6105, 1.75m SE of Duns. Easter-Sep. Daily, exc Tues (unless opened by prior arrangement), 10.00-18.00. Entrance charge. Parking available. Tel: (01361) 83268.
Over 60 varieties of farm animals and poultry including many rare breeds. Picnic areas.

Dawyck Botanic Gardens
Stobo, B712, 8m SW of Peebles. 15 Mar-22 Oct incl., daily 10.00-18.00. No animals (except

guide dogs). *Entrance charge. Tel: (01721) 6254.*

All year round colour from spring bulbs to autumn tints. Rare trees, including many very fine conifers, shrubs, rhododendrons and narcissi, among woodland walks. In the woods is Dawyck Chapel, designed by William Burn.

Devil's Beef Tub

A701, 6m N of Moffat. Free. Parking available. Can be seen from the road.

A huge, spectacular hollow among the hills, at the head of Annandale. In the swirling mists of this out-of-the-way retreat Border reivers hid cattle 'lifted' in their raids. Can be seen from the road.

Dryburgh Abbey

Off A68, 6m SE of Melrose. Opening standard. Entrance charge. Parking available. (HS). Tel:0131—244 3101.

Peacefully situated on the banks of the Tweed, Dryburgh Abbey is one of the four famous Border abbeys founded in the reign of David I by Hugh de Morville, Constable of Scotland. Though little save the transepts has been spared of the church itself, the cloister buildings have survived in a more complete state than in any other Scottish monastery, except Iona and Inchcolm. Much of the existing remains are 12/13th century. Sir Walter Scott is buried in the church.

Dryhope Tower

Off A708 near St. Mary's Loch, 15m W of Selkirk. Access all reasonable times. Free.

A stout little tower now ruinous, but originally four storeys high, rebuilt c 1613. Birthplace of Mary Scott, *The Flower of Yarrow,* who married the freebooter Auld Wat of Harden, 1576 - ancestors Sir Walter Scott was proud to claim.

Dunglass Collegiate Church

On estate road, W of A1 (signposted Bilsdean) 1m N of Cockburnspath. All reasonable times. Free. (HS). Tel: 0131-244 3101.

Founded in 1450, the church consists of nave, choir, transepts, sacristy and a central tower; richly embellished interior, in an attractive estate setting.

Duns Castle

16 miles W of Berwick-upon-Tweed on A6105. Open by private arrangement, groups of 8 or more. Charge for tour and refreshments. Parking available. Tel: (01361) 83211.

Duns Castle is a 14th century peel tower with Georgian additions, inhabited by the same family for 300 years. Its Gothic stone and

plasterwork are of the finest quality, and its furnishings reflect the Scottish, Dutch and French influences of its history. The castle is set in beautiful landscaped grounds with a lake, now a nature reserve, to the north.

Edinshall Broch

On the NE slope of Cockburn Law, off A6112 4m N of Duns. All reasonable times. Free. (HS). Tel: 0131-244 3101.

Listed among the ten Iron Age brochs known in lowland Scotland, its dimensions are exceptionally large. The site was occupied into Roman times.

Edrom Norman Arch

Off A6105, 3m ENE of Duns. All reasonable times. Free. (HS). Tel: 0131-244 3101.

Fine Norman chancel arch from church built by Thor Longus c 1105, now standing behind recent parish church.

Eyemouth Museum

Auld Kirk, Market Place, Eyemouth. Easter-Oct, Mon-Fri 10.00 to variable closing times. Sun 14.00. Entrance charge. Tel: (018907) 50678.

Opened in 1981 to commemorate the Great East Coast Fishing Disaster in which 189 fishermen were lost, 129 of them from Eyemouth. Displays include Eyemouth tapestry, and the wheelhouse of a modern fishing boat. Museum reflects the fishing and farming history of East Berwickshire.

Fast Castle

Off A1107, 4m NW of Coldingham. Parking available.

The scant, but impressive remains of a Home stronghold, perched on a cliff above the sea. Care should be taken on the cliffs.

Ferniehirst Castle

1.5m S of Jedburgh. Information centre: open May-Oct, Wed 13.30-16.30. Entrance charge. (Private apartments in castle, open by arrangemennt only. Additional fee. Contact Lothian Estates Office, Jedburgh). Tel: (01835) 62201. Parking available. Gift Shop.

Scotland's frontier fortress. 16th century Border Castle, ancestral home of the Kerr family, recently restored by the Marquis of Lothian, Chief of the Kerrs. A 17th century stable has been adapted to incorporate an information centre giving details on Border families and Border history.

Flodden Monument

Town Centre, Selkirk. All times. Free. Tel: (01750) 20096.

The monument was erected in 1913 on the 400th anniversary of the battle and is inscribed 'O Flodden Field'. The memorial is the work of sculptor Thomas Clapperton.

Floors Castle

B6089, signposted 1m N of Kelso. Easter weekend. End April, May, June, Sept, Sun-Thurs 10.30-17.30. July & Aug, daily 10.30-17.30. Oct, Sun & Wed 10.30-16.00. Last admission to house 45 mins before closing. Coach parties by arrangement in April & Oct. Entrance charges. Parking available. Gift shop. Licensed restaurant. Garden Centre open daily for plant sales. Tel: (01573) 223333.

A large and impressive mansion, built by William Adam in 1721, with additions in the 1840s by William Playfair. A holly tree in the grounds is said to mark the spot where James II was killed by the bursting of a cannon in 1460. Location of the film 'Greystoke'.

Lady Gifford Statue

Village clock, in West Linton. 17m SSW of Edinburgh. All reasonable times. Tel: (01968) 60346.

Statue on the front of the village clock at West Linton, carved in 1666 by the Laird Gifford, a Covenanter and skilled stonemason. The clock is on the site of a well, disused since Victorian times. Laird Gifford also executed panels (1660 and 1678) on a house opposite, depicting Lady Gifford and the entire family genealogy.

Gladstone Court Street Museum

A702 North Back Road, Biggar, 26m from Edinburgh, 12m from A74 (South). Easter-Oct, daily 10.00-12.30, 14.00-17.00; Sun 14.00-17.00; other times by arrangement. Parking available. (Biggar Museum Trust). Tel: (01899) 21050.

An indoor street museum of shops and windows. Grocers, photographers, dressmakers, bank, school, library, ironmonger, chemist, china merchant, telephone exchange, etc.

Grey Mare's Tail

Off A708, 10m NE of Moffat. (NTS). Tel: 0141—552 8391.

A spectacular 200-feet waterfall formed by the Tail Burn dropping from Loch Skene. The area is rich in wild flowers and there is a herd of wild goats.

NB. Visitors should keep to the path to the foot of the falls: there have been serious accidents to people scrambling up and care should be exercised.

Halliwell's House Museum and Robson Gallery

Off main square, town centre, Selkirk. Apr-Oct, Mon-Sat 10.00-17.00, Sun 14.00-16.00. Jul & Aug open daily until 18.00. Nov-Dec, daily 14.00-16.00. Free. Parking available. Gift shop. Tel: (01750) 20096.

This row of 18th-century dwelling houses has recently been extensively renovated and now houses an attractive and lively museum dealing with Selkirk's long and rich history. The building's history and its long link with the ironmongery trade are thoughtfully re-created. The Robson Gallery has constantly changing exhibitions. Listening post in ironmongers shop, and video in upstairs gallery.

Harestanes Countryside Visitor Centre

Harestanes, by Ancrum, 3 miles N of Jedburgh. Easter-Oct. Daily, 10.00-17.00. Free. Parking available. Gift shop. Book shop. Tearoom. Tel: (018353) 306.

Harestanes Countryside Visitor Centre is a group of converted farm buildings which house a variety of facilities designed to introduce the visitor to the Borders countryside. As well as interior displays, there are Ranger-led walks and other Ranger activities in the grounds of the estate. Games room, new play area adjacent.

Hawick Museum & Art Gallery

In Wilton Lodge Park, on western outskirts of Hawick. Apr-Sep, Mon-Sat 10.00-12.00 and 13.00-17.00, Sun 14.00-17.00; Oct-Mar, Mon-Fri 13.00-16.00, closed Sat, Sun 14.00-16.00. Entrance charge. Parking available. Cafe. Tel: (01450) 73457.

In the ancestral home of the Langlands of that Ilk, an unrivalled collection of local and Scottish Border relics, natural history, art gallery, etc. Situated in 107-acre Wilton Lodge Park, open at all times: riverside walks, gardens, greenhouses, recreations and playing fields. Small cafe.

Hermitage Castle

In Liddesdale, 5.5m NE of Newcastleton. Apr-Sept, opening standard. Oct-Mar, weekends only. Entrance charge. Parking available. (HS). Tel: 0131—244 3101.

This strikingly dramatic 13th-century castle was a stronghold of the de Soulis family and, after 1341, of the Douglases. It has had a vivid, sometimes cruel history; to here Mary, Queen of Scots made her exhausting ride from Jedburgh in 1566 to meet Bothwell, a journey which almost cost her her life. The building consists of four towers and connecting walls, outwardly almost perfect.

The Hirsel, Homestead Museum, Craft Centre and Grounds

On A697, immediately W of Coldstream. All reasonable daylight hours every day of the year. Parking available (small charge). Tel: (01890) 882834.

Museum housed in old farmstead buildings (with integrated Craft Centre) with history of estate, old tools, natural history. Walks in Leet Valley, round the grounds of Hirsel House (not open to the public). Famous rhododendron wood. Tearoom open Sun and bank holiday afternoons, and for groups by arrangement.

James Hogg Monument

By Ettrick 1m W of B7009. All times. Free. Parking available.

A monument on the site of the birthplace of James Hogg (1770-1835), known as 'The Ettrick Shepherd', friend of Scott. His grave is in the nearby church.

Jedburgh Abbey and Visitor Centre

High Street, Jedburgh. Opening standard. Entrance charge. Parking available. (HS). Tel: 0131—244 3101.

This Augustinian abbey is perhaps the most impressive of the four great border abbeys, founded by David I in 1138. The noble remains are extensive, the west front has a fine rose window, known as St. Catherine's Wheel, and there is a richly carved Norman doorway. Remains of other domestic buildings have been recovered recently.

Jedburgh Castle Jail & Museum

Castlegate, Jedburgh. Mon-Sat 10.00-17.00, Sun 13.00-17.00. Entrance charge. Parking available. Tel: (01835) 63254 or (0450) 73457.

On the site of Jedburgh Castle, a 'modern' reform jail was built in 1825. Rooms have been interestingly reconstructed to create the 're-formed' system of the early 19th century. A history of the Royal Burgh is interpreted. The jail is set in a grassy area, suitable for picnics, and forms part of the Jedburgh Town Trail.

Jedforest Deer and Farm Park

Mervinslaw Estate, Camptown, 5 miles S of Jedburgh on A68. Signposted. May-Oct. Daily 10.00-17.00 (May-Sept), 11.00-16.30 (Sept & Oct). Entrance charge. Parking available. Gift shop. Tearoom. Tel: (0183 54) 364.

Borders working farm with sheep, suckler cows, corn and red deer. Large display of rare breeds, including sheep, cattle, pigs, goats, poultry and waterfowl. Old and new breeds are compared. Emphasis on physical contact with animals and involvement with farm activities. Display boards with written, pictorial and hand-phone information. Daily bulletin board, coded walks, adventure land, conservation and wet areas. Tractor rides with commentary can be booked. Horse riding, educational resource material, guide book.

Kailzie Gardens

2m E of Peebles on B7062. Early Mar-Oct. Daily 11.00-17.30. Entrance charge. Parking available. Gift shop. Tearoom. Plant centre. Tel: (01721) 20007.

17 acres of garden surrounded by mature timber. Walled garden dated 1812 with greenhouses, laburnum alley, shrub borders and collection of shrub roses. Woodland and burnside walks. Also collection of waterfowl. Gift shop, art gallery and licensed tearoom.

Kelso Abbey

Bridge Street, Kelso. Opening standard. Free. (HS). Tel: 0131—244 3101.

This 12th-century Tironensian abbey, was one of the earliest completed by David I and was built on a plan unique to Scotland. It was one of the largest of the Border abbeys. When the Earl of Hertford entered Kelso in 1545 the abbey was garrisoned as a fortress and was taken only at the point of the sword; the garrison of 100 men, including 12 monks, was slaughtered, and the building was almost entirely razed. The tower is part of the original building.

Kelso Museum

Turret House, Abbey Court, off Bridge Street. Apr-Oct. Entrance charge. Parking available. Tel: (01573) 225470 or (01450) 73457.

Located in one of Kelso's oldest and most attractive buildings, owned by the National Trust for Scotland, the Museum interprets Kelso's history as a market town, concentrating on the skinning and tanning industry. Nearby car parking. Access to ground floor only for wheelchair visitors.

Kirk Yetholm

Off B6352, 8m SE of Kelso.

Attractive village, with Town Yetholm, once famous as the home of the Scottish gypsies, now the northern end of the Pennine Way.

Kittiwake Gallery

Entrance to St. Abbs Village at Head Start Visitor Centre. Easter-Sept, daily, 11.00-17.30. Oct-Easter, Sat & Sun 12.00-16.00. Free. Parking available. Gallery shop. Tearoom. Tel: (0189 07) 71504 or 71588.

Privately-owned gallery, displaying paintings

and limited edition prints, greeting cards by Frederick J. Watson, the gallery proprietor. From Easter to September, demonstrations of landscape and wildlife painting of local subjects.

Leyden Obelisk and Tablet
Denholm on A698 NE of Hawick. All times. Free.
The village was the birthplace of John Leyden (1776-1811), poet, orientalist and friend of Sir Walter Scott. An obelisk was set up in 1861 and a tablet on a thatched cottage records his birth there. Another famous son of Denholm was Sir James Murray, editor of the Oxford English Dictionary whose birth is commemorated on a tablet on a house in Main Street.

Hugh MacDiarmid Memorial Sculpture
At Whita Hill Yett, approx. 2m NE of Langholm on the Langholm to Newcastleton road. At any time.
Steel and bronze sculpture by Jake Harvey to commemorate the literary achievements of the Langholm-born poet and Scots Revivalist. Nearby is Malcolm Monument.

Ladykirk
4 miles E of Swinton and 0.5 miles from Norham off B6470. All reasonable times. Parking available.
Ladykirk was built in 1500 by James IV, in memory of 'Our Lady' who had saved him from drowning. As the Border was only 300 yards away and in constant dispute, he ordered it built to withstand fire and flood - hence the all-stone construction of the kirk with no wooden rafters and, until this century, stone pews. The Wardens of the East March met regularly in the parish to resolve disputes between Scotland and England. In 1560, a copy of the last peace treaty between them was signed in Ladykirk, marking the end of sporadic warfare.

Manderston
Off A6105, 2m E of Duns. Mid May-Sep, Thurs & Sun 14.00-17.30. Entrance charges for house and grounds. Shop. Tearoom. Tel: (01361) 83450.
This Edwardian country house is one of the last great classical houses to be built in Scotland. The house contains a silver staircase, thought to be unique. It also gives an insight into life 'below stairs'. It has extensive estate buildings and gardens particularly noted for their rhododendrons. Tearoom, shop, gardens, stables and marble dairy.

Marjoribanks Monument
At E entrance to Coldstream. All times. Free.

Obelisk with a stone figure of Charles Marjoribanks, elected the First Member of Parliament for Berwickshire after the passing of the Reform Act of 1832.

Mary, Queen of Scots House
Queen Street, Jedburgh. Easter-mid Nov, daily 10.00-17.00. Tel: (01835) 63331/(01450) 73457.
A 16th century bastel house in which Mary, Queen of Scots is reputed to have stayed in 1566 when attending the Court of Justice. Now a museum containing several relics associated with the Queen. Delightful gardens surround the house which also forms part of the Jedburgh Town Trail.

Mellerstain House
Off A6089, 7m NW of Kelso. Easter; 1 May-30 Sept, Sun-Fri 12.30-16.30. Admission charge. Parking available. Gift shop. Self-service tearoom. Tel: (0157 381) 225.
This is one of the most attractive mansions open to the public in Scotland, with exceptionally beautiful interior decoration and plaster work. Begun about 1725 by William Adam, it was completed between 1770 and 1778 by William's son Robert. There are attractive terraced gardens and pleasant grounds with fine views. Self-service tearoom, gift shop, lake, thatched cottage and garden.

Melrose Abbey
Main Square, Melrose. Opening standard. Entrance charge. Parking available. (HS). Tel: 031—244 3101.
This Cistercian Abbey is the finest and largest of the Border abbeys, founded in 1136 by David I. It is notable for its fine traceried stonework. It suffered the usual attacks of all the Border abbeys during English invasions, but parts of the nave and choir dating from a rebuilding of 1385 include some of the best and most elaborate work of the period in Scotland. In addition to the flamboyant stonework, note on the roof the figure of a pig playing bagpipes. There is an interesting museum in the Commendator's House, at the entrance.

Melrose Motor Museum
200 yards from Melrose Abbey, towards Newstead. Mid May-mid Oct, daily 10.30-17.30 or by arrangement. Part-time from Easter to mid May. Entrance charges. Parking available. Tel: (0189 682) 2624/(01835) 22356.
Private collection with vehicles on loan, mainly vintage from 1909 to the late 1960s. Excellent motorcycles and bicycles with a quantity of old signs and items of memorabilia. Display cases of toy cars, cigarette cards, etc. Shop.

Mertoun Gardens

St. Boswells. Apr-Sept, Sat, Sun & Mon Public Holidays 14.00-18.00 (last entry 17.30). Entrance charge. Parking available. Tel: (01835) 23236.

20 acres of beatiful grounds with delightful walks and river views. Fine trees, herbaceous borders and flowering shrubs. Walled garden and well preserved circular dovecote thought to be the oldest in the county. No dogs. No guide dogs.

Milnholm Cross

1 mile S of Newcastleton beside B6357. All times. Parking available.

Erected around 1320, and owned by the Clan Armstrong Trust, Milnholm Cross is a memorial to Alexander Armstrong who was murdered in Hermitage Castle some four miles away. It faces the ruin of Mangerton Castle, seat of the Armstrong chiefs for three hundred years. Nearby, in Newcastleton, is the Janet Armstrong House, museum and clan information centre of the Armstrongs, open from Easter to September.

Moat Park Heritage Centre

Biggar town centre. 1 Apr-31 Oct, daily 10.00-17.00, Sun 14.00-17.00. Entrance charge. Parking available. Gift shop. Tel: (01899) 21050.

This former church has been adapted to display the history of the Upper Clyde and Tweed Valleys, from the days of the volcano and the glacier right up to yesterday's newspapers. Fine collection of embroidery including the largest known patchwork cover, containing over eighty figures from the 1850's.

Moffat Museum

The Neuk, off High Street, Moffat. Easter week, Whit.-Sept, Mon-Sat, exc. Wed 10.30-13.00, 14.30-17.00, Sun 14.30-17.00. Entrance charge. Tel: (01683) 20868.

Situated in an old bakehouse in the oldest part of the town. The Scotch oven is a feature of the ground floor. No guide dogs.

Moffat Pottery

20 High Street, Moffat. Jan-Dec. Mon-Sat 09.00-17.00. Tel: (01683) 20793.

Studio pottery known as the home of Moffat's 'Singing Potter', Gerard Lyons. Pots, tapes and paintings of the potter, also metal sculptures by John McPhail and jewellery by Irene McPhail.

Museum of Border Arms and Armour

9m S of Hawick on A7 at Teviothead. All year, daily 09.00-19.00. Parking available. Tel: (0145 085) 237.

Former smithy with craft gallery. The museum houses a display of weapons and equipment from the 16th century.

Neidpath Castle

A72, 1m W of Peebles. Thurs before Easter until Sept 30. Mon-Sat 11.00-17.00, Sun 13.00-17.00. Oct, Tues only 11.00-16.00. Groups at other times by arrangement. Entrance charges. Parking available. Gift shop. Tel: (01721) 720333.

In a beautiful valley among wooded hills, Neidpath Castle is dramatically situated high above the River Tweed. This mediaeval castle, with walls nearly 12 feet thick, contains a rock-hewn well and pit prison, and two of the three original vaults. It is also an interesting example of how such a fortress could be adapted to the more civilised living conditions of the 17th century. There are fine views from several levels, right up to the parapet. The castle was once besieged by Cromwell and cannon damage is still visible.

Old Gala House and Christopher Boyd Gallery

Scott Crescent, Galashiels. On A7 northbound; fork left at St. Peter's Church School. Southbound: follow signs from War Memorial. Easter-Nov. Easter-Sept 10.00-16.00 (Sun 14.00-16.00); Oct 12.00-16.00 (Sun 14.00-16.00). Parking available. Sales point. Tearoom. Tel: (01750) 20096.

Dating from 1583, Old Gala House is the former home of the Lairds of Gala. Reopened in 1988 as an interpretation centre. Especially interesting painted ceiling (1635). Gardens, coffee room (seating 16-20), small sales point. Temporary Art Galleries.

Paxton House

5 miles W of Berwick upon Tweed on B6461. Easter-Oct. Daily. First tour 12.00, last tour 16.15. Entrance charge. Parking available. Gift shop. Licensed tearoom, daily in season 10.00-17.00. Tel: (01289) 86291.

Paxton House is a Georgian, Palladian country mansion set in 70 acres of gardens, parkland and woodland. The house was built for the Homes of Wedderburn, designed by the Adam family and furnished by Chippendale. The restored Regency picture gallery is an outstation of the National Galleries of Scotland. Tearoom has facilities for coach parties. Adventure playground.

Priorwood Gardens

In Melrose, by Abbey, on B6361. Open 2-30 Apr and 1 May-24 Dec, Mon-Sat 10.00-17.30; 1 May-31 Oct, Mon-Sat 10.00-17.30, Sun 13.30-

17.30. Admission by donation. Trust shop. (NTS). Tel: (0189 682) 2555.
A garden which specialises in flowers suitable for drying, also apple trees in variety. There is an NTS Visitor Centre. Picnic tables, orchard walk, dry flower garden, NTS shop.

Rennie's Bridge
Kelso. All times. Free. (Borders Regional Council).
A fine 5-arched bridge built over the River Tweed in 1803 by Rennie to replace one destroyed by the floods of 1797. On the bridge are two lamp posts from the demolished Old Waterloo Bridge in London, which Rennie built in 1811. There is also a fine view to Floors Castle.

Roxburgh Castle
Off A699, 1m SW of Kelso. All times. Free.
The earthworks are all that remain of the once mighty castle, destroyed by the Scots in the 15th century, and the walled Royal Burgh which gave its name to the county. The present village of Roxburgh dates from a later period.

St. Mary's Loch
Off A708, 14m ESE of Selkirk. Parking available.
Beautifully set among smooth green hills, this three-mile-long loch is used for sailing and fishing. On the neck of land separating it from Loch of the Lowes at the south end stands Tibbie Shiel's Inn, long kept by Tibbie Shiel (Elizabeth Richardson, 1783-1878) from 1823, and a meeting place for many 19th-century literati. Beside the road towards the north end of the loch is a seated statue of James Hogg, the 'Ettrick Shepherd', author of the Confessions of a Justified Sinner and a friend of Scott, who farmed in this district. Tearoom and two hotels nearby.

St. Ronan's Wells Interpretative Centre
Wells Brae, Innerleithen. Easter-Oct. Daily, 14.00-17.00. Parking available. Gift shop. Tearoom. Tel: (01721) 20123.
History of the site and building told in display of objects, photographs and documents relating to the well, made famous in Sir Walter Scott's novel of the same name. Herb garden, tearoom and the original well.

Scottish Museum of Woollen Textiles
Tweedvale Mill. On main road (A72) at Walkerburn, 9m ESE of Peebles. Apr-Oct, Mon-Sat 09.00-17.00. Free. Parking available. Large mill shop. Coffee shop. Tel: (0189 687) 619.
This display features the development of the woollen industry from a cottage industry to a major occupation of the Borders. Many interesting exhibits. Group bookings by arrangement. Coffee and tea shop.

Scott's View
B6356, 4m E of Melrose.
A view over the Tweed to the Eildon Hills, beloved by Scott; here the horses taking his remains to Dryburgh for burial stopped as they had so often before for Sir Walter to enjoy this panorama.

Scotus Statue, Duns
At Duns, in public park. All times. Free.
Duns was the birthplace of John Duns Scotus (1266-1308), a Franciscan who became a leading divine and one of the greatest medieval philosophers. It is said the word 'dunce' came into the English language as a result of criticism of his work after his death.

Selkirk Glass
Off A7 N of Selkirk. All year, Mon-Fri 09.00-17.00, Sat 10.00-16.30, Sun 12.00-16.00. Glass making: Mon-Fri 09.00-16.30. Free. Tel: (01750) 20954.
Visitors are welcome at factory and showroom to see a range of paperweights and watch craftsmen at work. Coffee shop.

Sir Walter Scott's Courtroom
Market Place, Selkirk. Jul-Aug, Mon-Fri 14.00-16.00, other times by appointment. By application to: Ettrick and Lauderdale District Council, Municipal Buildings, High Street, Selkirk. Free. Parking available. Tel: (01750) 20096.
The bench and chair from which Sir Walter Scott, as Sheriff of Selkirk, administered justice here for 30 years, are on display, with portraits of Scott, James Hogg, Mungo Park and Robert Burns, with ancient charters. Also displayed are watercolours by Tom Scott, RSA.

Smailholm Tower
Off B6404, 6m NW of Kelso. Opening standard, closed in winter. (HS). Tel: 031—244 3101.
An outstanding example of a 16th-century Border peel tower built to give surveillance over a wide expanse of country. It is 57 feet high, in a good state of preservation and houses an exhibition of costumed dolls and tapestries on the theme of Sir Walter Scott's 'Minstrelsy of the Scottish Border'. At nearby Sandyknowe Farm, Scott spent some childhood years.

Robert Smail's Printing Works
7/9 High Street, Innerleithen, 30m S of Edinburgh. Shop only: 1 May-midsummer daily,

except Tues & Sun. Restored Printing Works and Shop: daily midsummer-31 Oct, Mon-Sat 10.00-13.00 and 14.00-17.00, Sun 14.00-17.00. Parking available (NTS) Tel: (01896) 830206.

These buildings contain an office, a paper store with reconstructed water wheel, composing and press rooms. Visitors may view the printer at work. Victorian office contains many historic items. Trust Shop.

Swinton Kirk

Swinton, 6 miles from Coldstream, 6 miles from Duns on A6112. All reasonable times. Free. Parking available.

Although Swinton Kirk has been much altered, the south and east walls are 1,000 years old. It was originally a long, narrow building, with the altar at the east end, and the Aumbry which can still be seen. The bell is dated 1499 and was rung as a death knell after Flodden (1513). Behind the communion table is an effigy of Alan Swinton from 1200, while the oldest coat of arms in Britain (of the Swinton Family) is above the gallery door. A copy of one of the longest recorded family trees in Britain (Swinton) is in the kirk.

Teddy Melrose, Scotland's Teddy Bear Museum

The Wynd, Melrose. Jan-Dec, daily 10.00-17.00. Entrance charge, children free, must be accompanied by an adult. Parking available. Gift shop. Tearoom and tea garden. Tel: (0189 682) 2464.

Scotland's Teddy Bear museum informs and entertains visitors with its individual presentation of famous character bears, accompanied by the history of great British bears, manufacturers. Combined displays offer the most comprehensive collection of British bears in the world - including Rupert, Paddington, Winnie and Bully Bears. Access for disabled visitors through the Wynd. Braille panels accompany the displays.

Telford Memorial

At Westerkirk, B709, 6m NW of Langholm. All times. Free. Tel: (0138 73) 80976.

Memorial to Thomas Telford (1757-1834), the engineer who was born in the valley of the Meggat Water near Westerkirk. There are several reminders of him nearby at Langholm. Access for wheelchair users (next to road).

Thirlestane Castle

Lauder, 28m S of Edinburgh on A68. Easter. May, Jun, & Sep, Wed, Thu & Sun only; Jul & Aug, every day except Sat, 14.00-17.00. Last admission 16.30. Grounds: same dates, 12.00-18.00. Entrance charges. Parking available. Gift shop. Tearoom. Tel: (01578) 722430.

Fine castle steeped in Scottish history, still the home of the Maitland family after four centuries. Magnificent 17th-century state rooms. Tea room, gift shop, gardens, museum and castle. The Border Country Life Museum Trust was established in 1981 to set up a museum to depict country life in the Scottish Borders from prehistoric times to the present day. Displays reflect the traditions, folklore and land use of the Borders. Demonstrations of vintage tractors and traditional farming methods are organised periodically by the Border Vintage Agricultural Association.

Traquair House

B709, off A72, 8m ESE of Peebles. Easter week, May-Sept, daily 13.30-17.30 (10.30-17.30, July & Aug). Entrance charges. Parking available. Gift shop. Restaurant/tearoom. Tel: (01896) 830323.

Dating back to the 10th century, this is said to be the oldest continuously inhabited house in Scotland. 27 Scottish and English monarchs have visited it, including Mary, Queen of Scots, of whom there are relics. It was once the home of William the Lion who held court here in 1209. The well-known Bear Gates were closed in 1745, not to be reopened until the Stuarts should ascend the throne. Ale is regularly produced at the 18th-century brewhouse, and there are woodland walks and four craft workshops. Exhibitions are held during the summer months and the annual Traquair Fair is held the first weekend in August. Material available on cassette by arrangement. Restaurant/tearoom, gift shop, gallery, brewery, woodland and River Tweed walks and newly planted maze.

Tweed Bridge

A698 at Coldstream, 9m ENE of Kelso.

The 300 feet long bridge was built in 1766 by Smeaton and in the past was a crossing into Scotland for eloping couples taking advantage of Scotland's then-easier marriage laws.

Tweeddale Museum & Picture Gallery

High Street, Peebles. All year. Mon- Fri 10.00-13.00, 14.00-17.00. Also weekends, 14.00-17.00, Easter-Oct. Tel: (01721) 20123.

Housed in the Chambers Institution, which was given to Peebles in 1859 by William Chambers the publisher, the museum presents regularly changing displays on various themes of Tweeddale's heritage and culture.

Trimontium Exhibition

Ormiston Institute, The Square, Melrose. Apr-Oct. Daily, 10.30-16.30. Entrance charge. Gift shop. Tel: (0189 682) 2463.

The Trimontium Exhibition - 'A Roman Frontier Post and its People' - tells the story of the Celts and Romans at the 370-acre complex in the lee of the three Eildon Hills (Trimontium). Exhibition room has display panels and cases; video room, photographs, models of the Trimontium and Cappuck forts, and interesting finds. There is also a street corner with replica blacksmith's and potter's workshops; huge stones from the Langlee temple; replica legionary helmet, sword and armour. Visitors can 'join' the garrison and become troopers.

Tweedhope Sheep Dogs
At Moffat Fisheries. A708 on outskirts of Moffat. Easter-Oct, Mon-Fri 10.30-16.30. Demonstrations 11.00, 15.00. Weekends and winter by appointment. Entrance charge. Parking available. Craft shop. Tearoom. Tel: (01683) 21471.
Border Collie visitor centre shows working sheep dogs using their skills in a natural hillside setting. Demonstrations twice daily, plus special attractions such as 'Baa Baa Black Sheep'.

Union Suspension Bridge
Across River Tweed, 2m S of Paxton on unclassified road.
This suspension bridge, the first of its type in Britain, was built by Samuel Brown in 1820 and links England and Scotland.

Waterloo Monument
Off B6400, 5m N of Jedburgh. Easter-Oct. Free. No access to interior. Tel: (0183 53) 306.
This prominent landmark on the summit of Penielheugh Hill (741 feet) was built in 1815 by the Marquess of Lothian and his tenants. Can be seen from a walk from Harestanes Countryside Visitor Centre.

The John Wood Collection
Fishers Brae, Coldingham. Apr-Oct, 09.00-18.00, Mon-Sat. Free. Car parking only. Tel: (018907) 71259.
Photographic exhibition of Border life in the early 1900s. Printed from the original glass plates which were discovered in a potting shed.

Yarrow
A708, W from Selkirk. Parking available.
A lovely valley praised by many writers including Scott, Wordsworth and Hogg, who lived in this area. Little Yarrow Kirk dates back from 1640, Scott's great-great-grandfather was minister there. The nearby Deuchar Bridge (not now in use) was built in the 17th-century. On the hills around Yarrow are the remains of ancient Border keeps.

Adam Pottery
76 Henderson Row, corner of Saxe-Coburg Street. Jan-Dec exc Xmas, New Year and Easter periods. Mon-Sat 10.00-18.00. Charge for talk and throwing demonstration (3 days' notice). Pottery showroom and sales. Tel: 0131-557 3978.
'One-Woman' pottery where Janet Adam's wheelthrown stoneware and porcelain is made and sold. Delicate porcelain vases and bowls, large planters, bread crocks, jugs and decorative platters are all reduction-fired to 1300C, giving a wide palette of subtly colourful glazes. Visitors can watch the potter at work - advance notice is required for throwing demonstrations.

Ainslie Park Leisure Centre
Off Ferry Road, 0.25m E of Crewe Toll roundabout. Centre is on left after Northern General Hospital into Pilton Drive. All year. Charges variable according to activity. Parking available. Tel: 0131-551 2400.
Opened in 1989; superbly equipped, brightly designed building on leisure theme with swimming pools, flumes and a leisure complex. Function room for 150. Bar, cafe and audio visual library.

Brass Rubbing Centre.
Trinity Apse, Chalmers Close, Royal Mile. Jun-Sep, weekdays 10.00-18.00; Oct-May, weekdays 10.00-17.00; Suns during Festival 14.00-17.00. Free. A charge is made for every rubbing, which includes cost of materials and a royalty to the churches where applicable. Tel: 0131—556 4364.
Rubbings of the brass commemorating Robert the Bruce and the Burghead Bull, a Pictish incised stone c AD 700 are among the selection available. Instruction and materials supplied.

Butterfly and Insect World
Melville Nursery, 5m S of Edinburgh on A7 towards Dalkeith. Early Mar-Jan, exc. Xmas and New Year. 10.00-17.00 summer. 10.00-16.00 winter. Entrance charges. Parking available. Gift shop. Tearoom. Tel: 0131-663 4932.
The farm, housed in a large greenhouse with lush tropical plants, cascading waterfalls and lily ponds, provides the setting for butterflies from all over the world to fly freely around. Exotic insects, photographic displays, tearoom, garden centre, tropical fish shop, children's playground and picnic area. Free car parking.

Calton Gallery
10 Royal Terrace, NE shoulder of Calton Hill. Jan-Dec exc 24 Dec-5 Jan. Mon-Fri 10.00-18.00,

Sat 10.00-13.00. Tel: 0131-556 1010.
Family firm of fine art dealers established in 1980 in an elegant Georgian townhouse. Royal Terrace, on the northern face of Calton Hill, was designed by William Playfair around 1820 and is the longest unbroken facade in the New Town. Visitors see 19th and early 20th-century Scottish oil paintings, watercolours and prints in room settings on three floors. Landscapes and seapieces, still-life and figurative paintings. English and European paintings and bronzes.

Calton Hill
Off Regent Road at E end of city centre. All times. Free. (Edinburgh District Council) Tel: 0131—225 2424.
A city centre hill, 350 feet above sea level, with magnificent views over Edinburgh and the Firth of Forth. The monumental collection on top includes a part reproduction of the Parthenon, intended to commemorate the Scottish dead in the Napoleonic Wars; it was begun in 1824 but ran out of funds and was never completed. The 102 feet high Nelson Monument (completed 1815) improves the view from its high parapets. The buildings of the Royal Observatory (1744 and 1818) are open on application to: The Custodian, City Observatory, Calton Hill, Edinburgh.

Camera Obscura
Castlehill, at top of Royal Mile, next to Castle. Jan-Dec. Apr-Oct, daily 09.30-18.00 (later in Jul & Aug). Nov-Mar, daily 10.00-17.00. Entrance charge. Gift shop. Tel: 0131-226 3709.
High in the unusual Outlook Tower, an 1850s 'cinema' shows live images of Edinburgh. The scene changes as the guide operate the Camera's system of revolving lenses and mirrors, and tells the story of the city's historic past. Also 3-D International Holography Exhibition. Pinhole Photography. Victorian Edinburgh and Artists' Edinburgh exhibitions. Award-winning centre.

Cammo Estate
Approx. 4 miles from city centre. NW of Queensferry Road. Jan-Dec. Visitor Centre, May-Sep, Mon-Fri 08.00-17.00. Free. Parking available. Tel: 0131-317 8797.
Forty acres of mature woodland, pond and ruined buildings illustrate the fascinating history of a once-private estate. Owned by National Trust for Scotland, managed by Edinburgh District Council. Pleasant walks, River Almond walkway adjoins for walk to Cramond.

Canal Centre
Baird Road, Ratho, 8 miles W of Edinburgh.
Signposted. Jan-Dec. Charges for use of facilities. Parking available. Restaurant and bars. Tel: 0131-333 1320/1251.
Based at the Bridge Inn at Ratho, two luxury canal boat restaurants cruise the Union Canal. Exhibits of canal life in the past on view in Bridge Inn, souvenirs and canalware for sale. Dry dock and reception centre opened by the Seagull Trust in 1993 - free cruising for disabled visitors.

Canongate Kirk.
On the Canongate, Royal Mile.
The church, built by order of James VII in 1688, is the Parish Church of the Canongate and also the Kirk of Holyroodhouse and Edinburgh Castle. The church silver dates from 1611. Restored in 1951, the church contains much heraldry. The burial ground contains the graves of Adam Smith, the economist, 'Clarinda', friend of Robert Burns, and Robert Fergusson, the poet.

City Art Centre
Market Street. Open Jun-Sep, Mon-Sat, 10.00-18.00, Sun during Festival, 14.00-17.00. Oct-May, Mon-Sat 10.00-17.00, usually free, occasionally charges for special exhibitions. Tel: 0131-225 2424, ext. 3541.
The City of Edinburgh's Art Gallery. A converted warehouse on four floors with a programme of changing exhibitions and displays from the City's collection of paintings.

Collective Gallery
Cockburn Street, near Waverley Station. Jan-Dec exc Xmas and New Year. Tues-Sat 11.00-17.00. Extended hours at peak times. Free. Shop. Tel: 0131-220 1260.
'New Art' venue, showing contemporary Scottish work in exhibitions that change monthly. Educational programme of workshops, classes, talks and tours. Works available for sale, gallery shop specialising in innovative applied art and design.

Craigmillar Castle
A68, 3.5m SE of city centre. Opening standard exc. Oct-Mar, closed Thu (pm) and all day Fri. Entrance charge. Parking available. (HS). Tel: 0131—244 3101.
Imposing ruins of massive 14th-century keep enclosed in the early 15th century by an embattled curtain wall; within are the remains of the stately ranges of apartments dating from the 16th and 17th centuries. The castle was burnt by Hertford in 1544. There are strong connections with Mary, Queen of Scots, who frequently stayed here. While she was in residence in 1566 the plot to murder Darnley was forged.

Cramond

5m NW of city centre, on the shores of the Firth of Forth. Parking available.

This picturesque 18th century village is situated at the mouth of the River Almond. See particularly the Roman fort and medieval tower, the kirk, kirkyard and manse, the old schoolhouse and the iron mills. Conducted walks around the village start from The Maltings, June-Sep, Sun 15.00, free. Exhibition at The Maltings, Cramond Village, Jun-Sep, Sat & Sun 14.00-17.00, free.

Crystal Visitor Centre

Eastfield, Penicuik, 10m S of Edinburgh. All year. Tours Mon-Fri 09.00-15.30. Shop, Restaurant and Audio-Visual, 09.00-17.00 Mon-Sat and Sun 11.00-17.00. Entrance charge. Tour charge (except for disabled). Children under 8 years not admitted to factory tour. Tel: (01968) 675128.

Conducted tours are available, unveiling every aspect of the glassmaker's craft. Children under 10 years not admitted on factory tours. No photography. Audio-visual presentations Mon-Sat, 0900-1630. Licensed cafeteria, children's play area and picnic facilities.

Dean Village

Bell's Brae, off Queensferry Street, on Water of Leith.

There was grain milling in this notable village of Edinburgh for over 800 years. The view downstream through the high arches of Dean Bridge is among the most picturesque in the city. A walk along the waterside leads to St. Bernard's Well, an old mineral source (open by arrangement).

Edinburgh Castle

Castle Rock, top of the Royal Mile. Apr-Sep, daily 09.30-17.15 (last entry). Oct-Nov daily 09.30-16.15 (last entry). Castle closes 45 mins after last entry. Entrance charges. Parking available. (HS). Tel: 0131—244 3101.

One of the most famous castles in the world, whose battlements overlook the Esplanade where the floodlit Military Tattoo is staged each year, late August to early September. The castle stands on a rock which has been a fortress from time immemorial. The oldest part of the buildings which make up the castle is the 12th-century chapel dedicated to St. Margaret. In addition to the Great Hall built by James IV, with fine timbered roof, and the Old Palace, which houses the Regalia of Scotland and the Military Museum; the castle also holds the Scottish National War Memorial, opened in 1927.

Edinburgh Experience

City Observatory, Calton Hill. Car park at summit; pedestrian access by steps from Regent Road. Early Apr-late Oct. Mon-Fri 14.00-17.00. Sat & Sun 10.30-17.00. Jul & Aug, daily 10.30-17.00. Other times by arrangement. Entrance charge. Parking available. Tel: 0131-556 4365.

20 minute full-colour three-dimensional slide show, viewed through 3-D glasses. The story of Scotland's capital is told, from its volcanic birth to the present day.

Flying Colours Gallery

William Street, central Edinburgh. Feb-Dec, Tues-Fri 11.00-18.00, Sat 10.00-13.00. Free. Tel: 0131-225 6776.

Flying Colours Gallery shows work by living Scottish artists in a succession of solo exhibitions changing monthly. Lively and colourful work from established artists as well as young, unknown talent. All works for sale.

Fountain Brewery

Scottish & Newcastle Breweries plc, Gilmore Park. Tours Mon-Fri 10.15 & 14.15. Entrance charges. No children under 8 on tour. Parking available. Tel: 0131-229 9377 (10.00-16.00).

A tour of the complete brewing process and high-speed canning line, in the most fully automated brewery in Europe.

The Fruitmarket Gallery

29 Market Street. All year. Tues-Sat 11.00, also Sun during Festival 12.00-18.00. Free. Bookshop. Restaurant. Tel: 0131-225 2383.

An independent gallery hosting varied exhibitions of contemporary painting, sculpture, architecture & photography from Scotland and the international art world.

Edinburgh Gallery

18a Dundas Street. N of Hanover Street. Jan-Dec, Mon-Fri 11.00-17.00. Sat 10.00-13.00. Free. Tel: 0131-557 5227.

The Edinburgh Gallery holds regular exhibitions of contemporary works of art, with a bias towards Scottish figurative, landscape and still life.

Georgian House

No. 7 Charlotte Square. Apr-Oct, Mon-Sat 10.00-17.00. Sat 10.00-13.00. Free. Tel: 0131-225 2160.

The lower floors have been furnished as they might have been by their first owners, showing the domestic surroundings and reflecting the social conditions of that age. Charlotte Square itself was built at the end of the 18th century and is one of the most outstanding examples of its period in Europe. Bute House is the official residence of the Secretary of State for Scotland. The West side of the square is dominated by the green dome of St. George's Church, now West Register House.

General Register House
E end of Princes Street. Jan-Dec. Legal: 09.30-16.30. Historical: 09.00-16.45 (last admission 16.25). Exhibitions: 10.00-16.00. Free. Tel: 0131-556 6585.
This fine Robert Adam building, founded 1774, is the headquarters of the Scottish Record Office and the home of the national archive of Scotland. There is a branch repository at West Register House in Charlotte Square. In front is a notable statue of the Duke of Wellington. Alternative wheelchair access. Guide dogs admitted to exhibition area.

Gladstone's Land
477B Lawnmarket, Royal Mile. 1 Apr-31 Oct, Mon-Sat 10.00-17.00, Sun 14.00-17.00. Last admission 30 mins. before closing. (NTS). Tel: 0131—226 5856.
Completed in 1620, the six-storey tenement contains remarkable painted ceilings, and has been refurbished as a typical home of the period.

Gorgie City Farm Project
51 Gorgie Road. Jan-Dec exc. Xmas and New Year. Free. Car and minibus parking only. Tearoom. Tel: 0131-337 4202.
2.5 acres of land adjacent to Gorgie Road, Edinburgh. This city farm has a variety of animals, animal pens, a farm kitchen with workshop/craft facilities. Picnic and play area.

Greyfriar's Bobby
Corner of George IV Bridge and Candlemaker Row. All time. Free.
Statue of Greyfriar's Bobby, the Skye terrier who, after his master's death in 1858, watched over his grave in the nearby Greyfriars Churchyard for 14 years.

Greyfriars Kirk
Greyfriars Place, S end of George IV Bridge. Easter-Sept, Mon-Fri 10.00-16.00, Sat 10.00-14.00. Kirkyard 09.00-18.00. Free. Gift/bookshop. Tel: 0131-225 1900.
The Kirk, dedicated on Christmas Day, 1620, was the scene of the adoption and signing of the National Covenant on 28 February 1638. The Covenant is displayed at the church. The kirkyard, inaugurated in 1562, is on the site of a 15th century Franciscan Friary, and contains a fine collection of 17th century Scottish monu-ments. In 1679, 1,400 Covenanters were imprisoned in the kirkyard. There is a martyrs' Monument and a memorial to Greyfriars Bobby.

George Heriot's School
Lauriston Place. May be viewed from the grounds. Gates close 16.30. Tel: 0131-229 7263 (Trust Office).
Now a school, the splendid building was begun in 1628, endowed by George Heriot, goldsmith and jeweller to James VI and I, the 'Jingling Geordie' of Scott's novel *Fortunes of Nigel*.

Hermitage of Braid
Braid Road. 2.5 miles S of city centre. Jan-Dec. Visitor Centre Mon-Fri 09.00-17.00, park open all reasonable times. Tel: 0131-447 7145.
Tranquil woodland walks in 130 acres of ancient mature woodland, including Blackford Hills with excellent views across Blackford Pond and the surrounding city. Good area for birdwatching. Guided walks from May-Sept, environmental and educational activities are bookable.

Hillend Ski Centre
Biggar Road, S outskirts of Edinburgh. Apr-Sept, Mon-Fri 09.30-21.00. Oct-Mar, daily, 09.30-22.00. Closed Xmas & New Year's Day. Charge for chairlift. Session tickets for skiers are also available. Parking available. Restaurant. Tel: 0131—445 4433.
The largest artificial ski slope in Britain. Facilities include chairlift, drag lift, ski-hire, tuition, showers and changing rooms. Grass ski-ing available May to September. Fine views from top of chairlift (available to non-skiers) of the Pentland Hills, over Edinburgh and beyond. Refreshments and picnic area.

Huntly House
Canongate, Royal Mile. Jun-Sep, Mon-Sat 10.00-18.00; Oct-May, Mon-Sat 10.00-17.00; Sun during Festival 14.00-17.00. Free. Tel: 0131—225 2424, ext 6689.
Built in 1570, this fine house was later associated with members of the Huntly Family. It is now a city museum illustrating Edinburgh Life down the ages, and contains important collections of Edinburgh silver and glass and Scottish pottery.

Kingfisher Gallery
5 Northumberland Street Lane NW, right turn off Northumberland Street. Jan-Dec, Mon-Fri 10.30-16.30. Also Sat 10.30-16.30 from Jun-Aug. Free. Tel: 0131-557 5454.
Small mews art gallery specialising in Scottish

and international contemporary art - paintings, sculpture, ceramics and jewellery.

Kinloch Anderson Heritage Room
Commercial Street/Dock Street, Leith. Jan-Dec, Mon-Sat 09.00-17.30. Free. Parking available. Courtesy taxi service. Woollen shop. Tel: 0131-555 1371/1390.
The Heritage Room is a museum of historic items made or collected by Kinloch Anderson since the company's foundation in 1868. One cabinet features the Royal Tartans, others regimental and civilian uniforms and the history of kiltmaking. A viewing window allows visitors to see manufacturing in progress. A talk on the origin of the kilt and how it is made today can be arranged. Retail shop specialises in cashmeres and woollens, high quality clothing from Scotland, accessories and gifts. Highland Dress Room for men's kilt outfits.

King's Theatre
2 Leven Street. Tel: 0131-229 1201.
Opened in 1906. 4 licensed bars and coffee bars. Completely restored 1985. Seating 1350. Producing ballet, opera, comedy, farce, variety, drama, dance etc. Productions normally change weekly. Details and advance booking from Box Office.

John Knox House
45 High Street, Royal Mile. All year, Mon-Sat 10.00-17.00, last entry 16.30. Entrance charge. Tel: 0131—556 9579/2647.
A picturesque house, said to be the only 15th century house in Scotland, having traditional connections with John Knox, the famous Scottish reformer. The recent restoration programme has revealed the original walls, fireplaces and painted ceiling. There is also a 10-minute video film of John Knox's life in Geneva and Scotland.

Lady Stair's House
Off Lawnmarket, Royal Mile. Jun-Sept, Mon-Sat 10.00-18.00; Oct-May, Mon-Sat 10.00-17.00; Sun during Festival 14.00-17.00. Free. Gift shop. Tel: 0131-225 2424, ext. 6593.
Built in 1622, this is now a museum of Burns, Scott and Stevenson.

Lamb's House
Burgess Street, Leith. Visits by prior arrangement. (NTS). Tel: 0131-554 3131.
The restored residence and warehouse of Andrew Lamb, a prosperous merchant of the 17th century. Now an old people's day centre.

Lauriston Castle
N of A90 at Cramond Road South, 4m WNW of city centre. Apr-Oct, daily except Fri 11.00-13.00, 14.00-17.00; Nov-Mar, Sat and Sun only, 14.00-16.00. Entrance charge. Parking available. Tel: 0131-336 2060/225 2424, ext. 6682.
The original tower house built by Sir Archibald Napier, father of the inventor of logarithms was much extended by William Burn in the 1820's. The last occupant, W.R. Reid, owner of the prestigious Edinburgh furnishing firm of Morison & Co., completely refurbished the Castle in 1903 and his Edwardian interior has been carefully preserved. It includes a fine collection of eighteenth century Italian furniture, oriental rugs etc. Now administered by the City of Edinburgh. Car park.

Leith Waterworld
377 Easter Road. Also accessible from bottom of Leith Walk. Jan-Dec. Mon-Fri 12.00-21.30 (community programmes from 09.00-12.00). Sat and Sun 09.00-17.00. Entrance charge. Parking available. Cafe. Tel: 0131-555 6000.
Two flumes, a river run, bubble beds, spa pool, wave machine, shower curtains, waterfall, mushrooms, fast flow channel, beach area add up to water play for all ages.

Magdalen Chapel
Cowgate, off the Grassmarket. Jan-Dec. Mon-Fri 09.30-16.30. Other times by arrangement. Free. Gift shop. (Scottish Reformation Society). Tel: 0131-220 1450.
This 16th-century chapel, is notable for its stained-glass windows.

Museum of Antiquities
Jan-Dec. Mon-Sat 10.00-17.00. Sun 14.00-17.00. Tel: 0131-225 7534.
An intriguing and comprehensive collection of the history and everyday life of Scotland from the Stone Age to modern times. Also 'Dynasty' - the Royal House of Stewart exhibition traces 300 years of Stewart rule in Scotland through portraits and objects from the Scottish National Collection.

Museum of Childhood
High Street, Royal Mile. Jun-Sep weekdays 10.00-18.00; Oct-May weekdays 10.00-17.00; Sun during Festival 14.00-17.00. Free. Tel: 0131-225 2424, ext. 6645/6647.
This unique museum has a fine collection of toys, dolls, dolls' houses, costumes and nursery equipment. It has recently been extended into a former Georgian theatre and completely refurbished.

Museum of Fire

Lauriston Place. Visits by arrangement with Fire Brigade Headquarters. Free. (Lothians & Borders Fire Brigade). No Parking. Tel: 0131-228 2401.

Guided tours round the museum, with its collection of old uniforms, equipment and engines, subject to the availability of a Fireman Guide.

National Gallery of Scotland

The Mound. Mon-Sat 10.00-17.00 (extended hours during Festival); Sun 14.00-17.00. Free. Tel: 0131-556 8921.

One of the most distinguished of the smaller gallleries of Europe, the National Gallery of Scotland contains a comprehensive collection of old masters, impressionist and Scottish paintings. This includes masterpieces by Raphael, El Greco, Rembrandt, Constable, Titian, Velasquez, Raeburn, Van Gogh and Gauguin. Drawings, watercolours and original prints (Turner, Goya, Blake etc.) are shown on request (Mon-Fri 10.00-12.30, 14.00-16.30).

National Library of Scotland

George IV Bridge. All year, exc. first week in Oct. Reading Room: Mon, Tues, Thurs, Fri 09.30-20.30, Wed 10.00-20.30, Sat 09.30-13.00. Exhibitions: Mon-Fri 10.00-17.00 (10.00-20.30 during Festival), Sat 10.00-17.00, Sun 14.00-17.00. Free. Publications counter. Tel: 0131-226 4531.

Founded in 1689, this is one of the four largest libraries in Great Britain. Its unparalled collection on Scottish history and culture is available to researchers, and its frequently changing exhibitions are open to the general public.

Netherbow Arts Centre

43 High Street. All year, Mon-Sat 10.00-16.30 (also in evenings for theatre). Free. Cafe/refreshments. Tel: 0131-556 9579/2647.

A modern arts centre in Edinburgh's Old Town offering a range of exhibitions and performances with an emphasis on the Scottish arts. Open-air courtyard. Restaurant.

New Town Conservation Centre

13A Dundas Street. All year. Mon-Fri 09.00-13.00, 14.00-17.00. Free. Tel: 0131-557 5222.

Headquarters of committee which administers grants for the conservation of the Georgian 'New Town'. There is a display of work in progresss and a conservation reference library. Publications are on sale. There are guided walks from June to September and at other times by arrangement. Particulars from Conservation Centre.

Open Eye Gallery

75/79 Cumberland Street. Jan-Dec. Mon-Fri. 10.00-18.00, Sat 10.00-16.00. Free. Tel: 0131-557 1020.

Contemporary and fine arts gallery, with 17 exhibitions per year showing work by established artists as well as young contemporaries. Regular exhibitions of ceramics, sculpture and innovative jewellery. Print room specialising in early 20th century etchings.

Palace of Holyroodhouse

Foot of the Royal Mile. Apr-Oct 09.30-17.15, Sun 10.30-16.30; Nov-Mar 09.30-15.45 (not Sun). The Palace is also closed during Royal and State Visits and for periods before and after visits; check dates. Tel: 0131-556 7371/0131-556 1096 (recorded information).

The Palace of Holyroodhouse is the official residence of the Queen in Scotland. The oldest part is built against the monastic nave of Holyrood Abbey, little of which remains. The rest of the palace was reconstructed by the architect Sir William Bruce for Charles II. Here Mary, Queen of Scots lived for six years; here she met John Knox; here Rizzio was murdered, and here Prince Charles Edward Stuart held court in 1745. State apartments, house tapestries and paintings; the picture gallery has portraits of over 70 Scottish kings, painted by De Wet in 1684-86.

Parliament House

Parliament Square, behind the High Kirk of St. Giles, Royal Mile. All year, Tue-Fri 10.00-16.00. Free. Tel: 0131—225 2595.

Built 1632-39 this was the seat of Scottish government until 1707, when the governments of Scotland and England were united. Now the Supreme Law Courts of Scotland. See the Parliament Hall with fine hammer beam roof and portraits by Raeburn and other major Scottish artists. Access (free) to the splendid Signet Library on an upper floor is by prior written request only, to: The Librarian, Signet Library, Parliament House, Edinburgh. Outside is the mediaeval Mercat Cross, which was restored in 1885 by W E Gladstone. Royal proclamations are still read from its platform. Restaurant.

The People's Story

Housed in the Canongate Tolbooth, near the foot of Royal Mile. Mon-Sat 10.00-17.00 (June to Sept 10.00-18.00). During the Edinburgh Festival: Sun 14.00-17.00. Free. Tel: 0131-225 2424, ext 4057.

The Canongate Tolbooth, which was built in 1591, now houses The People's Story. The museum tells of the lives, works and leisure of ordinary people in the Scottish capital from the late 18th century to the present day. It has reconstructions of a cooper's workshop, a steamie, a 1940s kitchen and many more displays based on first hand accounts of Edinburgh life. Lift and adapted toilets for disabled visitors.

Royal Botanic Garden
Inverleith Row, Arboretum Place (car parking). Jan-Dec exc Christmas and New Year. Daily Sept-Oct 10.00-18.00. May-Aug 10.00-20.00. Mar-Apr 10.00-18.00. Nov-Feb 10.00-16.00. Free. Plant houses 10.00 (Sun 11.00) to 17.00, summer; 10.00 (Sun 11.00) to 30 minutes before sunset, winter. Free. Parking available. Terrace cafe. Specialist gifts and plants for sale. Tel: 0131-552 7171.
The Royal Botanic Garden has a world famous rock garden and probably the biggest collection of rhododendrons in the world. The unique exhibition plant houses show a great range of exotic plants displayed as indoor landscapes and a plant exhibition hall displays many aspects of botany and horticulture. Tearoom and publications counter.

Royal Commonwealth Pool & Nautilus Flume Complex
From Princes Street turn onto North Bridge, follow road for about 1m, turn left onto Salisbury Place, then right into Salisbury Road; pool is on left. All year. Entrance charge. Parking available. Cafeteria. Tel: 0131-667 7211.
50m swimming pool, diving pool, teaching pool, Nautilus Flume Complex (Europe's largest indoor flume). Cafeteria. Fitness centre.

Royal Lyceum Theatre Company
Grindlay Street. All year. Group rates. Tel: 0131-229 9697.
Resident company in fine Victorian theatre. Up to 12 plays a year. 3 bars, restaurant. Facilities: easy booking; disabled access; concessions; tours and more.

Royal Museum of Scotland
Chambers Street. Jan-Dec. Mon-Sat 10.00-17.00, Sun 12.00-17.00. Free. Tearoom. Tel: 0131-225 7534.
Part of the National Museums of Scotland in a fine Victorian building. Houses the national collections of decorative arts of the world, ethnography, natural history, geology, technology and science. Special exhibitions, lectures, gallery talks, films and other activities for adults and children. Tearoom.

Royal Observatory
Blackford Hill. Apr-Sept, Mon-Fri 10.00-16.00, Sat, Sun, holidays 12.00-17.00. Oct-Mar, daily 13.00-17.00. Entrance charge. Parking available. Gift Shop. Tel: 0131-668 8405.
Situated at the home of the Royal Observatory and University Department of Astronomy, the Visitor Centre demonstrates the work of astronomers, especially with telescopes in Australia and Hawaii. Also on show is the largest telescope in Scotland. Wide ranging bookshop, fine views of Edinburgh from hill. Alternative entrance for wheelchairs.

Royal Scottish Academy
At the foot of the Mound, on Princes Street. Mon-Sat 10.00-17.00, Sun 14.00-17.00. Entrance charge. Tel: 0131-225 6671.
The Academy has annual exhibitions and special Festival exhibitions. Ramped wheelchair entrance at side.

St. Cecilia's Hall
The Cowgate, off the Grassmarket. Jan-Dec, Wed, Sat 14.00-17.00. Sun 14.00-17.00. Entrance charge. Parking available. Gift shop. Tel: 0131-667 1011, ext 4577/4415.
This elegant concert hall was built for the Edinburgh Musical Society in 1762. Restored by the University of Edinburgh in 1968, it houses the Russell Collection of Early Keyboard Instruments.

St. Cuthbert's Church
Lothian Road. Open with guides Jun-Sep, Mon-Fri 10.30-15.30; other times by arrangement. Free. Tel: 0131-229 1142.
An ancient church, the 'West Kirk', rebuilt by Hippolyte Blanc in 1894. The tower is 18th century, and there is a monument to Napier of Merchiston, inventor of logarithms. Thomas de Quincey is buried in the churchyard. Coffee served Tuesday mornings.

St. Giles Cathedral
High Street, Royal Mile. Winter: Mon-Sat 09.00-17.00. Sun 12.00-17.00. Summer: Mon-Sat 09.00-19.00, Sun 13.00-17.00. Also open for services. Occasionally closed for weddings, ceremonies etc. Please check before travelling any distance. Free (donation for Thistle Chapel). Gift shop. Restaurant. Tel: 0131-225 9442.
There has been a church here since the 9th century. Of the present building, the tower is late 15th century. At one time, there were four churches here, and yet another served as a prison. See also the exquisite Thistle Chapel. In the street outside the west door is the Heart of Midlothian, a heart-shaped design in the cobblestones. It marks the site of the Old Tol-

booth, built 1466, which was stormed in the 1736 Porteous Riots and demolished in 1817. Restaurant.

St. John's Church
W end of Princes Street. All reasonable times. Free. Tel: 0131-229 7565.
An impressive 19th-century church, the nave of which was built in 1817 by William Burn. There is a fine collection of Victorian stained glass. SPCK bookshop, Peace and Justice Resource Centre, One World Shop, Corner Stone Restaurant and the International Voluntary Service.

St. Mary's Cathedral
In Palmerston Place, West End. Mon-Sat 07.30 (Morning prayers) 18.15, Sun 08.00-19.00. Occasionally later in summer. Shop. Tel: 0131-225 6293.
Built 1879, with the western towers added in 1917. The central spire is 276 feet high and the interior is impressive. Nearby is the charming Easter Coates House, built in the late 17th century with some stones filched from the old town; it is now St. Mary's Music School. Gardens with seats.

St. Triduana's Chapel
At Restalrig Church, in Restalrig district, 1.5m E of city centre. Opening standard. Free. (HS). Tel: 0131-244 3101.
From the late 15th century the shrine of St. Triduana was situated in the lower chamber of the King's Chapel built by James III, adjacent to Restalrig Church. The design, a two storey vaulted hexagon, is unique. The lower chapel of St. Triduana survives intact but the upper chamber was demolished in 1560.

The Scotch Whisky Heritage Centre
354 Castlehill, The Royal Mile. Jan-Dec, exc. Xmas and New Year's Day. Daily, 10.00-17.00. Extended hours June-Sept. Entrance charge. Whisky and gift shop. Tel: 0131-220 0441.
A visit brings the story of Scotch Whisky to life. Find out how and where whisky is made from a guided tour and audio-visual show. Travel in a whisky barrel through the history of Scotch Whisky with sound effects, aromas and commentary (choice of 7 languages). Whisky and gift shop.

Scott Monument
In Princes Street Gardens. Oct-Mar, Mon-Sat 10.00-15.00; Apr-Sept, Mon-Sat 10.00-18.00. Entrance charge. Small shop. Tel: 0131-225 2424.
Completed in 1844, a statue of Sir Walter Scott

and his dog Maida, under a canopy and spire 200 feet high, with 64 statuettes of Scott characters. Fine view of the city from the top.

Scottish Agricultural Museum
Ingliston, nr. Edinburgh Airport. May-Sept, Mon-Fri 10.00-17.00. Jun-Aug, also Sat 10.00-17.00. Oct-Apr, Wed only 10.00-17.00. Open to groups outside normal hours/season. Parking available. Shops. Tearoom. Tel: 0131-333 2674 or 0131 225 7534, ext. 313.
Scotland's national museum of country life. Farming, old trades and skills, social and home life. Fascinating displays, old photographs, audio visual presentation. Teas, shop, parking, disabled facilities and access.

Scottish Experience and Living Craft Centre
High Street, opposite John Knox's House. Jan-Dec, exc Xmas and New Year. Daily, 10.00-18.00. Entrance charge. Shops. Restaurant. Tel: 0131-557 9350.
Scottish craftspeople in a small complex of workshops, weaving tartan, making kilts and Aran sweaters, making pottery - visitors can try throwing a pot - working Scottish jewellery and sgian dhubhs. Bagpipe workshop shows how pipes are made and how to play them - pipes and chanters for sale. Ancestral research undertaken, information about Scottish clans and tartan history. Exhibition of Highland dress through the ages. Film theatre and Scottish fare.

Scottish National Gallery of Modern Art
Belford Road. All year, Mon-Sat 10.00-17.00, Sun 14.00-17.00 (extended hours during Festival). Prints and Drawings room open by arrangement between 10.00-12.00, 14.30-16.30 Mon-Fri. Free. Parking available. Cafe. Tel: 0131-556 8921.
Scotland's collection of 20th-century painting, sculpture and graphic art, with masterpieces by Derain, Matisse, Braque, Hepworth, Picasso and Giacometti; and work by Hockney, Caulfield and Sol Le Witt. Also Scottish School. Cafe.

Scottish National Portrait Gallery
E end of Queen Street. Mon-Sat 10.00-17.00 (extended hours during Festival), Sun 14.00-17.00. Free. Print Room and Reference Section open 10.00-12.00, 14.30-16.30 Mon-Fri. Cafe. Tel: 0131-556 8921.
Illustrates the history of Scotland through portraits of the famous men and women who contributed to it in all fields of activity from the 16th century to the present day, such as Mary, Queen of Scots, James VI and I, Flora MacDonald, Robert Burns, Sir Walter Scott, David

Hume and Ramsay MacDonald. The artists include Raeburn, Ramsay, Reynolds and Gainsborough. Reference section of engravings and photographs including calotypes by Hill and Adamson.

Scout Museum
Valleyfield Street, Tollcross. Jan-Dec exc public hols. Mon-Fri 09.30-16.30. Please check opening times by telephone. Free. Donation box. Tel: 0131-229 3756.
Based within Area Scout offices, an exhibition of the history of the Scout movement in Edinburgh and worldwide, with photographs, books, uniforms and badges.

Stills
105 High Street, halfway down Royal Mile. Up small flight of steps. Jan-Dec, exc public hols. Tues-Sat 11.00-17.30. Free. Tel: 0131-557 1140.
Stills is a photography gallery showing Scottish and international photography, with an emphasis on contemporary work. Education activities support exhibitions, and there is a specialist photography bookshop.

Talbot Rice Gallery
University of Edinburgh, Old College, South Bridge. Tues-Sat 10.00-17.00. Usually free. Closed certain Sats if no special exhibition, check press or Tel: 0131-650 2210/1/2/3.
Edinburgh University's Torrie Collection and changing exhibitions are on public display in this fine building, part of the University of Edinburgh, begun by Robert Adam in 1789 and completed by William Playfair around 1830. Visitors are invited to view the fine architecture of Robert Adam and William Playfair in the Old College building.

Sir Jules Thorne Historical Museum
At rear of Royal College of surgeons of Edinburgh, 18 Nicolson Street. Jan-Dec exc public hols. Mon-Fri 14.00-16.00. Free. Donations invited. Tel: 0131-556 6206.
Historic exhibition of 'Edinburgh and Medicine'. Lower floor of the hall illustrates the history of surgery in general, and Edinburgh's special contribution from 1505 to the present. Facsimiles of many precious records are displayed, such as the Queen Mary Charter of 1567, and artefacts connected with notable Edinburgh figures in early medical history. Sections are devoted to distinguished surgeons such as Sir Charles Bell, Liston and Syme, and to less worthy personalities such as Burke and Hare.

369 Gallery
233 Cowgate. Jan-Dec. Tues-Sat 12.00-18.00. Free. Tel: 0131-225 3013.
Art gallery, mounting new exhibitions every month.

Traverse Theatre
Cambridge Street, next to Usher Hall and Lyceum. Jan-Dec. Daily 10.00-01.00. Bar 12.00-24.00 (Fri, Sat 01.00). Charge for performances. Restaurant and bar. Inductive loop. Tel: 0131-228 1404.
Britain's acclaimed theatre for new writing has pioneered work by new writers for the last thirty year, and has launched the careers of many actors, directors and writers. Now in a new theatre in the heart of the city.

University Collection of Historic Musical Instruments
Reid Concert Hall, Bristo Square. All year, Wed 15.00-17.00, Sat 10.00-13.00. Free. Tel: 0131-447 4791 & 0131-650 2423.
The collection now consists of over 1,000 instruments and is maintained by the University for the purposes of research, performance and support for teaching. Some 350 are woodwind, over 150 are brass, about 250 stringed and the rest percussion, bagpipes, ethnographic and acoustical instruments. Study room by arrangement.

Usher Hall
From West End of Princes Street, turn onto Lothian Road; Usher Hall is on left. Please contact the Usher Hall for further details. Tel: 0131-228 1155.
Edinburgh's premier concert hall which offers a wide and exciting range of concerts and dance performances.

West Register House
W side of Charlotte Square. Mon-Fri. Exhibitions: 10.00-16.00. Search Room: 09.00-16.45. Free. Tel: 0131-556 6585.
Formerly St. George's Church, 1811, this now holds the more modern documents of the Scottish Record Office. Permanent exhibition on many aspects of Scottish history, including the Declaration of Arbroath, 1320. No guide dogs.

White Horse Close
Off Canongate, Royal Mile.
A restored group of 17th-century buildings off the High Street. The coaches to London left from White Horse Inn (named after Queen Mary's Palfrey), and there are Jacobite links.

Zoo
Entrance from Corstorphine Road, 3 miles W of city centre on A8. Open every day of the year.

April-Sept 09.00-18.00. Oct-Mar 09.00-16.30. (Sundays open 09.30). Entrance charges. Parking available. Gift shops. Restaurant. Tearoom. Cafeteria. Kiosks in summer months. Bar. Children's play area. Tel: 0131-334 9171.

Established in 1913 by the Royal Zoological Society of Scotland, this is one of Britain's leading zoos, with a large and varied collection of mammals, birds and reptiles in extensive grounds on Corstorphine Hill. Edinburgh Zoo is world famous for its large breeding colony of Antarctic Penguins. Restaurants, bars, adventure playground and shops.

LOTHIAN

Abercorn Church
Off unclassified road 2m N of A904, by Hopetoun, South Queensferry. All year, daily. Free. Tel: 0131-331 1869.

Ancient church dedicated to St. Serf, founded in 5th century. Abercorn was the first bishopric in Scotland dating from AD 681. Present building, on site of 7th century monastery, dates from 12th century (see Norman Arch in S wall), reconstructed in 1579 and 1893. Display of 8th century Anglian crosses and hogback monuments; Duddingston aisle 1603; Binns aisle 1618. Also Hopetoun gallery and retiring rooms: 1704.

Almond Valley Heritage Centre
Millfield, Kirkton North at western edge of Livingston off A705. Jan-Dec. Daily 10.00-17.00. Entrance charge. Parking available. Shop. Tearoom. Tel: (01506) 414957.

Through museum displays and a range of open-air features extending over 16 acres, the Heritage Centre brings West Lothian's past to life. Traditional farm steading with friendly animals, working watermill, oil worker's cottage and 'mine' in the shale oil museum. Old farm machinery and narrow gauge railway. Horse-drawn cart rides to outlying fields, nature trail, play park, picnic area.

Almondell and Calderwood Country Park
On B7015 (A71) at East Calder or off A89 at Broxburn. 12m SSW of Edinburgh. Visitor Centre opening hours. Apr-Sept Mon-Wed 09.00-17.00, Thur 09.00-16.00, Sun 10.30-18.00. Oct-Mar Mon-Thur 09.00-17.00, Sun 10.00-16.30 closed for lunch 12.00-13.00. Free except for barbecues (small booking charge). Parking available. Tel: Mid Calder (01506) 882 254.

Extensive riverside and woodland walks in former estate, with large picnic and grassy areas. Visitor Centre housed in old stable block has large freshwater aquaria, displays on natural and local history, and short slide show.

Ranger Service, guided walks programme in summer.

Antonine Wall
From Bo'ness to Old Kilpatrick, best seen off A803 E of Bonnybridge, 12m S of Stirling. All reasonable times. Free. (HS). Tel: 0131—244 3101.

This Roman fortification stretched from Bo'ness on the Forth to Old Kilpatrick on the Clyde. Built about AD 142-143, it consisted of a turf rampart behind a ditch, with forts about every two miles. It was probably abandoned about AD 163. Remains are probably best preserved in the Falkirk/Bonnybridge area, notably Rough Castle, and at Bearsden.

Athelstaneford Church
Off B1343, 4m N of Haddington. All reasonable times. Free; donations. Tel: (0162088) 249 or (0162088) 378.

The plaque by the church tells the story of the origins of St Andrews Cross (the Saltire), which was first adopted as the Scottish flag at this place. A floodlit flag flies permanently on the site.

Bass Rock
Off North Berwick. Boat trips from North Berwick go round the Bass Rock. Tel: (01620) 2838 (boat trips) or (01620) 2197 (Tourist Information Centre).

A massive 350-feet-high rock, 1 mile in circumference, 3.25 miles ENE of North Berwick whose many thousands of raucous seabirds include the third largest gannetry in the world. Once a Covenanters' prison. Accessible on SW side only.

Beecraigs Country Park, Linlithgow
From Linlithgow take Preston Road S for 2m, signposted on left. Country Park open all year; Visitor Centre all year, 08.30-17.00. Free. Tel: (01506) 844516.

700 acre country park with nature trails, trout farm, deer farm, country crafts, trim course and plenty of opportunities for a variety of sporting pursuits.

Birkhill Clay Mine
From Bo'ness take A706 towards Linlithgow, right at crossroads at top of hill, 2m to Upper Kinneil Farm, turn right down unclassified signposted road. Early Apr-late Oct, weekends only. Mid-July-Aug, daily 11.00-16.00 (last tour). Entrance charge. Openings coincide with Bo'ness & Kinneil Railway. Parking. Tel: (01506) 825855 (24 hrs).

Fireclay mine. Discover the secrets of fireclay

deep in the underground tunnels at the heart of the mine. See 300-million-year-old fossils, learn how miners worked the clay. Meadow walk, ancient woodlands. Small shop selling confectionary/refreshments. Mine tour not accessible to disabled visitors.

Blackness Castle
B903, 4m NE of Linlithgow. Opening standard, except Oct-Mar closed Thur afternoon and Fri. (HS). Tel: 0131—244 3101.
Interesting 15th century castle built out of the shore of the Forth, suggesting a fortified ship in appearance. Once it was one of the most important fortresses in Scotland and was one of the four castles which by the Articles of Union were to be left fortified. Since then it has been a state prison in Covenanting time, a powder magazine in the 1870's, and more recently, for a period, a youth hostel.

Bo'ness & Kinneil Railway
Off Union Street, Bo'ness. Leave M9 at Junction 3 or 5. Open weekends, Apr-Oct, Dec. Also holiday Mons, Apr, May, Aug. Also Wed-Fri, June. Daily, mid Jul-Aug. Check timetable for exact dates and times. Entrance charge. Buffer-stop Cafe. Sales stand. Picnic area. Parking available. Tel: (01506) 822298.
Working steam railway system, with historic locomotive and rolling stock. Live steam and authentic station buildings. Refreshments and sales stand. Buffer Stop Cafe (snacks), picnic area, visitor trail and visitor centre. Free car parking. Steam trains run summer weekends from 12.00-17.00.

Borthwick Church
Off A7, 13m SE of Edinburgh. Parking available. Tel: (01875) 20653.
Nearby is Borthwick Castle (seen from outside only), built about 1430, with twin towers and two wings, one of the strongest and biggest of Scotland's tower houses. Mary, Queen of Scots visited the castle after her marriage to Bothwell. Borthwick Church, largely Victorian with an aisle and a vault dating from the 15th century, an apse originating in the 12th century, 18th and 19th century memorials (particularly Dundas family), and two 15th century effigies thought to be the best preserved in Scotland. Associated with Borthwick family and Clan.

Cairnpapple Hill
Off B792, 3m N of Bathgate. Apr-Sept, standard opening, closed Oct-Mar. Entrance charge. (HS). Tel: 0131-244 3101.
Sanctuary and burial cairns. Originally a Neolithic sanctuary remodelled in the Early

Bronze Age (c 1800 BC) as a monumental open-air temple in the form of a stone circle with enclosing ditch. Later (c 1500 BC) it was despoiled and built over by a Bronze Age Cairn, considerably enlarged several centuries later. Now excavated and laid out.

Castlelaw Fort
Off A702, 7m S of Edinburgh. Open all reasonable times. Free. (HS). Tel: 0131-244 3101.
A small Iron Age hill fort consisting of two concentric banks and ditches. In the older rock-cut ditch an earth-house is preserved. Occupied into Roman times (2nd century AD).

The Chesters Fort
1m S of Drem, unclassified road to Haddington, East Lothian. All times. Free. (HS). Tel: 0131-244 3101.
The Chesters is one of the best examples in Scotland of an Iron Age fort with multiple ramparts.

Crichton Castle
B6367, 7m SE of Dalkeith. Opening standard, Apr-Sept. Closed Oct-Mar. Entrance charge. Parking available. (HS). Tel: 0131—244 3101.
The keep dates from the 14th century, although today's ruins are mostly 15th/17th century. This castle, elaborate in style, has an arcaded range and impressive Italianate facade, including piazza. The upper frontage of which is wrought with faceted stonework and was erected by the Earl of Bothwell in the 16th century. The little Collegiate Church, 0.5m north, dating from 1499 and still in use, is notable for its tower and barrel vaulting. Signposted walk to Borthwick.

Dalkeith Park
At E end of Dalkeith High Street, 7m S of Edinburgh on A68. Apr-Oct, daily 10.00-18.00. Entrance charge. Parking available. Shop. Tearoom. Tel: 0131-663 5684 (11.00-18.00) or 0131-665 3277 outwith these hours.
Woodland walks beside the river in the extensive grounds of Dalkeith Palace. Tunnel walk, adventure woodland play area, nature trails, 18th century bridge and orangery.

Dalmeny House
By South Queensferry, 7m W of Edinburgh, take A90 then B924. May-Sep, Sun 13.00-17.30. Mon & Tues 12.00-17.30. Last admission 16.45. Other times by arrangement only. Entrance charge. Parking available. Tearoom. Tel: 0131-331 1888.
The Primrose family, Earls of Rosebery, have lived here for over 300 years. The present house dates from 1815, in Tudor Gothic style,

built by William Wilkins. Interior Gothic splendour of hammerbeamed hall, vaulted corridors and classical main rooms. Magnificent collection of 18th-century British portraits, French furniture, tapestries, porcelain from the Rothschild Mentmore collection, the Napoleon collection and other works of art. Lovely grounds and 4.5-mile shore walk from Cramond to South Queensferry.

Dalmeny Kirk
Off A90, 7m W of Edinburgh, 2m E of South Queensferry in Dalmeny. All year, daily on request. Free. Tel: 0131-331 1869.
Dedicated to St. Cuthbert, Dalmeny Kirk has been described as the most complete example of a Romanesque (Norman) church in Scotland. Built C1130-50, the church consists of a modern West Tower (1934); the original nave, chancel and semi-circular apse; the South Doorway with exquisitely carved arches. On the north side is the Rosebery aisle and crypt built in 1671 by Sir Archibald Primrose. The stained glass windows in the apse were gifted by a Polish army officer at the end of World War II. The church was restored in 1927-37, and in 1992.

Deep-Sea World
North Queensferry. Follow signs to Forth Road Bridge. From S, take first exit to North Queensferry. From N, take exit 1 and follow signs to North Queensferry. Jan-Dec exc Xmas and New Year. Daily 09.00-18.00. Entrance charges. Parking available. Gift shop. Shark Bite Restaurant. Tel: (01383) 411411.
Visitors have a 'diver's eye view' of thousands of fish as they travel along transparent tunnels on an underwater safari beneath the Firth of Forth. Wet and dry interactive exhibits in this, the largest single fish display in the northern hemisphere, include octopus display, corals, tropical fish, rock pools, audio visual.

Dirleton Castle
A198, 8m W of North Berwick. Opening standard. (HS). Tel: 0131-244 3101.
Near the wide village green of Dirleton, these beautiful ruins date back to 1225 with 15th/17th century additions. The castle had an eventful history from its first siege by Edward I in 1298 until its destruction in 1650. The 'clustered' donjon dates from the 13th century and the garden encloses a 17th century bowling green surrounded by yews.

Dunbar Leisure Pool
Castlepark, Dunbar. May-Sep, daily 10.00-20.00. Oct-Apr, 10.00-17.00 (Thur, Fri 20.00). Entrance charges. Parking available. Restaurant/tearoom. Tel: (01368) 65456.
Sited on a clifftop near Dunbar Castle, attractive complex has 25-metre, 6-lane swimming pool with water features, health suite, function and activity hall. Indoor beach area for waterplay for swimmers of all ages, yellow, 'banana' flume with speedometer so that swimmers can check the speed of their descent.

Forth Bridges
Queensferry, 10m W of Edinburgh.
For over 800 years travellers were ferried across the Firth of Forth. Queensferry was named from Queen Margaret who regularly used this passage between Dunfermline and Edinburgh in the 11th century. The ferry ceased in 1964 when the Queen opened the Forth Road Bridge, a suspension bridge then the longest of its kind in Europe (1,993 yards). Also here is the rail bridge of 1883-90, one of the greatest engineering feats of its time. It is 2,765 yards long.

Gleneagles Crystal
37 Simpson Road, East Mains Industrial Estate, Broxburn. Jan-Dec exc Xmas and New Year. Mon-Sat 10.00-17.00, Sun 12.00-17.00. Free. Parking available. Shop. Coffee. Tel: (01506) 852566.
Factory where production of Gleneagles of Edinburgh hand-cut crystal can be seen from the viewing gallery. Factory shop with large selection of glass.

Glenkinchie Distillery
From Pencaitland village, take Lempockwells road past farm, then right at crossroads. Distillery can be seen in glen. Jan-Dec exc Xmas and New Year. Mon-Fri 09.30-16.30. Parking available. Gift shop. Tel: (01875) 340451.
Set in a tiny valley, Glenkinchie, the only remaining malt whisky distillery close to Edinburgh, shows aspects of all the traditional distilling crafts, from malt storage to warehousing the whisky. The original floor maltings now house a collection of whisky artefacts, including a scale model of a malt distillery made for the British Empire Exhibition of 1924.

Gosford House
Longniddry. Jun & Jul, Wed, Sat & Sun 14.00-17.00. Parking available. Tel: (0187 57) 201.
In fine setting on the Firth of Forth. Central part of the house by Robert Adam, 1800. North and south wings by William Young, 1890. South wing contains celebrated marble hall. Ornamental waters with wildlife including

(since 1983) nesting wild geese. Prior notice preferred for disabled visitors.

Hailes Castle
Off A1, 5m E of Haddington. Keykeeper monument. (HS). Tel: 0131-244 3101.
13th/15th century stronghold in oddly low-lying situation. Here Bothwell brought Mary, Queen of Scots on their flight from Borthwick Castle in 1567. There is a fine 16th-century chapel.

The Heritage of Golf
West Links Road, Gullane, 14m ENE of Edinburgh. Open by appointment. Free. Tel: (0187 57) 277.
The exhibition shows how the game of golf developed after it arrived in Scotland from Holland in the 15th century. The visitor can see the simple origins, the natural materials and the skill of the early makers; and the development of golf from early days to the present.

Hopetoun House
W of South Queensferry, Easter-Sept, daily 10.00-17.00 (last admission 16.45). Tel: 0131—331 2451 (09.00-17.00).
This great Adam mansion is the home of the Hope family, Earls of Hopetoun and later Marquesses of Linlithgow. Started in 1699 to the designs of Sir William Bruce, it was enlarged between 1721-54 by William Adam and his son, Robert. The mansion still contains much of the original furniture from the 1760's and many portraits, which include, Rubens, Rembrandt and Canaletto. The extensive grounds include deer parks with fallow and red deer and St Kilda sheep. Also sea walk, formal rose gardens, educational day centre and stables museum featuring 'Horse and Man in Lowland Scotland'. Nature trail, licensed restaurant. Family museum, rooftop viewing platform. Free parking.

The House of the Binns
Off A904, 4m E of Linlithgow. Easter weekend, May-Sept, daily. exc Fri, 14.00-17.00. Last tour 16.30. Entrance charges. Guided tours only. Parking available. (NTS) Tel: (0150 683) 4255.
Occupied for more than 350 years, The Binns dates largely from the time of General Tam Dalyell, 1615-1685, and his father. It reflects the early 17th-century transition in Scottish architecture from fortified stronghold to gracious mansion. There are magnificent plaster ceilings, fine views across the Forth and a visitor trail.

Inchcolm Abbey
On Inchcolm Island in the Firth of Forth; check South Queensferry for boat trips or hire. Apr-
Sept, opening standard. Oct-Mar, closed. Entrance charge. Parking available. (HS). Tel: 0131-244 3101.
The monastic buildings, which include a fine 13th century octagonal chapter house, are the best preserved in Scotland.

Inveresk Lodge Garden
S of Musselburgh, A6124, 7m E of Edinburgh. All year, Mon-Fri 10.00-16.30, Sun 14.00-17.00. (NTS). Tel: 0131-226 5922.
This garden of a 17th-century house (not open to the public) displays a range of plants suitable for the small garden. Good shrub rose border and selection of climbing roses.

Kinneil Museum and Roman Fortlet
In Bo'ness, 16m WNW of Edinburgh on A904 (adjacent to Kinneil House). Apr-Sept, Mon-Sat 10.00-17.00, Sun (Jun, Jul, Aug only) 10.00-17.00. Oct-Apr, Sat only 10.00-17.00. Free. Museum shop. Tel: (01324) 24911, ext. 2472.
Converted 17th century stables, with displays of Bo'ness Pottery and cast iron work. An exhibition entitled '2000 years of history' provides an insight into the estate's colourful history and provides guidance for viewing the remaining monuments, including a consolidated Roman fortlet, medieval house, church & village remains,and James Watt's cottage. History tours of the estate by costumed interpreters is available by calling (0506) 824318.

Lennoxlove House
On B6369, 1m S of Haddington. Easter Weekend and May-Sept, Wed, Sat, Sun 14.00-17.00. Entrance charges. Parking available. Gift shop. Tearoom. Gardens. Tel: (01620) 823720.
Originally named Lethington, it was owned for centuries by the Maitlands, one of whom was Secretary to Mary, Queen of Scots. In 1672 the Duchess of Lennox, (La Belle Stewart who was the model for Britannia on the coinage), bought and bequethed it to Lord Blantyre, stipulating that it be renamed "Lennoxlove" in memory of her devotion to her husband. House has a threefold interest: its historic architecture; the association of the proprietors with the Royal House of Stewart; and the Hamilton Palace collection of portraits, furniture and porcelain. Gardens. Tearoom.

Linlithgow Palace
S shore of loch, Linlithgow. Opening standard. Entrance charge. Parking available. (HS). Tel: 0131—244 3101.
The splendid ruined Palace overlooking the loch is the successor to an older building which was burned down in 1424. The Chapel and

Great Hall are late 15th-century and the fine quadrangle has a richly-carved 16th-century fountain. In 1542 Mary, Queen of Scots was born here while her father, James V, lay dying at Falkland Palace. In 1746 the palace was burned, probably by accident, when occupied by General Hawley's troops. George V held a court in the Lyon Chamber here in 1914. This now roofless palace still represents one of the most remarkable achievements in Scottish mediaeval architecture.

Livingston Arena
5 Almondvale West, centre of Livingston, West Lothian. Aug-Apr. Daily 10.00-22.00. Entrance charges. Parking available. Cafeteria. Lounge bar/restaurant. Tel: (01506) 462222.
Olympic-size ice pad for curling, skating, and ice hockey, one of Scotland's most modern ice sports facilities, with 800 pairs of skates for hire. Host for national and international events.

Luffness
1m E of Aberlady on A198. By arrangement. Free. Parking available. (Luffness Ltd). Tel: (0187 57) 218.
A 16th-century castle with a 13th-century keep built on the site of a Norse camp. There are extensive old fortifications, an old moat and gardens.

Maid of the Forth
Hawes Pier, South Queensferry, 7 miles W of Edinburgh. Easter-Sept. Daily. Sailing schedule on request. Charge for cruises. Parking available. Gift shop, tearoom and bar on board. Tel: 0131-331 4857.
Boat trip under the Forth Bridge and downriver to Inchcolm Island to visit 12th-century Augustinian abbey. Bird Sanctuary, seals may also be seen. Full commentary on the way. Cruise time 2.5 hours, including 1.5 hours on Inchcolm.

Malleny House Gardens
In Balerno, off A70, 7.5m SW of Edinburgh. Gardens: open all year, daily 10.00-sunset. Parking available. (NTS). Tel: 0131-226 5922.
Adjoining a 17th-century house (not open) is a garden with many interesting plants including a good collection of shrub roses. The National Bonsai Collection for Scotland is housed here. No dogs.

John Muir Country Park
W side of Dunbar, East Lothian. Jan-Dec. All times. Free. Parking available. Tel: (01368) 63886.
Country park, established 1976 and named after John Muir who lived in Dunbar before

emigrating to America. He was in the forefront of the movement to establish the National Parks in America - Yosemite, Sequoia and General Grant National Parks. The country park extends for 8.5 miles from Dunbar Castle, with a variety of natural habitats to explore including cliffs, dunes, saltmarsh and woodlands. Clifftop trail gives access to the coastline.

John Muir House
126-128 High Street, Dunbar. Jun-Sept or by arrangement with Dunbar T.I.C. Free. Parking available. Tel: (01368) 63353 (T.I.C.).
Birthplace of John Muir, famous American conservationist and author. The top flat has been restored to the period (1838).

Museum of Flight
By East Fortune Airfield, off B1347, 4.5m S of North Berwick. Apr-Sept, daily 10.30-16.30, and several open days. (NMS). Tel: (0162 088) 308.
Aircraft on display at this World War II former RAF airfield range from a supersonic Lightening fighter to the last Comet 4 which was in airline service. The varied collection also includes a Spitfire, a 1930 Puss Moth and a 'Blue Streak' rocket. Special exhibitions relate to the development of fighter aircraft from 1914 to 1940 and to the airship R34 which flew from East Fortune to New York in 1919. Toilets, picnic area. Free car and coach park.

Myreton Motor Museum
Off A198, 17m from Edinburgh and 6m SW of North Berwick. May-Oct, daily 10.00-18.00; Nov-Apr, daily 10.00-17.00. Parking available. Tel: (0187 57) 288.
A varied collection of road transport from 1897, including motor cars, cycles, motorcycles, commercials, World War II military vehicles and automobilia. Catalogue and children's quiz book.

Niddry Castle
10m W of Edinburgh, turn off A89 1m W of Newbridge. May-Sept, Sun only 14.00-16.30. At other times by arrangement for groups. Donations. Tel: (01506) 890 753.
Late 15th-century Scottish Castle, a refuge for Mary, Queen of Scots, now being restored from a crumbling ruin to its former splendour. Also archaeological dig.

North Berwick Law
S of North Berwick, off B1347. All times. Free.
The 613-ft volcanic rock is a fine viewpoint and is crowned by a watch tower dating from

Napoleonic times, and an archway made from the jawbone of a whale.

North Berwick Museum
School Road. Easter-end May, Sat and Mon 10.00-13.00, 14.00-17.00, Fri and Sun 14.00-17.00. Jun-mid Sept, Mon-Sat 10.00-13.00, 14.00-17.00, Sun 14.00-17.00. Mid Sept-late Oct, Sat & Mon 10.00-13.00, 14.00-17.00, Fri & Sun 14.00-17.00. Free. Tel: (01620) 3470.
A compact museum with galleries devoted to natural history, archaeology and the life of the North Berwick area, housed on the upper floor of a former school. Special exhibitions are arranged in June to August.

Ormiston Market Cross
At Ormiston, B6371, 2m S of Tranent. (HS). Tel: 0131-244 3101.
A 15th century cross in the main street.

Polkemmet Country Park
From Whitburn take B7066 W for 2m. Signposted on right-hand side. All year. Facilities vary according to season and weather. Park free, charge for activities. Restaurant. Bar. Parking available. Tel: (01501) 43905.
Converted stables and barn. Remnants of old mansion house owned previously by the Baillie family. Restaurant, bar, visitor centre. 9-hole golf course and floodlit driving range. Woodland walks.

Preston Market Cross
0.5m S of Prestonpans, 8m E of Edinburgh. All times. Free. (HS). Tel: 0131-244 3101.
An outstanding Scottish market cross, the only one that still stands where and as it was built. The tall shaft, surmounted by a unicorn, stands on a circular structure with niches and a parapet. It was probably erected by the Hamiltons of Preston after they obtained the right to hold a fair in 1617.

Preston Mill and Phantassie Doocot
Off A1 at East Linton, 6m W of Dunbar. 1 Apr-30 Sept, Mon-Sat 11.00-13.00, 14.00-17.00, Sun 14.00-17.00; 1-31 Oct, Sat 11.00-13.00, 14.00-16.30, Sun 14.00-16.00 (last tour 20 mins before closing). Parking available. (NTS) Tel: (01620) 860426.
A picturesque water-mill, possibly the only one of its kind still in working condition in Scotland. Nearby is Phantassie Doocot (dovecot), originally containing 500 birds, and the Rennie Memorial, which contains a part of John Rennie's Waterloo Bridge.

Preston Tower and Gardens
Prestonpans, 8 miles E of Edinburgh on B1361.

Tower, by arrangement, all year. Gardens open daily, dawn-dusk, all year. Car parking only. Tel: (01875) 810232 (Mon-Fri) for access to tower.
An imposing 15th-century tower house with a two-storey 17th-century addition. The original three-storeys consist of basements (with dungeon), hall and bedrooms. The upper storeys contain more living accommodation. New stairs exist between the basement and first floor, where once there was only a sealable trap door. The gardens have been restored with elements of Scottish 17th and 18th-century gardens, including laburnum arch, topiary, old-fashioned roses beside seating alcoves, a herb garden and a dovecot.

Prestonpans Battle Cairn
E of Prestonpans on A198. All times. Free. Parking available.
The cairn commemorates the victory of Prince Charles Edward over General Cope at the Battle of Prestonpans in 1745.

Rosslyn Chapel
At Roslin, off A703, 7.5m S of Edinburgh. 1 Apr-31 Oct, Mon-Sat 10.00-17.00, Sun 12.00-16.45. Entrance charge. Coffee shop. Crafts. Tel: 0131—440 2159.
This 15th century chapel is one of Scotland's lovliest and most historic churches, renowned for its magnificent sculpture and Prentice Pillar. It is situated in a beautiful wooded setting near the village of Roslin. Coffee shop and craft shop.

St. Mary's Collegiate Church
Sidegate, Haddington. Apr-Sept, Mon-Sat 10.00-16.00. Sun 13.00-16.00. Donations accepted. Parking available. Gift shop. Tearoom. Tel: (0162 082) 5111.
14th-century medieval church, built on the scale of a cathedral. Choir and transepts badly damaged at siege of Haddington, completely retored (1971-73). Features include fibreglass ceiling, Burne Jones and Sax Shaw windows, East Lothian tapestries, Lauderdale Aisle. The home church of Scots Reformer, John Knox. Nearby, St. Mary's Pleasance.

St. Michael's Parish Church
Beside Linlithgow Palace, on S shore of the loch, Linlithgow. Oct-May, Mon-Fri 10.00-12.00, 14.00-16.00. Jun-Sept, daily 10.00-12.00, 14.00-16.00. Free. Car parking only. Gift shop. Tel: (01506) 842188.
One of the finest examples of a medieval parish church in Scotland. Contemporary 'golden'

crown by Geoffrey Clarke replaced the medieval crown which collapsed in 1820.

Scottish Mining Museum
Prestongrange, on B1348 between Musselburgh and Prestonpans. Apr-Sept. Daily, 11.00-16.00 (last tour 15.00). Entrance charges. Parking available. Gift shop. Refreshments. Tel: 0131—663 7519.
Exhibitions: 'The Miner's Skill and 'Cutting the Coal', on mechanical coal extraction. Cornish beam pumping engine house. Self-drive Coal Heritage Trail to Lady Victoria Colliery. Also on view are steam locomotives, a steam crane, a colliery winding engine and remains of a Hoffman kiln. Special 'Steam Days' on first Sunday of each month, April to October.

Stevenson House
2 miles E of Haddington, signposted from A1. House: 6-week open period, July-mid Aug: Thurs, Sat, Sun 14.00-17.30. Other times by arrangement, Apr-Oct. Guided tour takes minimum 1 hour. Charge. Under 7's free, must be accompanied. Garden: open all year. Honesty box. Parking available. Self-service tea and coffee. Tel: (01620) 823376.
Although the mansion house dates from the 13th century, the present house dates mainly from the 16th century. It was altered both structurally and in decoration during the 18th century. The guided tour includes details of the history, furniture, pictures and china. Well landscaped gardens (both House Garden and Walled Kitchen Garden).

Suntrap
At Gogarbank, between A8 and A71, 6m W of Edinburgh. Garden all year, daily 09.30-dusk. Advice centre all year, Mon-Fri 09.30-16.30; except when staff member is on holiday. 1 Apr-30 Sept also Sat and Sun 14.30-17.00. Parking available. Tel: 0131-339 7283.
A gardening advice centre, of particular interest to owners of small gardens, offering courses of instruction. Outlying department of Oatridge Argicultural College. Special section for disabled gardeners.

Tantallon Castle
A198, 3m E of North Berwick. Opening standard, exc Oct-Mar closed Thur pm and all day Fri. Entrance charge. Parking available. (HS). Tel: 0131-244 3101.
Very impressive fortification in magnificent clifftop setting. Earliest parts date from 14th century. Associated with the Earls of Douglas. Although the castle withstood a regular siege by James V in 1528, it was eventually destroyed by General Monk in 1651.

Torness Power Station
By A1, 6m SE of Dunbar. May-Sept. Guided tours, weekdays and Sats, between 10.00 and 16.00. Free. Refreshments available. Parking available. Tel: (01368) 63500, ext. 3871/2.
Nuclear Power Station. This plant, the most modern power station in Britain, is operated by Scottish Nuclear Ltd and produces a quarter of all the electricity consumed in Scotland.

Torphichen Preceptory
B792, 5m SSW of Linlithgow. Open summer standard, closed in winter. (HS). Tel: 0131-244 3101.
Once the principal Scottish seat of the Knights Hospitallers of St. John. An exhibition depicts the history of the Knights in Scotland and overseas.

Whitekirk
St. Mary's Parish Church: on A198 approach from A1 or from North Berwick. Free. Early-morning-late evening. Sunday worship: 11.30 (unless stated otherwise). Visitors welcome. Parking available. Printed guide available.
The history and architecture of the church date back to 6th century. Large red sandstone building with high square tower (Norman). Famed for pilgrimages in medieval times and a healing well. The tithe barn behind the church is one of the oldest still standing. Its history is linked to St. Baldred.

Winton House
B6355, 6m SW of Haddington. Open by prior arrangement to parties of 10 and over and exceptionally to others. Tel: (01875) 340222.
A gem of Scottish Renaissance architecture dating from 1620. Associations with Charles I and Sir Walter Scott. Beautiful plaster ceilings, unique carved stone chimneys, fine pictures and furniture. Terraced gardens, fine trees, in springtime masses of daffodils. Personally conducted tours.

Wool Stone
In Stenton, B6370, 5m SW of Dunbar. All reasonable times. Free. Parking available.
The medieval Wool Stone, used formerly for the weighing of wool at Stenton Fair, stands on the green. See also the 14th-century Rood Well, topped by a cardinal's hat, and the old doocot.

Yester Parish Church
Gifford, B6369, 5m SSE of Haddington. All reasonable times. Free.
The Dutch-looking church dates from 1708, and in it is preserved a late medieval bell, and also a 17th century pulpit. A tablet near the church

commemorates the Rev John Witherspoon (1723-94), born at Gifford, principal of Princeton University, USA, and the only cleric to sign the American Declaration of Independence. No guide dogs.

FIFE

Abbot House Heritage Centre
Maygate, Dunfermline. All year, daily 10.00-17.00. Abbot's Kitchen restaurant. Book and gift shop. Tel: (01383) 733266.
A heritage centre in one of Scotland's oldest town houses, parts of which date from 1460, in the heart of Scotland's ancient capital. Abbot House, beside historic Dunfermline Abbey where kings and queens including St. Margaret and Robert the Bruce are buried, has been restored and developed to tell the story of Dunfermline and Scotland in an entertaining and interesting way.

Aberdour Castle
At Aberdour, A921, 5m E of Forth Bridge. Opening standard, except closed Thurs pm & Fridays in winter. (HS) Tel: 0131-244 3101.
Overlooking the harbour at Aberdour, the oldest part is the tower, which dates back to the 14th century. To this other buildings were added in succeeding centuries. A fine circular doocot stands nearby, and here also is St. Fillan's Parish Church, part Norman, part 16th century.

Alexander III Monument
By A921 S of Kinghorn at Pettycur Promontory. All times. Free. Parking available.
On the King's Crag, a monument marks the place where Alexander III was killed in a fall from his horse in 1286.

Sir Douglas Bader Garden for the Disabled.
Duffus Park, Cupar. Daily during daylight hours. Tel: (01334) 53722 ext 437.
The garden has raised beds, rock gardens, shrub border, fountains, waterfalls and sheltered seating.

Balbirnie Craft Centre
In Balbirnie Park, Markinch, on eastern outskirts of Glenrothes New Town. All year, exact times vary, but usually Mon-Fri, 10.00-17.00, Sat 12.00-17.00; Sun 13.00-17.00. Free. Parking available. Tel: (01592) 755975.
Craft Centre has seven workshops of potter, leatherworker, jeweller and silversmith, modern furniture maker, stained glass artist, fashion designer and original paintings.

Balcaskie House and Gardens
2 miles W of Pittenweem on B942 Jun-Aug, Sat-Wed 14.00-18.00 (last entry 17.00). Entrance charge. Parking available. Refreshments. Tel: (01333) 311202.
Owned by Sir Ralph Anstruther of That Ilk, Bart., Balcaskie has been in the Anstruther family for nine generations since 1698. The architect Sir William Bruce bought the estate and the existing tower house in 1665. He built the present house and terraced garden, which offers fine views of the Firth of Forth and the Bass Rock, and laid out the formal park and avenues along strong axial vistas.

Balgonie Castle
By Markinch Fife. 2m E of Glenrothes on B921 off A911. All year. Parking available. Tel: (01592) 750119.
14th-century castle with additions to 1702. 17th-century home of Field Marshall Sir Alexander Leslie, made Lord General of the Scottish Covenanting Army and 1st Earl of Leven. Garrisoned by Rob Roy McGregor with 200 clansmen in January 1716. Recently restored 14th-century chapel. 2-acre wildlife garden. Leather carver's workshop and tapestry weaver's studio. Continuing restoration of this family home, and living museum. Educational centre for school visits (no charge).

Balmerino Abbey
On S shore of River Tay on unclassified road 5m SW of Newport. View from outside only. Entrance charge (honesty box). (NTS). Tel: 0131-336 2157.
Cistercian abbey founded in 1229 by Queen Ermingade, second wife of William Lyon. Ruined during period of reformation. Set in particularly peaceful gardens.

British Golf Museum
Opposite Royal & Ancient Golf Club in St. Andrews. May-Oct, daily, 10.00-17.30; Nov, Thur-Tue 10.00-16.00; Dec-Feb, Thur-Mon 11.00-15.00; Mar-Apr, Thur-Mon, 10.00-17.00. Entrance charge. Parking available. Shop. Tel: (01334) 78880.
Interesting memorabilia for all golfing enthusiasts dating back to the time when the now world-famous game was originated in this historic town.

Michael Bruce's Cottage
Kinnesswood off A911, 4m E of Milnathort. Apr-Sept, daily 10.00-18.00. (Keys at The Garage, Kinnesswood). Admission by donation. (Michael Bruce Memorial Trust).
A cottage museum in the birthplace of the Gentle Poet of Loch Leven (1746-1767), who

wrote and improved some of the Scottish paraphrases.

Burleigh Castle
Off A911, 2m NE of Kinross. Opening standard. Free: key-keeper at farm opposite. (HS). Tel: 0131-244 3101.
A fine tower house dating from about 1500. The seat of the Balfours of Burleigh, several times visited by James VI.

Burntisland Museum
Above library, High Street. Open library hours. Parking nearby. Free. Tel: (01592) 260732.
New display - "Burntisland Edwardian Fair". Walk through the sights and sounds of the town's Fair as it was in 1910. Also view local history gallery.

Andrew Carnegie Birthplace Museum
Moodie Street, Dunfermline. Apr-Oct, Mon-Sat 11.00-17.00, Sun 14.00-17.00; Nov-Mar, daily 14.00-16.00. Free. Parking available. Tel: (01383) 724 302.
Weaver's cottage, birthplace of Andrew Carnegie in 1835, and linked Memorial Hall. The displays tell the fascinating story of the weaver's son who emigrated to America and became one of the world's richest men and who then gave away 350 million dollars for the benefit of mankind.

Cowdenbeath Leisure Centre
Pitt Road, Cowdenbeath. 6 miles from Dunfermline. Jan-Dec, Mon-Fri 07.00-21.00. Sat & Sun 09.00-16.30. Entrance charge. Parking available. Tel: (01383) 514520.
Opened in June 1987, Centre has 25-metre main swimming pool and 11-metre toddlers' pool kept at a constant 84 degrees. Multi-gym with free weights and life rower, life cycle power jog and climbmax; sunbeds and sauna.

Crail Museum and Heritage Centre
62-64 Marketgate, Crail. Easter period, Jun-mid Sept, Mon-Sat 10.00-12.30, 14.30-17.00. Sundays and weekends outside main opening period, afternoons only. Free. Parking available. Tel: (01333) 50869.
Exhibits include relics of golf, HMS Jackdaw, the Royal Burgh, the Collegiate Church, local architecture, the old harbour, crafts and Crail past and present. Heritage Centre and Information Office.

Crail Tolbooth
Marketgate, Crail. 9m SE of St. Andrews. Tel: (01333) 50310.
The Tolbooth dates from the early 16th century, displaying a fish weather vane, and a coat of arms dated 1602. In the striking Dutch Tower is a bell dated 1520, cast in Holland. There have been 18th and 19th century additions. Elsewhere in this picturesque fishing village which is the oldest Royal Burgh in the East Neuk of Fife, see the Collegiate Church dating back to the 13th century, the Mercat Cross topped by a unicorn, the harbour and the crowstepped, red-tiled houses. The Tolbooth is a library and Town Hall.

Crawford Arts Centre
93 North Street, St. Andrews. Gallery. All year. Mon-Sat 10.00-17.00, Sun 14.00-17.00. Gallery free. Tel: (01334) 74610.
Arts Centre with exhibition galleries and Studio Theatre. Children's workshops are regularly organised and exhibitions change monthly. Coffee available in galleries. Sculpture Court.

Crook of Devon Fish Farm
5 miles W of Kinross on A977 to Kincardine Bridge. Mar-Oct, then weekends up to Xmas. Daily 10.00-18.00 (20.00 in summer). Entrance and permit charges. Parking available. Shop. Restaurant. Tel: (01577) 840297.
Working trout farm stocking 50,000 rainbow trout in ponds. Bank fishing available. Visitors can feed the trout and visit the "Commando-style" adventure park.

Robinson Crusoe Statue
Lower Largo. All times.
Bronze statue of Alexander Selkirk, the real life mariner on whom Daniel Defoe based his famous character. The statue has stood on the site of his home for over 100 years.

Crystals Arena
Viewfield Road, Glenrothes. Aug-May 09.00-24.00. Entrance charges. Refreshments. Tel: (01592) 773774.
Leisure centre with ice skating, ice hockey, curling, carpet bowls, snooker tables.

Culross
7.5 miles W of Dunfermline. Parking available.
Culross, on the north shore of the River Forth, is a most remarkable example of a small town of the 16th and 17th centuries which has changed little in 300 years. The small 'palace' (NTS) was built between 1597 and 1611 by Sir George Bruce, who developed the sea-going trade in salt and coal from Culross. With crowstepped gables and pantiled roofs, the 'palace' also has outstanding painted ceilings. Other buildings which must be seen include the Study, the Town House, the 13th-century Abbey (HS), the Ark and the Nunnery.

Dogton Stone
Off B922, 5m NW of Kirkcaldy. All reasonable times. Free. Entry by Dogton Farmhouse. (HS). Tel: 0131-244 3101.
An ancient Celtic Cross with traces of animal and figure sculpture.

Dunfermline Abbey and Palace
Monastery Street, Dunfermline. Opening standard exc Oct-Mar, closed Thurs pm and all day Fri. Entrance charge. (HS). Tel: 0131—244 3101.
This great Benedictine house owes its foundation to Queen Margaret, wife of Malcolm Canmore (1057-93) and the foundations of her modest church remain beneath the present nave, a splendid piece of late Norman work. At the east end are the remains of St. Margaret's shrine, dating from the 13th century. Robert the Bruce is buried in the choir, his grave marked by a modern brass. Of the monastic buildings, the ruins of the refectory, pend and guest-house still remain. The guest-house was later reconstructed as a royal palace, and here Charles I was born.

Dunfermline District Museum and Small Gallery
Viewfield Terrace, Dunfermline. All year except public and local holidays. Mon-Sat 11.00-17.00. Free. Small shop. Parking available. (Dunfermline District Council). Tel: (01383) 721814.
The museum, housed in a Victorian villa, has an interesting local history collection, particularly of weaving and linen damask material, the industry that made Dunfermline famous. Special exhibitions are on show regularly. The small gallery which is contained in this museum has a monthly turnover of photographic, art and crafts exhibitions.

Earlshall Castle & Gardens
1m E of Leuchars, off A92, 6 miles from St.Andrews. Apr-Oct, daily 13.00-18.00. Entrance charge. Free admission to garden for visitors in wheelchairs. Gardens, gift shop, tearoom, picnic facilities, woodland walks. Parking available. Tel: (01334) 839205.
Built in 1546 by Sir William Bruce, ancestor of present owners - private family home. Jacobite relics, military trophies and special exhibitions.

East Sands Leisure Centre
In St. Andrews immediately adjacent to East Sands beach. Jan-Dec, Mon-Fri 09.00-22.00, Sat & Sun 09.00-18.00. Entrance Charges. Parking available. Tel: (01334) 76506.
Leisure centre and pool with 50-metre water slide and all facilities.

Falkland Palace and Gardens
A912, 11m N of Kirkcaldy. Apr-Sept, Mon-Sat 10.00-18.00, Sun 14.00-18.00; Oct, Mon-Sat 10.00-17.00, Sun 14.00-17.00. Last tour of palace 1 hour before closing. Entrance charges. Shop. (NTS). Tel: (0133 757) 397.
A lovely Royal Palace in a picturesque little town. The buildings of the Palace, in Renaissance style, date from 1501-41. This was a favourite seat of James V, who died here in 1542, and of his daughter Mary, Queen of Scots. The Royal Tennis Court of 1539 is still played on. The gardens are small but charming.

Fife Folk Museum
At Ceres, 3m SE of Cupar. Apr-Oct, daily (except Fri) 14.15-17.00. Entrance charge. Small Museum Shop. Parking available. Tel: (0133 482) 380 (outwith opening hours).
Situated in the 17th-century Weigh House, near an old bridge in an attractive village, this museum is a growing collection in a unique setting, showing the agricultural and rural life of Fife in bygone times. Countryside annexe opened in 1983. Nearby is the attractive Ceres Church (1806) with a horse-shoe gallery. Alternative wheelchair entrance.

Hill of Tarvit
A916, 2m S of Cupar. House: open weekends during Easter weekend & Apr, Sat & Sun 14.00-18.00; 1 May-30 Sep, daily 14.00-18.00 (last admission 17.30). Garden: grounds open all year, 10.00-sunset. (NTS). Tel: (01334) 53127.
An Edwardian country house of 1696, designed by Sir Robert Lorimer for Mr. Frederick Boner Sharp, an art collector of note. Fine collection of furniture, portraits, paintings, tapestries, chinese porcelain and bronzes. Tearoom (weekends only, Apr, May, Jun, Sep, Oct and daily July, Aug). Lovely gardens, woodland walk to hilltop viewpoint.

Isle of May
Access by boat from Anstruther. Contact Lynn or Jim Raeper, Anstruther Pleasure Trips, 30 Dreelside, Anstruther, Fife. May-Sept. Daily, weather permitting. Kiosk at Anstruther Harbour open 30 mins before sailing times. Charge for trip. Parking on pier. Tel: (01333) 310103.
The Isle of May is a nature reserve with a colony of grey seals and thousands of breeding birds including puffins, razorbills, kittiwakes, guillemots, eider ducks, shags and terns, as well as the remains of a 12th-century chapel. Anstruther Pleasure Trips also take coastal and fishing trips.

Kellie Castle and Gardens
On B9171, 3m NNW of Pittenweem, 10m S of St. Andrews. Castle: Weekends in April 14.00-18.00. Easter, May-Sept, daily 14.00-18.00. Oct, daily 14.00-17.00 (last tour 16.15). Garden and grounds daily 10.00-sunset. Entrance charges. Parking available. Tearoom (NTS) Tel: (013338) 271.

Fine architecture of the 16th/17th centuries, though the earliest parts date from the 14th century. Owned by the Oliphants for over 250 years, then by the Earls of Mar and Kellie, it was restored nearly a century ago by Professor James Lorimer. His grandson, the sculptor Hew Lorimer, is resident custodian. Notable plaster work and painted panelling. 4 acres of fine Victorian gardens.

Kirkcaldy Museum and Art Gallery
By railway station. All year, exc. public holidays, Mon-Sat 11.00-17.00, Sun 14.00-17.00. Free. Tel: (01592) 260732.

Visit this award-winning museum to see the heritage of Kirkcaldy District in a unique collection of fine Scottish paintings, a fascinating new historical display and a full programme of changing art, craft and local history exhibitions. Gallery shop for crafts, cards and local publications.

Kirkcaldy Ice Rink
Rosslyn Street, Kirkcaldy. Signposted, Jan-Dec 09.00-24.00. Entrance charges. Parking available. Gift shop. Restaurant, refreshments. Tel: (01592) 52151.

Ice rink, established 1938, home of Scottish Curling Championships. Multi-purpose facility used for concerts, shows and other events.

Kirkcaldy Swimming Pool
Esplanade, near town centre. Jan-Dec. Mon & Tue 08.00-18.30, Wed & Thur 08.00-20.00, Fri 08.00-19.00, Sat & Sun 08.00-16.00. Fitness room and Sauna suite open to 20.00, Mon-Fri. Entrance charges. Car parking only. Cafe. Tel: (01592) 265366.

Opened in 1971, this building is a popular activity centre offering casual and competitive swimming, sauna, sunbeds, fitness room. Kirkcaldy residents used to swim in the harbour before the pool opened.

Knockhill Racing Circuit
By Dunfermline, 5 miles N of M90 on A823. Jan-Dec. Entrance charges. Parking available. Restaurant, cafe. Tel: (01383) 723337 or 622090.

Racing track featuring motor and motorcycle events almost every Sunday from April to mid-October. High speed racing action, trackside parking, adventure playground, music.

Laing Museum
High Street, Newburgh, Fife. Apr-Sept, weekdays 11.00-18.00. Sat-Sun 14.00-17.00; Oct-Mar, Wed, Thur 12.00-16.00, Sun 14.00-17.00. Free. Tel: (01334) 53722, ext. 141.

Museum with displays on the theme of Victorian Scotland - self help, emigration, the antiquarian movement, geology and recreated Victorian study. Temporary exhibitions and historical reference library.

Letham Glen
Leven, off A915. Glen open all year, daily, dawn-dusk. Nature Centre, Jan-Dec. Xmas and New Year. Mon-Fri 12.00-15.00. Summer: Sat 14.00-16.00, Sun 14.00-16.30. Winter: Sat 13.00-15.00, Sun 13.00-15.30. Free. Car parking in summer. Tel: (01333) 429231.

This picturesque glen has a variety of educational and recreational facilities for visitors. Rustic bridges, a doocot, putting green and pets' corner. In the heart of the glen is the Alpine-style Nature Centre where exhibitions are staged throughout the year, and where students demonstrate crafts in summer. (Easy access for disabled visitors). Mile-long nature trail from the centre to the far end of the Glen. Information booklets available.

Leuchars Parish Church
Main Street, Leuchars, 5 miles from St. Andrews on A919 to Dundee. Mar-Oct. Daylight hours up to 19.00. Visitors are also welcome to join services. Other times by arrangement. Free, donations welcome. Parking available. Tours and tearoom on Tuesdays. Teas, coffees by arangement on other days. Tel: (Church officer's house) (01334) 838884.

Leuchars Parish Church comprises an ancient Norman chancel and apse, richly ornamented, with a fine 17th-century bell tower. The rest of the church is Victorian. Many and varied stone carvings inside and outside, with masons' marks. Handbook available.

Levenmouth Swimming Pool and Sports Centre
Promenade, Leven. Jan-Dec, exc Xmas and New Year. Mon, Wed, Fri 08.00-22.00. Tues, Thur 07.00-22.00. Sat, Sun 08.00-21.00. Charges for activities. Parking available. Sports shop. Cafeteria. Tel: (01333) 429866.

Centre has leisure pool with wave-making machine, water cannons, flume, whirlpool spa, water jets and geysers. Four-court gameshall, fitness room, sunbeds, sauna and other facilities.

Loch Leven Castle
On an island on Loch Leven, Kinross. Access

by boat from Kinross. Apr-Sept, opening standard. Oct-Mar closed. Entrance charge. Parking available. (HS). Tel: 0131-244 3101.

The tower is late 14th or early 15th century. Mary, Queen of Scots was imprisoned here in 1567 and from it escaped eleven months later.

Pittencrieff House Museum

Pittencrieff Park, Dunfermline. May-Oct, daily except Tues 11.00-17.00. Free. Parking available. Tel: (01383) 722935 (May-Oct only) or (01383) 721814.

The house, standing in a fine park, was built in 1610 for the Lairds of Pittencrieff, and was bought by Andrew Carnegie in 1902. There are displays of local history, costumes, and an art gallery.

Ravenscraig Castle and Park

On a rocky promontory between Dysart and Kirkcaldy. Daily, Oct-Apr 10.00-15.00, May-Sept 10.00-19.00. Accessible from shore at all reasonable times. Tel: (01592) 642090.

Imposing ruin of a castle founded by James II in 1460. Later it passed into the hands of the Sinclair Earls of Orkney. It is perhaps the first British castle to be symmetrically designed for defence by firearms.

St. Andrew's Castle

Shore at St. Andrews. Opening standard. (HS). Tel: 0131—244 3101.

This ruined castle, which has been rebuilt at several periods, overlooks the sea and was founded in 1200 as a fortress and principal residence of the Bishop of St. Andrews. Here Cardinal Beaton was murdered in 1546, and the first round of the Reformation struggle was fought out in the siege that followed. The impressive bottle dungeon and secret passage - a mine and counter-mine - are notable features.

St. Andrew's Cathedral

In St. Andrews. Charge for museum and St. Rule's (Regulus') Tower. Opening standard. (HS). Tel: 0131—244 3101.

Founded in 1160 and consecrated in 1318, St. Andrew's Cathedral was once the largest church in the country. Its design is said to have exceeded the capacity of the builders of the day to construct it. The remains include parts of the east and west gables, the south wall of the nave, and portions of the choir and south transept. There is a fascinating museum and St. Rule's Tower, dating from 1127, gives a magnificent view of the town.

St. Andrews Museum

Kinburn Park, Doubledykes, St. Andrews. Apr-Sept, daily 11.00-18.00; Oct-Mar, Mon-Fri 11.00-16.00. Sat & Sun 14.00-17.00. Free. Car parking only. Gift shop. Tearoom. Tel: (01334) 77706.

Display - with sounds and smells - of the history of the town of St. Andrews from medieval to modern times. Temporary exhibitions programme; children's activity room; children's events during school holidays. Gallery talks and other events for adults.

St. Andrews Preservation Trust Museum

12 North Street, St. Andrews. Easter weekend, mid June-mid Sept, daily 14.00-16.30. Also 30 Nov (St. Andrew's Day). Donations. Gift shop. Tel: (01334) 77629.

Converted fishermen's houses. Collection comprises items of interest from St. Andrews including displays from a well-known grocer's shop and also a chemist, fishing equipment and photographs. Features work of the Trust in conservation and renovation.

St. Andrews Sealife Centre

The Scores, St. Andrews. All year, daily 10.00-18.00 (21.00 in July and Aug). Entrance charges. Gift shop. Restaurant. Tel: (01334) 74786.

A new world beneath the waves. The superb setting of St. Andrews Bay makes the Sealife Centre an experience for anyone visiting the east coast of Scotland. Hundreds of exciting sea creatures are on display and multi-level viewing gives the chance to come face to face with them, in displays designed to recreate their natural environment. There is now also an outdoor seal pool and British shark display. Oysters, the restaurant, offers meals throughout the day with panoramic views of the sea.

St Andrews University

St Andrews town centre. Tel: (01334) 76161.

The oldest university in Scotland, founded in 1412. See the 15th-century Church of St Salvator, now the chapel for the united colleges of St Salvator (1455) and St Leonard (1512); St Mary's College (1537) with its quadrangle; and the 16th-century St Leonard's Chapel. Also in the town are St Mary's House built in 1523 and now St Leonard's School Library, and Holy Trinity Church with a 16th century tower and interesting interior features. Guided tours operate twice daily through the summer.

St. Bridget's Kirk

Dalgety Bay, off A92, 2m SW of Aberdour. Open all reasonable times. (HS). Free. Tel: 0131-244 3101.

Ruins of an ancient church dedicated to St. Bridget in 1244.

St. Fillan's Cave

Cove Wynd, Pittenweem, near harbour, 9m SSE of St. Andrews. All year, 10.00-17.00. Charge for adults only.

St Fillan's Cave gave Pittenweem (Pictish for The Place of The Cave) its name. Situated behind the harbour and now surrounded by houses, with tiny well and stone staircase. Augustinian monks from the Isle of May established the Priory, the Great House and the Prior's lodging above the cave, cutting through the rock from the garden to the holy cave-shrine below. Restored and rededicated in 1935.

St. Monan's Church

In St. Monan's, A917, 12m S of St. Andrews. All reasonable times. Free.

Possibly a Ninianic foundation, c 400 AD. A place of healing from early times. David I was reputedly cured of an arrow wound here. It became a Royal Votive Chapel perhaps at that time. Alexander III initiated new building work c 1265. David II repaired and remodelled the Choir area in 1362 as a thanksgiving for deliverance from a storm at sea. James III gifted it to the Dominicans c 1460 and it became the Parish Church in 1646.

Scotstarvit Tower

Off A916, 3m S of Cupar. Opening standard. Free. (HS). Tel: 0131-244 3101.

A fine tower known to have been in existence in 1579.

Scottish Deer Centre

On A91, 3m W of Cupar, 12m W of St. Andrews. All year except Christmas and New Year. Apr-Oct 10.00-17.00. Later in summer. Special tours by arrangement, all year. Entrance charge. Parking available. Craft shop. Winery selling Scottish wines and foods. Tel: (0133781) 391.

The centre offers a unique opportunity to see many species of deer: feed, stroke and photograph during a ranger-led tour. Audio-visual show and walk through multi-media exhibition. Giant outdoor adventureland, treetop canopy walk and maze. Rare breeds of deer. Farm walk and picnic sites. Winery and wine exhibition, craft centre, restaurant and snack bar. Free parking, modern toilets.

Scottish Fisheries Museum

At Anstruther harbour, 10m SSE of St. Andrews. Apr-Oct, Mon-Sat 10.00-17.30, Sun 11.00-17.00. Nov-Mar, Mon-Sat 10.00-16.30, Sun 14.00-16.30. Entrance charges. Parking available. Gift shop. Tearoom. Tel: (01333) 310628.

16th to 19th century buildings housing marine aquarium, fishing and ships' gear, model and actual fishing boats (including 'Fifie' and 'Zulu' in harbour). Well presented museum documenting the life of the east coast fisher folk. Reference library, tearoom.

Adam Smith Theatre

Bennochy Road, Kirkcaldy. Tel: (01592) 260498.

Theatre with performances all year, named after Adam Smith, the economist who was born in Kirkcaldy in 1723.

John McDouall Stuart Museum

Rectory Lane, Dysart, 2m N of Kirkcaldy. 1 Jun-31 Aug, daily exc. public holidays 14.00-17.00. Free. Tel: (01592) 260732.

A 17th-century building restored by the NTS as part of their 'little houses' scheme. Birthplace of the explorer John McDouall Stuart (1815-1866) who crossed Australia's desert heart in 1861. Permanent display relating to the explorer. Nearby are other NTS 'little houses' and the picturesque harbour.

Swilken Golf Visitor Centre

Argyll Business Park, Largo Road, 1 mile from centre of St. Andrews. Jan-Dec. Mon-Fri 09.00-17.00, Sat 10.00-16.00 (shop only). Free. Parking available. Shop. Tel: (01334) 72266.

Specialised golf visitor centre with showroom and computerised club fitting bay. Craftsmen in the factory produce quality golf clubs from traditional hickory-shafted putters to the latest boron metal woods. Resident professional. Computerised swing analysis.

Vane Farm Nature Reserve

On the S shore of Loch Leven, on B9097, off M90 and B996, 4.5m S of Kinross. Apr-Oct, daily 10.00-17.00, Nov-Mar, daily 10.00-16.00, except Christmas/New Year. (RSPB). Tel: (01577) 62355.

The Nature Centre is a converted farm building equipped with displays designed to interpret the surrounding countryside and the loch. Between the last week of September and April, the area is a favourite feeding and resting place for vast numbers of wild geese and duck, and binoculars and telescopes are provided for observation. Also observation hide and nature trail. Shop selling wide range of RSPB gifts. Car park with picnic space. Path up Vane Hill through birchwoods with impressive views.

Wemyss Caves

East Wemyss, 5 miles E of Kirkcaldy on A955. Signposted. Jan-Dec. Open access to some caves, for others, request key in advance from

Wemyss Environmental Education Centre, East Wemyss. Weekdays 10.00-15.00 exc public hols. Free. Parking available. Tel: (01592) 714479.

Several caves, cut into the sandstone cliffs by sea erosion during the last Ice Age, show evidence of prehistoric and recent occupation. They contain a fine set of wall inscriptions, some possibly showing Bronze Age influence, while others are attributable to the Picts and Norsemen. The more famous inscriptions include a Viking longship and the god Thor, as well as animal illustrations of horse, salmon and swan - the swan being incorporated in the coat of arms of the Earl of Wemyss to this day.

The West Port
St. Andrews, at W end of South Street. All times. Free. (HS). Tel: 0131-244 3101.

One of the few surving city gates in Scotland. Its building contract is dated 1589 although it was completely renovated in 1843. It now consists of a central archway protected from above by battlements between two semi-octagonal turrets with gun loops.

PERTHSHIRE

Aberfeldy Distillery
On A827 E of Aberfeldy. Jan-Dec (exc. Xmas and New Year). Mon-Fri 09.30-16.30. Restricted opening in winter. Free. Parking available. Tel: (01887) 820330.

Malt distillery and maturation warehouse built by the Dewar family in 1898 in their home town of Aberfeldy. Shop and reception.

Aberfeldy Water Mill
Mill Street. Easter-Oct. Mon-Sat 10.00-17.30, Sun 12.00-17.30. Entrance Charge. Parking available. Shop. Restaurant Tel: (01887) 820803.

Working oatmeal mill with interpretative gallery and video presentation. Tours stress the importance of mills and milling in the social history of Scotland.

Abernethy Round Tower
At Abernethy, A913, 9m SE of Perth. Free apply to Keykeeper. (HS). Tel: 0131-244 3101.

A round tower, 74 feet high, dating from the 11th century. Tradition has it that Malcolm Canmore did homage to William the Conqueror here. Beside it is a Pictish symbol stone.

Achray Forest Drive
Off A821, 4m N of Aberfoyle. Easter-Oct. Daily 1000-1800. Entrance charge per car. Tel: (0187 72) 258.

Scenic drive on Forestry Commission roads with fine views of the Trossachs. Walks, picnic places, play area and toilets.

Alyth Museum
Off A94, 3m N of Meigle. May-Sep, Wed-Sun 13.00-17.00. Free. Tel: (01738) 32488 (Perth Museum).

A collection of rural agricultural and domestic artefacts.

Amulree Parish Church
On A822 between Crieff and Dunkeld or Aberfeldy. Jan-Dec. Daily, during daylight hours. Door is at end of church furthest from gate. From Jul-Sept, Sunday services weekly at 09.45; from Oct-June, fortnightly at 14.15. Free. Parking available.

Amulree Parish Church was founded in 1743 as a Mission Church by the Society for the Propagation of Christian Knowledge (SPCK), when it was realised there was no regular preacher and no place of worship for 12 miles in any direction. Over the years, the population has shrunk - some emigrated to Ontario, Canada, and a display in the church, together with family lists, helps people looking for family roots.

Ardblair Castle
On A923 1m W of Blairgowrie. Jan-Dec, by appointment only. Entrance charge. Parking available. Tel: (01250) 873155.

Mainly 16th-century castle on 12th-century foundations, home of the Blair Oliphant family. Jacobite relics and links with Charles Edward Stuart. Room containing relics of Lady Nairne (nee Oliphant), author of Charlie is My Darling and other songs.

Atholl Country Collection
Blair Atholl. Easter, June-mid Oct. Daily, 13.30-17.30. From 09.30, Mon-Fri, July-Sept. Entrance charge. Parking available. Tel: (01796) 481232.

Folk museum with blacksmith's 'smiddy' and crofter's stable and byre. Emphasis on the importance of flax growing and spinning to the economy of the district. Road, rail and postal services, the school, the kirk, the vet and gamekeeper are all featured. Picnic area and adjacent to Blair Castle Craft Centre.

Auchingarrich Wildlife Centre
Glascorrie Road, Comrie. 2 miles S of Comrie on Braco road. Jan-Dec. Daily 10.00-dusk. Entrance charge. Special rates for handicapped people. Parking available. Shop. Coffee shop. Tel: (01764) 679469.

Set in 100 acres of Perthshire hill scenery, Auchingarrich has one of the largest bird collections in Scotland, with 17 ponds and over 100 species of waterfowl, ornamental and game birds. Highland cattle, wild deer, goats, 47-stone Rosie the pig, wallabies, llamas and a host of smaller animals. Visitors can handle young chicks in wild bird hatchery. Play area include 'child-sized' rabbit burrow. Woodland walks, viewpoints, picnic benches and barbecue sites.

Bell's Cherrybank Gardens
In Perth off A9 Glasgow Road at Arthur Bell Distillers office. Free. Parking available. Tel: (01738) 27330/21111.
Beautifully landscaped garden. Children's play area, cafe facility (light refreshments).

Black Watch Regimental Museum
Balhousie Castle, Perth. Entrance from Hay Street or North Inch. Jan-Dec exc Xmas and New Year period. Easter-Sep, Mon-Fri 10.00-16.30, Sun & public hols 14.00-16.30, Oct-Easter, Mon-Fri 10.00-15.30. Free. Parking available (Hay Street). Garden. Shop. Advance notice required for groups. Tel: (01738) 21281, ext. 8530.
Balhousie Castle houses the Regimental Headquarters and Museum of the Black Watch (Royal Highland) Regiment, and displays the history of this famous regiment from 1740 to the present.

Blair Athol Distillery Visitor Centre
S of Pitlochry centre. Open all year round, Mon-Sat 09.30-17.00. Sundays, Easter to Oct 12.00-17.00. Seating up to 90 persons. Licensed. Parking available. Tel: (01796) 472234.
Attractive group of distillery buildings with new Visitor Centre, audio-visual and shop. Restaurant.

Blair Atholl Mill
Turn off A9 for Blair Atholl, 5 miles N of Pitlochry. Apr (or Easter)-Oct, Mon-Sat 10.30-17.30, Sun 12.00-17.30. Entrance charge. Parking available. Shop. Tearoom, uses mill products. Tel: (01796) 481321 or 483317.
Built in 1613, this water mill produces oatmeal and flour which are on sale, and some is used in the small wholemeal bakery at the mill. Guide dogs in tearoom only.

Blair Castle
Near A9, 7m NNW of Pitlochry. Apr-late Oct. Daily 10.00-18.00 (last entry 17.00). Entrance charge. Parking available. Shop. Restaurant. Tel: (01796) 481207.
A white turreted baronial castle, seat of the Duke of Atholl, chief of Clan Murray. The oldest part is Cumming's Tower, 1269. Mary,

Queen of Scots, Prince Charles Edward Stuart and Queen Victoria stayed here. When the castle was in Hanoverian hands in 1746, General Lord Murray laid siege to it on the Prince's behalf, making it the last castle in Britain to be besieged. The Duke is the only British subject allowed to maintain a private army, the Atholl Highlanders. There are fine collections of furniture, portraits, lace, china, arms, armour, Jacobite relics and masonic regalia. Licensed restaurant, gift shop, deer park, pony-trekking, nature trails, picnic areas and caravan park. Free car and coach parks.

Bolfracks Garden
2m W of Aberfeldy on A827 to Kenmore. Gates on left. Apr-Oct. Daily 10.00-18.00. Donation box. Parking available. Tel: (01887) 820207.
Garden overlooking Tay Valley. Good collection of trees, shrubs and perennials. Open under Scotland's Gardens Scheme.

Branklyn Garden
Dundee Road (A85) Perth. 1 Mar-31 Oct, daily 0930-sunset. (NTS). Tel: (01738) 25535.
Described as the finest two acres of private garden in the country, this outstanding collection of plants, particularly rhododendrons, alpines, azaleas, herbaceous and peat garden plants, attracts gardeners and botanists from all over the world. Worth visiting for the Meconopsis blue poppies alone!

Bygones Museum and Balquhidder Visitor Centre
Stronvar House, Balquhidder, 2.5 miles W of A84 between Lochearnhead and Strathyre. Follow Thistle signs to Rob Roy's Grave. Mar-Oct. Daily 10.30-17.00. Free car park open all year for walkers. Entrance charge. Shop. Tearoom. Tel: (0187 74) 688.
A collection of everyday items and curios of yesteryear, displayed in a Scottish laird's baronial mansion overlooking Loch Voil and the Braes o' Balquhidder. Stronvar House was built by David Bryce in 1850, for David Carnegie. Balquhidder was the home of Rob Roy Macgregor, and his grave can be seen in the village churchyard.

Caithness Glass (Perth)
Inveralmond, Perth. On A9 north of the town. All year. Free. Factory shop: Mon-Sat 0900-1700, Sun 1300-1700, Sun 1100-1700 (Easter-end Sep). Factory viewing: Mon-Fri 0900-1630. (Caithness Glass plc.). Tel: (01738) 37373.
Visitors are welcome at the factory to see the fascinating process of glass-making. Factory shop, paperweight museum and gallery, and licensed restaurant. Ample car/coach parking.

Castle Menzies

On B846, Weem, 1m W of Aberfeldy. Apr-mid Oct, Mon-Sat 10.30-17.00, Sun 14.00-17.00. (Menzies Charitable Trust). Tel: (01887) 820982.

Outstanding 16th century Z-plan fortified tower house exemplifying the transition between earlier strongholds and later mansions. Seat of chiefs of Clan Menzies. Involved in the turbulent history of the Central Highlands. Prince Charles Stuart stayed here on his way to Culloden in 1746. Walled gardens, tearoom, gift shop.

Clan Donnachaidh Museum

Bruar Falls, Calvine, 4m W of Blair Atholl. Mid Apr-mid Oct, weekdays (ex Tues) 10.00-13.00, 14.00-17.00, Sun 14.00-17.00. At other times by arrangement. Free. Parking available. Tel: (01796) 483264.

Clan Donnachaidh comprises Reid, Robertson, MacConnachie, Duncan, MacInroy and others. Old and new exhibits include items associated with the Jacobite Risings of 1715 and 1745. Restaurant nearby.

Cluny House Gardens

3.5 miles from Aberfeldy on Weem-Strathtay road. Mar-Oct. Daily 10.00-18.00. Entrance charge. Car parking available, coaches by arrangement. Plant stall. Tel: (01887) 820795.

Cluny is a 2.5 hectare wild woodland garden growing mainly Himalayan plants. The garden holds the National Collection of Asiatic primulas and has a wide range of other groups of plants such as meconopsis, lilies, nomocharis, trilliums and rhododendrons. There are fine examples of specimen trees including the widest sequoia gigantea in Britain. April, May and June are spectacular flowering months, while September and October bring lovely autumn colours.

Crieff Visitors' Centre

On the A822 leading south from Crieff on Muthill Road. All year, daily 09.00-late, (09.00-17.00 winter). The factories are only open on working days. Free. Children's play area. Tel: (01764) 4014.

A large modern visitors' centre containing 180 seat restaurant, adjoining showroom and two walk round craft factories enabling visitors to see paperweights and pottery being made.

Culcreuch Castle and Country Park

Fintry, 6 miles S of Kippen on B822. Jan-Dec 12.00-23.00. Free. Parking available. Shop. Restaurant, tearoom and bar in Castle. Tel: (0136 086) 228.

Culcreuch Castle and its 1600-acre parkland lie between the Campsie Fells and the Fintry Hills at the head of the Endrick Valley. Visitors are welcome to explore the grounds including river banks, two small lochs and a magnificent pinetum planted in 1842. The castle, now a hotel, dates back to 1296 and is well-preserved. It is the ancestral home of the Galbraith clan, and since 1699 has been the home of the Barons of Culcreuch.

Drummond Castle Gardens

Muthill, 3 miles S of Crieff on A822. May-Sept. Daily 14.00-18.00 (last entry 17.00). Entrance charge. Cards and brochures for sale. Parking available. Gardens only open to public. Tel: (0176481) 257.

The Gardens of Drummond Castle were originally laid out about 1630 by John Drummond, 2nd Earl of Perth. In about 1830, the parterre was Italianised and embellished with fine figures and statues from Italy. Probably one of the most interesting pieces of statuary is the Sundial, designed and built by John Mylne, Master Mason to King Charles I.

Drummond Fish Farms

Aberuchill, 1 mile W of Comrie. All year. Jun-Aug 10.00-20.00. Sept-May 10.00-17.00. Entrance charges. Car parking, limited coach parking. Farm shop. Picnic facilities. Tel: (01764) 70500.

Fish farm open to view with explanatory notes and boards around farm. Fish feed included in admission charge. Four ponds, including beginners' pond, for fishing. Rods and tuition available.

Dunkeld Bridge

Over the River Tay at Dunkeld. Free access at all times.

One of Thomas Telford's finest bridges, built in 1809. An attractive riverside path leads from here downstream to the famous *Birnam Oak*, last relic of Macbeth's Birnam Wood, and then around the village of Birnam. Best view is from riverside garden. Wheelchair users should approach from the square through the archway. Hotel and tearoom adjacent.

Dunkeld Cathedral

High Street, Dunkeld, 15m NNW of Perth. Opening standard. Free. (HS). Tel: 0131-244 3101.

Refounded in the early 12th century on an ancient ecclesiastical site, this cathedral has a beautiful setting by the Tay. The choir has been restored and is in use as the parish church. The nave and the great north-west tower date from the 15th century.

Dunkeld Little Houses

Dunkeld, A9 15m N of Perth. Tourist Information Centre with audio-visual presentation. Open Apr-Dec. Free. Parking available. (NTS). Tel: (01350) 727460.

The houses date from the rebuilding of the town after the Battle of Dunkeld, 1689. Charmingly restored by NTS and Perth County Council, they are not open to the public but may been seen from the outside and information on them gained from the Visitor Centre or from the National Trust for Scotland's representative at the Ell shop.

Earthquake House

Off A85 just W of Comrie. Apr-Oct. Free. Exhibits can be seen through window and glazed doors at any reasonable time. Car parking only.

The village of Comrie lies close to the Highland boundary fault and has a history of earth tremors. Tiny Earthquake House was built in 1874 as a recording station, but a period of low seismic activity and the installation of more sophisticated equipment elsewhere in Scotland meant that it gradually fell into disrepair. Restored in 1986, this is one of the nation's smallest listed buildings. It contains a model of the original seismometer, and modern seismological equipment provided by the British Geological Survey. Records of recent local, national and international earthquakes are on display.

Edradour Distillery

2.5m E of Pitlochry. Mar-Oct, Mon-Sat, 09.30-17.00. Nov-Feb, Sat 10.00-16.00 (shop only). Other times by arrangement. Parking available. Tel: (01796) 472095.

The smallest distillery in Scotland, established 1825. A visit includes a guided tour, audio-visual presentation and tasting.

Elcho Castle

On River Tay, 3m SE of Perth. Opening standard. Closed in winter. (HS). Tel: 0131-244 3101.

A preserved fortified mansion notable for its tower-like jambs or wings and for the wrought-iron grills protecting its windows. An ancestral seat of the Earls of Wemyss; another castle, on or very near the site, was a favourite hide-out of William Wallace.

Fair Maid's House Gallery

North Port, Perth. Scottish Craft Shop. Open daily 1000-1700 (except Sun) all year. Free. Tel: (01738) 25976.

One of the oldest buildings in Perth, now housing contemporary Scottish crafts and a gallery. Exhibition changes each month, covering painting, embroidery, tapestry, sculpture, etching and print-making.

Fairways Heavy Horse Centre

Walnut Grove, by Perth. 2m E of Perth, off A85. Daily, Apr-Sept, 10.00-18.00. Entrance charge. Tel: (01738) 32561/25931.

This Centre is both a working and breeding establishment for Clydesdale horses. There are forty brood mares during the summer months and two premium stallions and newly born foals. Enjoy a ride in a wagon pulled by a team of Clydesdales. See a video show featuring the heavy horses at work throughout the year. A video shows the blacksmith at work at his anvil and the horses being shod.

Falls of Dochart

Killin. Free.

Dramatic waterfalls rushing through the centre of this picturesque highland village. On the island of Inchbuie on the river is the burial ground of Clan McNab. Access key to this island and to the graveyard available from Tourist Information Centre in Killin.

Farm Life Centre

Dunaverig, Ruskie, Thornhill. 8 miles E of Aberfoyle on A873. June-Oct. Daily, 10.00-18.00. Entrance charges. Parking available. Gift shop. Farm tearoom. Shop. Tel: (0178 685) 277.

Dunaverig is a small family farm of the enclosure period, circa 1800, traditionally run with sheep, cattle and crops. The Farm Life Centre traces the history of Dunaverig from earliest times using models, photographs, charts, tools and implements housed in the original buildings. Animals indoors and outdoors, adventure playground, picnic areas, nature walks with fine views.

Fergusson Gallery

Marshall Place, by South Inch, Perth. Jan-Dec. Mon-Sat, 10.00-17.00. Free. Gift shop. Tel: (01738) 441944.

Art Gallery devoted to the works of the famous Scottish Colourist painter JD Fergusson, housed in a converted historic water works.

Fortingall Yew

Fortingall, 9m W of Aberfeldy. All times. Parking available.

The great yew in an enclosure in the churchyard is over 3,000 years old, perhaps the oldest tree in Britain. The attractive village, which was rebuilt in 1900 with many thatched cottages is claimed to be the birthplace of Pontius Pilate.

Glengoulandie Deer Park

8m NW of Aberfeldy on B846 to Kinloch Rannoch. May-Oct. Daily, 09.00-1 hour before sunset. Entrance charges. Parking available. Gift shop. Tel: (01887) 830261/830306.

Native animals housed in a natural environment. Many endangered species are kept, and there are fine herds of red deer and Highland cattle. No guide dogs.

Glenturret Distillery

From Crieff take A85 to Comrie for 1m, then turn right at crossroads for 0.25m. Mar-Dec, Mon-Sat 09.30-16.30, Sun 12.00-16.30. Jan, Feb, Mon-Fri 11.30-14.30. Entrance charge. Parking available. Smugglers Restaurant, Pagoda Room restaurant, whisky tasting bar. Whisky/souvenir shop. Tel: (01764) 2424.

Scotland's oldest distillery, with guided tour and free taste. Award-winning heritage centre, audio-visual and 3-D exhibition museum. Good facilites for blind visitors.

The Hermitage

Off A9, 2m W of Dunkeld. All reasonable times. Car park. (NTS).

A picturesque folly, built in 1758, restored in 1952, and again in 1986. It is set above the wooded gorge of the River Braan. There are nature trails in the area.

Huntingtower Castle

Off A85, 3m WNW of Perth. Opening standard except Oct-Mar, closed Thur pm and all day Fri. Entrance charge. (HS). Tel: 0131-244 3101.

A 15th century castellated mansion until 1600 known as Ruthven Castle. This was the scene of the Raid of Ruthven in 1582; James VI, then 16, accepted an invitation from the Earl of Gowrie to his hunting seat and found himself in the hands of nobles who demanded the dismissal of the royal favourites. When the king tried to escape, his way was barred by the Master of Glamis. The Ruthven conspirators held power for some months, but the Earl was beheaded in 1584. There are fine painted ceilings.

Hydro-Electric Visitor Centre

Pitlochry Power Station, on River Tummel at Pitlochry. Apr-Oct, daily 09.40-17.30. Entrance charge. Car parking only. Gift shop. Tel: (01796) 473152.

Exhibition describing Hydro Electric as a generator, transmitter and distributor of electricity. Displays, videos, computer interactive displays and one touch-screen educational game. Salmon ladder with viewing chamber. Viewing gallery for power station interior. Dam.

Inchmahome Priory

On an island in the Lake of Menteith, A81, 4m E of Aberfoyle. Access by boat from lakeside, Port of Menteith. Opening standard, except closed Oct-Mar. Entrance charge. Parking available. (HS). Tel: 0131-244 3101.

The ruins of an Augustinian house, founded in 1238, where the infant Mary, Queen of Scots was sent for refuge in 1547.

Innerpeffray Library

B8062, 4m SE of Crieff. Apr-Sept Mon-Sat 10.00-12.45, 14.00-16.45, Sun 14.00-16.00. Oct-Mar 10.00-12.45, 14.00-16.00, Sun 14.00-16.00. Closed all day Thurs. Entrance charge. Parking available. Tel: (01764) 2819.

The oldest library still in existence in Scotland, founded 1691, housed in a late 18th-century building. The nearby church was built in 1508.

Keathbank Mill

Balmoral Road, Blairgowrie, 0.5 mile north of town on A93. Apr-Oct. Daily 10.00-18.00. Entrance charge. Parking available. Gift shop. Coffee shop. Tel: (01250) 872025.

Built in 1864 on the bank of the River Ericht, the mill boasts Scotland's second largest working water wheel, an 1862 steam engine and 1937 diesel model. Heraldic workshops are now housed in the mill. These can be viewed, as well as a display of coats of arms, clan crests and shields. Outside, half a mile of model railway.

Leighton Library

The Cross, Dunblane, 6 miles N of Stirling on M9. May-Oct. Mon-Fri 10.30-12.30, 14.30-16.30. Free. Parking available.

The Leighton Library is said to be the oldest private library in Scotland. Built in 1684, it contains 4,500 books from 1,500 onwards, in around 50 languages. The collection covers a very wide range of subjects, now used as an international working library. The building and its contents were almost forgotten for 150 years until restoration in 1989-90, and full opening to the public in 1991.

Loch of the Lowes

Off A923, 2m NE of Dunkeld. Visitor Centre open Apr-Sept. Observation Hide is open permanently. Free. Parking available. (SWT). Tel: (01350) 727337.

This Scottish Wildlife Trust reserve is famous for its breeding osprey pair; visitors can watch these birds on the nest from a special hide. Visitor centre, staff ranger and observation hill. Wide range of provision for visitors with special needs.

Loch Tay Pottery
Loch Tay, Fearnan, 3 miles W of Kenmore.
Jan-Dec. Daily, 09.00-18.00 (occasionally
closed for holidays, Oct-Mar: please telephone).
Free. Car parking only. Pottery shop. Tel:
(01887) 830 251.
The pottery and showroom occupy an original
croft house overlooking Loch Tay. An
individual and wide-ranging selection of
pottery, all hand-thrown, decorated with the
owners' own glazes - some including ash from
their own fires. Ovenware and tableware, plus
customers' own commissions. All pottery sold
solely on these premises.

Megginch Castle Gardens
A85, 10m E of Perth. Apr-June and Sept, Wed
only 14.00-17.00, Jul and Aug, Mon-Fri 14.00-
17.00. Parking available. Tel: (01821) 642222.
The gardens around the 15th-century castle
have daffodils, rhododendrons and 1,000-year-
old yews. There is a double-walled kitchen
garden, 16th-century rose garden and 19th-
century flower parterre as well as the Gothic
courtyard with pagoda-roofed dovecote. There
is also an interesting example of topiary,
including a golden yew crown. An 18th-century
physic garden is currently being restored and a
new astrological garden has just been created.

Meikleour Beech Hedge
A93, just S of Meikleour, 12m NNE of Perth.
Parking available.
Listed as the highest of its kind in the world,
the Beech Hedge was planted in 1746 and is
now 580 yards long and 100 feet high.
Information board.

Melville Monument
1m N of Comrie, 6m W of Crieff. Access by
footpath from parking place on Glen Lednock
road. All times. Free. Parking available.
The obelisk in memory of Lord Melville (1742-
1811) stands on Dunmore, a hill of 840 feet,
with delightful views of the surrounding
country. The access path is linked to the scenic
4 mile Glen Lednock Circular Walk, running
from Comrie and back through varied
woodland (signposted).

Muthill Church and Tower
At Muthill, A822, 3m S of Crieff. All reasonable
times. Free. (HS). Tel: 0131-244 3101.
Ruins of an important church of the 15th
century, incorporating a 12th-century tower.

Muthill Museum
In centre of Muthill Village beside Muthill
Church and Tower. Easter and June-Sept, Tues,

Thurs, Sat and Sun 14.30-17.00. Free.
Small Folk Museum/Heritage Centre housed in
Georgian cottage (c.1760) in conservation
village.

Pass of Killiecrankie
Off A9, 3m N of Pitlochry. NTS Visitor Centre:
Apr-Oct, daily 10.00-17.00. Jun-Aug, daily
09.30-18.00. Site open all day. Entrance charge
for adults. Children free. Parking available.
Trust shop. Snack bar. (NTS). Tel: (01796)
473233.
A famous wooded gorge where in 1689 the
Government troops were routed by Jacobite
forces led by 'Bonnie Dundee'. Soldier's Leap.
NTS centre features the battle, natural history
and ranger services. The Pass is on the network
of Garry-Tummel walks, which extend for 20
miles in the area. Snack bar.

Perth Art Gallery and Museum
George Street. All year, Mon-Sat 10.00-17.00.
Free. Tel: (01738) 32488.
Collections of local history, fine and applied
art, natural history, archaeology and
ethnography. Changing programme of
temporary exhibitions.

Perth Repertory Theatre
High Street, Perth. Group concessions available,
but variable. Tel: (01738) 21031.
An intimate Victorian theatre, built in 1900 in
the centre of Perth, offering a variety of plays,
musicals, etc. Induction loop for hard of
hearing. Coffee bar and restaurant open during
day and for performances.

Pitlochry Festival Theatre
Off A9 bypass at Pitlochry local access. May-
Oct, open all day for refreshments and art
exhibitions. (Box Office) Tel: (01796) 2680.
Scotland's 'Theatre in the Hills' is now
rehoused in a magnificent new building by the
River Tummel. Opened by Prince Charles in
1981, it is a must for all holidaymakers.
Catering and bar facilities. Coffee shop open
from 10.00; lunch 12.00-14.00; restaurant 18.30-
20.00. Magnificent view from foyer and
restaurant.

Beatrix Potter Garden and Exhibition
Birnam Institute, Station Road, Birnam, 12
miles N of Perth off A9. Exhibition: June-Sept.
Mon-Sat 10.00-12.00, 14.00-16.00, Sun 14.00-
16.00. Gardens open all year. Free, donations
accepted.
Beatrix Potter drew much of the inspiration for
her renowned children's books from the area
around Dunkeld, where she spent many family
holidays. The garden includes animal figures

based on Potter's characters, and a children's rabbit warren, while the exhibition tells the story of her visits to Perthshire.

Queen Elizabeth Forest Park Visitor Centre
Off A821, 1m N of Aberfoyle. Easter-Oct, daily *10.00-18.00. Free. Parking available. Shop. Cafeteria. (FE). Tel: (0187 72) 258.*
In this 45,000 acres of forest, moor and mountainside there are many walks. On A821 is the David Marshall Lodge, a picnic pavilion and information centre. 'Duke's Road' from Aberfoyle to the Trossachs has fine views.

Queen's View Centre, Loch Tummel
6 miles NW of Pitlochry on B8019. Apr-Oct. Daily 10.00-17.30. Free. Parking available (charge). Gift shop. Tearoom. (FE). Tel: (01796) 473123.
Forestry exhibition about Tay Forest Park, with information, audio visual, shop, tearoom. Picnic tables. Guided walks through ancient woodland or magnificent mature forests. Forest walks, paths and cycle routes. Views along Loch Tummel to the peak of Schiehallion; Queen Victoria visited the spot in 1866.

Rumbling Bridge
A823 at Rumbling Bridge. Free. All reasonable times.
The River Devon is spanned here by two bridges, the lower one dating from 1713, the upper one from 1816. A footpath from the north side gives good access to spectacular and picturesque gorges and falls, one of which is known as the Devil's Mill. Another, Cauldron Linn, is a mile downstream, whilst Vicar's Bridge is a beauty spot a mile beyond this.

St. John's Kirk
St. John Street, Perth. Daily, exc Thurs pm. Holy Communion, Sun 09.30. Tel: (01738) 21755/23358.
Consecrated in 1242, this fine cruciform church largely dates from the 15th century, and was restored in 1923-28 as a war memorial. Here John Knox in 1559 preached his momentous sermon urging the 'purging of the churches of idolatry'. The 'Town Kirk' of Perth, St. John's is a venue for musical and dramatic productions from time to time. Wheelchair access via south door.

St. Mary's Church, Grandtully
At Pitcairn Farm, 3m ENE of Aberfeldy, off A827. All times. Free. (HS). Tel: 0131-244 3101.
A 16th century church, with remarkable 17th century painted wooden ceiling of heraldic and symbolic subjects.

Scone Palace
Off A93 (Braemar Road), 2m NE of Perth. Easter-mid Oct, Mon-Sat 09.30-17.00; Sun 13.30-17.00 (Jul & Aug 10.00-17.00), other times by arrangement. Entrance charges. Parking available. Produce and gift shop. Restaurant, coffee shop, banqueting facilities. Tel: (01738) 52300.
The present castellated palace, enlarged and embellished in 1803, incorporates the 16th-century and earlier palaces. It has notable grounds and a pinetum and is still a family home. The Moot Hill at Scone, known in the 8th century and earlier, was the site of the famous coronation Stone of Scone, brought there in the 9th century by Kenneth MacAlpine, King of Scots. In 1296 the Stone was seized by the English and taken to Westminster Abbey. The ancient Abbey of Scone was destroyed by followers of John Knox. Magnificent collection of porcelain, furniture, ivories, 18th-century clocks and 16th-century needlework. Full catering facilites. Coffee shop, restaurant, produce and gift shop, gardens, playground, banqueting, pinetum. Parties of disabled visitors welcome.

The Scottish Horse Museum
The Cross, Dunkeld. Easter to Sept, daily exc Tues & Wed, 10.00-12.00, 14.00-17.00. Entrance charge (children free). Parking available. Tel: (0135 02) 296.
Exhibits, uniforms, photographs, maps and rolls of all those who served in this Yeomanry Regiment.

Scottish Tartans Museum
Drummond Street, Comrie, 6m W of Crieff. Apr-Oct, Mon-Sat 10.00-18.00, Sun 11.00-17.00; Nov-Mar, check times with office. Entrance charge. Tel: (01764) 670779.
The Scottish Tartans Society is the custodian of the largest collection in existence of material relating to tartans and Highland dress, historic costumes and artefacts; weavers cottage; dye plant garden. There is a research service on surnames, clans and tartans, and an archive of every known tartan.

Scottish Wool Centre
Off main street, Aberfoyle. Jan-Dec exc Xmas and New Year. Daily 10.00-18.00. Entrance charge. Parking available. Large retail area. Restaurant, tearoom. Tel: (0187 72) 850.
Opened in 1992, the Scottish Wool Centre is a custom-built all weather visitor centre

presenting the 'Story of Scottish Wool' from the sheep to the shops. 'Sheep Spectacular' presented daily in 170-seat amphitheatre, craft area features carding, spinning and weaving as well as traditional Shetland knitting; 'Kids Farm' tells the story of cashmere, along with cashmere kids and baby lambs.

Stuart Crystal Strathearn Glass Works
Muthill Road, Crieff. Jan-Dec exc Xmas and New Year, daily 09.00-19.00. Free. Parking available. Coffee shop. Crystal shop. Tel: (01764) 4004.
Manufacturer of Scottish crystal. Visit the factory to view the traditional skills involved in the production and decoration of the full lead crystal displayed in the factory shop. Video on glass making, picnic area and large car park.

Tay Forest Park
Tay and tummel valleys - Forest Enterprise area near Dunkeld, Kenmore, Pitlochry, Tummel Bridge and Rannoch. All times. Free. Parking available. Gift shop. Tearoom. (FE) Tel: (01350) 727284.
Spectacular forests with superb views from six waymarked forest walks with a choice of route, two waymarked mountain bike trails and several peaceful picnic sites. Forest campsite. Guided walks can be arranged at Queen's View Centre in the heart of the park; forest exhibition, shop and tearoom.

Tombuie Smokehouse and Nature Trail
2.5 miles NE of Aberfeldy on Weem/Strathtay road. Apr-Oct. Daily, 11.00-18.00. Entrance charge, children free. Car parking only. Farm shop. Tel: (01887) 820127.
South-facing farm, overlooking the River Tay at Aberfeldy. Picnic areas, nature trail. Large collection of cheese presses, a three-horse mill gang, one of the few remaining in Scotland, and a standing stone. The farm shop sells products from the Smokehouse.

Tourist Island, The Highland Motor Heritage Centre
Off A9 at Bankfoot, 6 miles N of Perth. Jan-Dec. Easter-Sept, daily, 08.30-20.30. Oct-Easter, Mon-Fri 10.00-18.00, weekends 08.30-20.30. (Exc weekends Nov-Feb, 08.30-18.00). Entrance charges. Parking available. Gift shop. Licensed restaurant. Tel: (01738) 87696.
A collection of classic and vintage cars, costumes and memorabilia is displayed using authentic period settings. Other attractions in the museum include a driving game, free slot car racing and motor heritage videos.

Tullibardine Chapel
Off A823, 6m SE of Crieff. All reasonable times. Free. Apply adjacent farmhouse. (HS). Tel: 0131-244 3101.
Founded in 1446, this is one of the few rural churches in Scotland which was entirely finished and still remains unaltered.

Tullochville Farm Heavy Horse Centre
5 miles W of Aberfeldy on B846. Easter-Oct, daily, 10.00-17.00. Entrance charge. Parking available. Refreshments. Tel: (01887) 830365.
Display of farm implements used on a small hill farm (Tullochville), and once pulled by horses, with a collection of harness and memorabilia from the same period. Clydesdale horses, sometimes with foal. Smaller ponies used for pony trekking.

Wade's Bridge
On B846, north of Aberfeldy. All times. Free. Parking available.
The bridge across the River Tay was begun in 1733 by General Wade with William Adam as architect. It is considered to be the finest of all Wade's bridges. The Black Watch Memorial is a large cairn surmounted by a kilted soldier, erected close to the bridge in Queen Victoria's Jubilee Year (1887). Easy access across lawn to river bank.

ANGUS

Aberlemno Sculptured Stones
At Aberlemno, B9134, 6m NE of Forfar. All times. Free. (HS). Tel: 0131—244 3101.
In the churchyard is a splendid upright cross-slab with Pictish symbols; three other stones stand beside the road.

Angus Folk Museum
Off A94 at Glamis, 5m SW of Forfar. Easter Weekend, May-Sept. Daily 11.00-17.00, last tour 16.30. Entrance charge. Parking available. (NTS). Tel: (0130 7) 840288.
Kirkwynd Cottages, a row of 19th century cottages with stone-slabbed roofs, containing relics of domestic and agricultural life in the county in the 19th century and earlier. In the agricultural annexe are farming implements and a Bothy Exhibition, including tape recorded information.

Arbroath Abbey
In Arbroath. Opening standard. (HS). Tel: 0131—244 3101.
Founded in 1178 by William the Lion and dedicated to St Thomas of Canterbury, it was from here that the famous Declaration of Arbroath asserting Robert the Bruce as King

was issued in 1320. Important remains of the church survive; these include one of the most complete examples of an abbot's residence.

Arbroath Art Gallery
Arbroath Library, Hill Terrace. All year, Mon, Wed 09.30-20.00; Tues, Thurs 09.30-18.00; Fri, Sat 09.30-17.00. Free. Shop. Tel: (01241) 75598.
Changing exhibitions of paintings by local artists and others. Special interest exhibits.

Ardestie and Carlungie Earth-Houses
N of A92, Ardestie: about 6m E of Dundee, at junction with B962. Carlungie: 1m N on unclassified road to Carlungie. All times. Free. (HS). Tel: 0131-244 3101.
Two examples of large earth-houses attached to surface dwellings. At Ardestie the gallery is curved and 80 feet in length: the Carlungie earth-house is 150 feet long, and is most complex; used in first centuries AD.

Barnhill Rock Gardens, Dundee
Broughty Ferry Esplanade, via Broughty Ferry town centre and Bridge Street, off Dalhousie Road. Jan-Dec. Free. Parking available.
5 acres of well-maintained rock garden overlooking River Tay and of interest throughout the year with collections of antipodean plants and an extensive water feature.

Barrack Street Museum, Dundee
City centre. All year, exc Xmas and New Year. Mon-Sat 10.00-17.00. Free (prior notice of groups preferred). Shop. Tel: (01382) 23141, ext. 65162.
Dundee's museum of natural history. Main displays on wildlife of Tayside including highlands. Also geology. Also on show the skeleton of the Famous Tay Whale. New Art and Nature Gallery devoted to temporary exhibitions exploring the influence of nature on the Arts. Small shop, toilets.

Barrie's Birthplace
9 Brechin Road, Kirriemuir. Easter weekend, May-Sept, Mon-Sat 11.00-17.30, Sun 14.00-17.30. Entrance charge. Tearoom. Books and souvenirs for sale. Tel: (01575) 72646. (NTS).
Here in this white-washed cottage playwright, Sir John M Barrie was born in 1860. Manuscripts, personal possessions and mementoes of actors and producers associated with his plays are shown in the museum.

Barry Mill
Barry, off A930, 2 miles W of Carnoustie. Easter weekend, May-mid Oct. Daily 11.00-
13.00, 14.00-17.00. Entrance charge. Parking available. (NTS). Tel: (01241) 56761.
A working water mill running on a demonstration basis, where visitors can follow the milling process from the arrival of the oats to the bagging of the meal. Displays highlight the importance of the mill in the local community, on a site where there has been milling since the 15th century. Orchard picnic area and lade-side walkway.

Brechin Museum
In Library, St. Ninian's Square. All year, Mon, Wed 09.30-20.00; Tues, Thur 09.30-18.00; Fri, Sat 09.30-17.00. Free. Car parking only. Tel: (01307) 68813/64123.
Housed in Public Library. New displays include archaeology, medieval burgh and Cathedral, civic and industrial history, folk life and paintings by local artist David Waterson.

Brechin Round Tower
At Brechin. Viewed from the churchyard. All reasonable times. (HS). Tel: 0131—244 3101.
12th century cathedral, partially demolished in 1807, restored 1900-02. Attached to the cathedral are one of the two remaining round towers of the Irish type in Scotland, dating back to the 11th or 12th century.

Broughty Castle Museum, Dundee
Broughty Ferry, 4m E of city centre. Mon-Thu & Sat 10.00-13.00 and 14.00-17.00 (closed Fri). Sun, (Jul-Sep only) 14.00-17.00. Free. Tel: (01382) 76121.
Former estuary fort, now museum. Local history gallery includes sections on fishing, lifeboat, ferries and growth of town. Important collection of relics from Dundee's former whaling industry including harpoons, knives and scrimshaw. Wildlife of sea-shore. Display of arms and armour, and military history of castle. Small shop.

Broughty Ferry Harbour, Dundee
Adjacent to Broughty Castle Museum on waterfront. Parking available. Tel: (01382) 23141, ext. 4282.
Recently renovated, the harbour provides a focus for water-based activities - water skiing, a watering facility for yachts, sea and river swimming, the Dundee Water Festival in early August, with raft races. Water sports equipment for hire. Parking facilities for disabled visitors.

Camperdown House and Country Park, Dundee
Off A923, near junction with A972, 3m NW of

city centre. Tel: (01382) 23141.

A mansion of c. 1829 for the 1st Earl of Camperdown, son of Admiral Lord Duncan, victor of the Battle of Camperdown, 1797. The Mansion is situated in 395 acres of beautiful parkland containing many rare trees (including Camperdown Elm). Golf, tennis, horseriding, putting, caravan park. Mansion houses a self-service restaurant. Award-winning "Battle of Camperdown" Adventure Play Park and Wildlife Centre in grounds too.

Camperdown Wildlife Centre, Dundee

Off A923, near junction with A972, 3m NW of Dundee. Jan-Dec, Apr-Sept, daily 10.00-16.30 (last admission 15.45). Oct-Mar, daily 10.00-15.30 (last admission 14.45). Entrance charge. Snack bar, souvenir shop, restaurant in park. Parking available. Tel: (01382) 623555.

Indigenous wildlife collection including deer paddocks, wildcats, pinemartens, European brown bear, lynx, wolves, arctic foxes, pheasants, golden eagle and buzzards. Wildfowl ponds, bantams and large selection of domestic stock. Guided tours for educational parties. Snack bar and souvenir shop, restaurant 250 yards away, large play complex adjacent (free). Free parking.

The Caterthuns

5m NW of Brechin. All times. Free. (HS). Tel: 0131-244 3101.

These remains of Iron Age hill forts stand on hills on either side of the road from Balrownie to Pitmudie, beyond Little Brechin. The Brown Caterthun has four concentric ramparts and ditches; the White Caterthun is a well-preserved hill fort with massive stone rampart, defensive ditch and outer earthworks.

Clatto Country Park, Dundee

Dalmahoy Drive, off A972 from Dundee city centre. All year, 10.00-dusk. Free. Parking available. Tel: (01382) 89076.

Reservoir area with 24 acres of water protected by a shelter belt of conifer and mixed woodland. Particularly popular for windsurfing, canoeing and dinghy sailing (instruction available). Rowing boats, windsurfing, canoeing and sailing equipment for hire. Barbecue facilities. Children's adventure play area.

Claypotts Castle, Dundee

S of A92, 3 m E of city centre. Apr-Sept, opening standard. Oct-Mar closed. Free. (HS). Tel: 0131-244 3101.

Now in suburban surroundings, this is one of the most complete of tower houses, laid out on

a Z-plan. It bears the dates 1569 and 1588 and was built for the Strachan family.

Crombie Country Park

Monikie, near Broughty Ferry. 11.5 miles E of Dundee on A92. Turn left at Muirdrum Crossroads, signposted thereafter. Jan-Dec, 10.00-dusk. Free. Parking available. Tel: (0124 16) 360.

Victorian reservoir with the appearance of a natural loch. Extensive conifer woodland and some broadleaf and specimen trees in 250 acres of land. Wildlife hides, trails, display and interpretation centre. Ranger Centre with environmental displays, woodland and lochside walks. Guided walks, talks, picnic and barbecue areas, children's play park and conservation areas.

Damside Garden Herbs and Arboretum

Situated 2 miles inland off the A92 between Montrose and Stonehaven by Johnshaven. Follow signs. Apr-24 Dec. Tues-Sun 10.00-17.00. Evening by arrangement, groups. Entrance charge. Parking available. Tearoom and licensed shop. Tel: (01561) 61496.

Herb garden of over 8 acres showing the history of Celtic, Roman, Monastic and Formal Herbs. Newly planted arboretum. Information area. Tearoom seating 36. Shop (not licensed).

Discovery Point, Dundee

Discovery Quay, close to Tay Bridge. All year. Mar-Oct, Mon-Sat 10.00-17.00, Sun 11.00-17.00. Nov-Feb, Mon-Sat 10.00-16.00, Sun 11.00-16.00.

Major attraction entertains visitors with the story of the Royal Research Ship Discovery, Captain Scott's famous Antarctic exploration vessel, built in Dundee in 1901. The centre tells why she was built in Dundee, of her launching and voyages to Antarctica. Audio-visual recounts the rescue of the Discovery from the ice by Dundee whaler *Terra Nova,* and the *Morning.* Visitors can also tour the ship in her new berth - sections never before seen by the public have been opened up.

Duntrune Demonstration Garden, Dundee

Duntrune Terrace, off Claypotts Road, turn off from A85. Jan-Dec. Mon-Fri 08.00-16.00. Demonstration Apr-Sep every Wed pm and alternative Sat am. Parking available. Tel: (01382) 23141, ext. 4299.

A year-round display and advice centre on all aspects of gardening.

Eassie Sculptured Stone

In Eassie Kirkyard, 7m WSW of Forfar. All

reasonable times. Free. (HS). Tel: 0131-244 3101.

A fine example of an early Christian monument, elaborately carved.

Edzell Castle and Garden
Off B966, 6m N of Brechin. Opening standard exc Oct-Mar, closed Thurs pm and all day Friday. Entrance charge. (HS). Tel: 0131-244 3101.

The beautiful pleasance, a walled garden, was built by Sir David Lindsay in 1604; the heraldic and symbolic sculptures are unique in Scotland, and the flower-filled recesses in the walls add to the outstanding formal garden, which also has a turreted garden house. The castle itself, an impressive ruin, dates from the early 16th century, with a large courtyard mansion of 1580.

Errol Station Railway Heritage Centre
Errol Station, between Dundee and Perth. May-Sept, Sun only 12.00-17.00. Entrance charges. Parking available. Refreshments. Tel: (0157 54) 222.

Preserved railway station on the Dundee-Perth railway line, which is still operational. Original building of 1847 has booking office, general waiting room, ladies' waiting room and porter's house - all restored to 1920s appearance. Slide show of Dundee-Perth railway.

Glamis Castle
A94, 5m SW of Forfar. Easter, early Apr- early Oct, daily 10.30-17.30, other times by prior arrangement only. Entrance charge. Parking available. Gift shop. Gallery shop. Garden produce stall. Self-service restaurant. Tel: (0130 784) 242/243.

This famous Scottish castle, childhood home of Her Majesty Queen Elizabeth The Queen Mother and birthplace of The Princess Margaret, owes its present appearance to the period 1675-87. Portions of the high square tower, with walls 15 feet thick, are much older. There has been a building on the site from very early times and Malcolm II is said to have died there in 1034. The oldest part of today's castle is Duncan's Hall, legendary setting of Shakespeare's famous play 'Macbeth'. There are also fine collections of china, painting, tapestry and furniture. Gift shop, gallery shop (selling pictures, prints and antiques); garden produce stall, self-service restaurant (serving light lunches and a range of home-baked items).

House of Dun
On A935 4m W of Montrose. Grounds and courtyard buildings open Easter weekend, May-Oct, daily 11.00-17.30. Entrance charge. Parking available. (NTS). Tel: (0167 481) 264.

Palladian house overlooking the Montrose Basin, built in 1730 for David Erskine, Lord Dun, to designs by William Adam. Exuberant plasterwork in the saloon. Courtyard buildings include a potting shed and gamekeeper's room. Also Angus Weavers giving displays of weaving linen tableware on traditional looms. Woodland walks.

Howff Burial Ground, Dundee
Meadowside. Daily, closes 17.00 or dusk if earlier. Tel: (01382) 23141.

Formerly the gardens of the Greyfriars' Monastery, the Howff was granted to Dundee as a burial ground by Mary, Queen of Scots. Used as a burial ground between the 16th and 19th centuries, it contains many finely carved tombstones. It was also used as a meeting place by Dundee's Incorporated Trades until 1778, hence the name 'howff'.

Kerr's Miniature Railway
In Arbroath, on the seafront 600 yds from parking beside Hotel Seaforth on A92. Apr-Sept, Sat and Sun 14.00-17.00. July and first half of Aug, daily 14.00-17.00. Tel: (01241) 79249.

Steam and petrol-hauled trains (four locos). Runs for 400yds alongside BR Edinburgh to Aberdeen main line. Tunnel, footbridge and platforms, turntable and loco shed. Miniature bus and fire engine give trips for children along promenade.

Kirriemuir R.A.F. Museum
Bellies Brae, Kirriemuir, 5 miles NE of Glamis Castle. Apr-Sept. Mon-Thur, Sat 10.00-17.00, Fri & Sun 11.00-17.00. Donations accepted. Parking available. Tel: (01575) 73233.

Wartime Royal Air Force memorabilia, including war relics, uniforms, diaries and books, ejection seats, medals and instruments, flying suits.

William Lamb Memorial Studio
24 Market Street, Montrose. Jul, Aug, Sat 14.00-17.00. Free. Car parking only. Gift shop. Tel: (01674) 73232.

Studio of William Lamb, ARSA (1893-1951), noted Montrose sculptor and etcher, containing a selection of his works including heads of HM Queen Elizabeth and HRH Princess Margaret as girls, and HM The Queen Mother as Duchess of York. His workrooms with tools, and living room with his own designs of furniture, are also featured.

The Law, Dundee

All reasonable times. Car park at top of hill. Floodlit at night.

The Law is the highest point in the city, and takes its name from the old Scots word for a hill. It is the remains of a volcanic plug and was later the site of an ancient hill fort. Atop the Law is Dundee's War Memorial with a beacon which is lit four times a year. Magnificent panoramic views across Dundee and the surrounding countryside to Fife and the northern mountains.

McManus Galleries, Dundee

Albert Square, city centre. All year, exc Xmas and New Year. Mon-Sat 10.00-17.00. Free. Shop. Tel: (01382) 23141, ext. 65136.

Dundee's principal museum and art gallery. Local history displays including major new galleries on trade and industry, social and civic history. Archaeology gallery under redevelopment. Art galleries contain important collection of Scottish and Victorian paintings; and silver, glass, ceramics, furniture. Regular touring exhibitions. Shop.

Meigle Museum

In Meigle, on A94, 12m WSW of Forfar. Apr-Sept, opening standard. Closed Oct-Mar. Entrance charge. (HS). Tel: 0131-244 3101.

This magnificent collection of 25 sculptured monuments of the Celtic Christian period, all found at or near the old churchyard, forms one of the most notable assemblages of Dark Age sculpture in Western Europe.

Meffan Institute

20 West High Street, Forfar. Jan-Dec. Mon-Sat 10.00-17.00. Free. Gift shop. Tel: (01307) 68813 or 64123.

Art gallery and museum has two exhibition galleries, one exhibiting works from the permanent collection of Angus District Council, and the other staging touring exhibitions, which feature works by major Scottish and international contemporary artists in a wide-ranging programme. The museum is designed to tell the story of Forfar.

Mills Observatory, Dundee

Balgay Park, north side of the city. Apr-Sep, Mon-Fri 10.00-17.00, Sat 14.00-17.00; Oct-Mar, Mon-Fri 15.00-22.00, Sat 14.00-17.00. Closed Xmas and New Year. Free. (Booking essential for large groups and for entry into the planetarium). Parking available. Shop. Tel: (01382) 67138.

A public astronomical observatory with telescopes, displays on astronomy and space exploration, lecture room with projection equipment, and small planetarium. Viewing of sky subject to weather conditions. Balcony with fine views over River Tay. Audio-visual programme. Small shop and toilets.

Monikie Country Park

Off B962, 1m N of Newbigging, 10m N of Dundee. All year, exc Xmas and New Year, 10.00-dusk. Parking available. Souvenirs. Tearoom (May-Sept). Tel: (0182 623) 202.

Country park situated on a reservoir complex of three areas of water, constructed by the Dundee Water Company over a span of 20 years from 1845. Ground consists of parkland and mixed woodlands, and covers 185 acres. Countryside Ranger Service, woodland walks, watersports including canoeing, sailing and windsurfing courses. Children's play area, rowing, sailing and windsurf hire, picnic areas with barbecue sites. Tearoom in summer.

Montrose Museum and Art Gallery

Panmure Place. Jan-Dec, Mon-Sat 10.00-17.00. Free. Car parking only. Gift shop. Tel: (01674) 73232.

Extensive local collections cover the history of Montrose from prehistoric times to local government reorganisation, the maritime history of the port, the natural history of Angus and local art. Pictish stones, Montrose silver and pottery; whaling artefacts; Napoleonic items (including a cast of his death mask). Paintings by local artists and local views, sculpture by W. Lamb.

Red Castle

Off A92, 7m S of Montrose. All times. Free.

This red stone tower on a steep mound beside the sandhills of Lunan Bay probably dates from the 15th century when it replaced an earlier fort built for William the Lion by Walter de Berkely. Robert the Bruce gave it to Hugh, 6th Earl of Ross, in 1328.

Restenneth Priory

Off B9113, 1.5m ENE of Forfar. All reasonable times. Free. (HS). Tel: 0131-244 3101.

A house of Augustinian canons, probably founded by David I on the site of an earlier church in an attractive setting. A feature of the ruins is the tall square tower, with its shapely broach spire, and an early doorway at its base.

St. Cyrus National Nature Reserve

Old Lifeboat Station, Nether Warburton. From Montrose take A92 north: after crossing North Esk River take first right for 0.5m. From St. Cyrus take A92 for 1m, turn left before crossing North Esk bridge and proceed for 0.5m. May-

Sept, Tues-Sun 09.30-17.30. Free. Parking available. Tel: (0167 48) 3736.
The reserve has many botanical and ornithological interests while the visitor centre houses displays on local history, natural history, salmon fishing and wildlife. There are children's games, a salt water aquarium and an audio visual. Guide dogs not allowed.

St. Vigean's Museum
0.5m N of Arbroath. Open all reasonable times. (HS). Tel: 0131-244 3101.
A cottage musum containing Pictish gravestones which are among the most important groups of early Christian sculpture in Scotland. Attractive St. Vigean's Church nearby.

Shaw's Sweet Factory, Dundee
Fulton Road, west end of Kingsway by NCR factory. May-Sept, Mon-Fri 11.30-16.00 (closed last week Jul/first week Aug). Oct-Apr (exc Xmas & New Year). Wed only 13.30-17.00. Free. Coach parties or large groups Mon-Fri any time by phone (1 hour's notice). Factory shop. Parking available. Tel: (01382) 610369.
1940's style sweet factory, producing old fashioned sweets using traditional methods. The sweet-maker will demonstrate and explain the precedure. Factory shop and mini-museum of sweet making.

Tay Bridges, Dundee
The present Railway Bridge carries the main line from Edinburgh to Aberdeen. Built between 1883 and 1887, it replaces the first Tay Railway Bridge which was blown down by a storm in 1879 with the loss of a train and 75 lives after being in use for less than 2 years. The Rail Bridge is the longest in Europe. The Road Bridge was opened in 1966, spanning the River Tay from Dundee to Newport-on-Tay, a distance of 1.5 miles. It is made of box girders resting on 42 concrete piers, and took over 3 years to build. No disabled access to Road Bridge walkway.

Templeton Woods, Dundee
Signposted, N of A92 Coupar Angus road, opposite Camperdown Park. Jan-Dec. Ranger Centre open daylight hours in winter, 10.00-17.00 Apr-Sept. Parking available. Picnic and barbecue tables. Tel: (01382) 623555.
150 acres of mixed woodland is a major focus for the Dundee Countryside Ranger Service, who operate out of the award-winning Ranger Centre. The centre has an ongoing ecology-based exhibition, and is the start for a wide variety of guided walks.

University Botanic Garden, Dundee
Off Riverside Drive. Mar-Oct, Mon-Sat 10.00-16.30, Sun 11.00-16.00. Nov-Feb, Mon-Sat 10.00-15.00, Sun 11.00-15.00. Entrance charge. Parking available. Refreshments. Tel: (01382) 66939.
A teaching collection of native and exotic plants in 9 hectares of naturalistically landscaped garden, tropical and temperate planthouses. Award winning visitors centre.

ABERDEEN
Amusement Park
Beach Boulevard, Aberdeen. Easter-Sept. Open daily during Easter holidays, Jul, Aug. Entrance charge. Parking available. Beach bus. Gift shop. Tel: (01224) 581909.
Largest amusement park in Scotland with ten major rides, eight children's rides, large adventure playground, arcades, video games, roller coaster. Wristband ticket gives use of all rides and attractions.

Arts Centre Gallery
33 King Street. Jan-Dec. Mon-Sat, 10.00-17.00. Inductive loop. Tel: (01224) 635208.
Exhibitions, mainly by local artists, photographers and craftsmen. Exhibitions change monthly, additional smaller displays from time to time.

Art Gallery and Museums
Schoolhill. All year. Mon-Sat 10.00-17.00 (Thu 10.00-20.00), Sun 14.00-17.00. Free. Tel: (01224) 646333.
Permanent collection of 18th, 19th and 20th century art with the emphasis on contemporary works. A full programme of special exhibitions. Music, dance poetry, events, film, coffee shop, gallery shop, reference library, print room. Disabled access: A lift is available in the Gallery for disabled visitors which takes them to the first floor galleries and also gives access to the McBey print room and reference library. Guide dogs permitted.

Beach Leisure Complex
Beach Promenade. Jan-Dec. Daily. Parking available. Public transport. Beach Leisure Centre. Creche, cafe and bar. Inductive loop. Tel: (01224) 647647.
Beach Leisure Centre has exotic leisure pool, jacuzzi, four flumes, including one of the longest enclosed flumes in the world. Health suite and fully-equipped sports hall including 25ft practice climbing wall. Linx Ice Arena, 56 metres by 26 metres, provides curliing, discos, professional instruction, ice hockey and skating clubs, as well as open skating. Spectator seating for 1,000.

Bridge of Dee

Built in 1520's by Bishop Gavin Dunbar in James V's reign. Its seven arches span 400 feet and it formerly carried the main road south. The mediaeval solidity of the structure is enlivened by heraldic carvings.

Brig O'Balgownie

At Bridge of Don, N of Aberdeen, upstream of main A92 bridge.

Also known as the 'Auld Brig o' Don', this massive arch, 62 feet wide, spans a deep pool of the river and is backed by fine woods. It was completed c. 1320 and repaired in 1607. In 1605 Sir Alexander Hay endowed the bridge with a small property, which has so increased in value that it built the New Bridge of Don (1830), a little lower down, at a cost of £26,000, bore most of the cost of the Victoria Bridge, and contributed to many other public works. Now closed to motor vehicles.

Crombie Woollen Mill

Signposted of Great Northern Road (A96) at Woodside. Open 7 days, Mon-Sat 09.00-16.30, Sun 12.00-16.30. Closed Xmas and New Year. Free. Licensed restaurant and coffee shop. Parking available. Tel: (01224) 483201.

Visit the original home of the famous Crombie cloth, coats etc. Award-winning museum and visitor centre. Audio-visual display. A chance to buy cloth, wool and ready-made clothes at the picturesque former mill by River Don in Aberdeen. Fishing and riverside walks.

Cruickshank Botanic Gardens

Chanonry. All year, Mon-Fri 09.00-16.30, also May-Sep, Sat and Sun 14.00-17.00. Free. Tel: (01224) 272704.

Extensive collection of shrubs, herbaceous and Alpine plants, heather and succulents. Rock and water gardens.

James Dun's House

Schoolhill. All year. Mon-Sat 10.00-17.00. Free. Tel: (01224) 646333.

This former residence of James Dun, master and rector of Aberdeen Grammar School, is now a museum featuring special temporary exhibitions of particular interest to families. Museum shop.

Duthie Park and Winter Gardens

Polmuir Road/Riverside Drive. All year daily, 10.00 until 30 mins before dusk. Free. Restaurant and dining room. Plant shop. Tel: (01224) 585310.

One of Aberdeen's many parks - and one of the favourites with the residents. It features an all-year round display of colour in the Winter Gardens, as well as the unique 'rose hill' where the city's enthusiasm for roses is best seen. Westburn, Seaton, Hazlehead also well worth a visit.

Family History Shop

152/164 King Street. Jan-Dec. Mon-Fri 10.00-16.00, Sat 10.00-13.00. Tel: (01224) 646323.

Bookshop and advice centre for members of the public starting research into family history, attached to library (private) of Aberdeen and North-East Scotland Family History.

Fishmarket

Off Market Street. Tel: (01224) 897744.

Aberdeen is one of the major fishing ports of Britain, landing hundreds of tons of fish daily. Every morning (Mon-Fri) the fishing fleets unload their catches, which are auctioned off amid tense bustle. Best visited 0730-0930.

Gordon Highlanders' Regimental Museum

Viewfield Road. May-Sept. Tues & Thurs, 13.00-16.30, third Sun in month, 14.00-16.00. Other times by appointment. Free (donation box). Car parking available. Shop. Tel: (01224) 318174.

Displays of regimental uniforms, colours, weapons, silver and pictures.

His Majesty's Theatre

Rosemount Viaduct in city centre. Entrance charges vary according to performance. Parking nearby. Inductive loop. Tel: Box Office (01224) 641122.

Fine theatre building, designed by Frank Matcham and opened in 1906. Wide range of productions from opera and ballet to summer revue and the annual pantomime. Organised tours for schools, workshops and talks.

Jonah's Journey

Rosemount Place, Aberdeen. Apr-Sept, Mon-Fri 10.00-16.00; Oct-Mar, Mon-Fri 10.00-14.00. Sat/Sun by arrangement. Closed public holidays. July, please check with Aberdeen Tourist Information Centre. Parking available. Coffee lounge. Shop. Tel: (01224) 647614.

The Gallery forms activity-based learning centre on aspects of life in Bible times; ideal for children as they can dress-up, grind grain, spin, weave. Also they can visit a well, a nomad's tent, Israelite house, workshop, etc. Coffee lounge, shop (Mon-Sat 10.00-12.00). Street market, Sat 10.00-12.00.

King's College

High Street, Old Aberdeen. Free. (University of Aberdeen).

Founded 1494. The chapel, famous for its rich woodwork, is 16th century and the notable 'crown' tower is 17th century.

Kirk of St. Nicholas

On a site bounded by Back Wynd, Schoolhill, Correction Wynd and Union Street. May-Sept (main door access) Mon-Fri 12.00-16.00, Sat 13.00-15.00. Oct-Apr (access through office) Mon-Fri 10.00-13.00. Sunday service, Jan-Dec 11.00. Free (donation box). Small shop. Tel: (01224) 643494.

St. Nicholas, the original parish church (locally known as 'the mither kirk'), is still an active place of worship. Although much damaged at the Reformation, the fabric of the church still incorporates 12th century masonry in the transepts, a 15th century vaulted lower church, the rebuilt nave (part of the West Kirk, designed by James Gibbs in 1755), the rebuilt choir (East Kirk, 1837-1874). Features include medieval effigies, wall and floor monuments, 17th century needlework panels, woodwork from the 16th to the 20th centuries. The north transept was refurbished in 1990 by the oil industry, winning a Saltire Society award. The 48-bell carillon is regularly heard throughout the city centre.

Marischal Museum

Marischal College, Broad Street. Jan-Dec, Mon-Fri, 10.00-17.00, Sun, 14.00-17.00. Free. Tel: (01224) 273131.

An imposing granite structure of the 19th century. In the quadrangle, entered by a fine archway, are older buildings of 1836-44, with the graceful Mitchell Tower. The Marischal Museum houses local, classical, Egyptian and Chinese antiquities, and a general ethnographic collection.

Peacock Printmakers

21 Castle Street. Jan-Dec, exc 2 weeks over Xmas. Mon-Sat 09.30-17.30. Free. Shop. Tel: (01224) 639539.

Printmaking workshop, gallery showing art related to North-East Scotland, small museum, shop selling prints and maps. Tours and demonstration of printmaking facilities on request.

Provost Ross's House/Maritime Museum

Shiprow. NTS Visitor Centre open May-Sept, Mon-Sat 10.00-16.00. Free. Tel: (01224) 572215. Maritime Museum open Jan-Dec, Mon-Sat 10.00-17.00. Shop. Special exhibitions Oct-Mar. Tel: (01224) 585788.

Built in 1593, Provost Ross's House is the third oldest house in Aberdeen. NTS Visitor Centre includes a presentation on the Trust's Grampian properties. Aberdeen Maritime Museum, within Provost Ross's House, uses models, paintings and audio-visual displays to tell the story of local shipbuilding, the fishing industry, and North Sea oil and gas developments.

Provost Skene's House

Guestrow, off Broad Street. All year. Mon-Sat 10.00-17.00. Free. Parking available. Tel: (01224) 641086.

Erected in the 16th century, this house bears the name of its most notable owner, Sir George Skene, Provost of Aberdeen 1676-1685. Remarkable painted ceilings and interesting relics. Period rooms suitably furnished and displays of local history. A video gives an introduction to the house and its history. Provost Skene's kitchen (for tea, coffee and light meals).

St. Machar's Cathedral

Chanonry. All year, 09.00-17.00. Free. Tel: (01224) 485988.

This granite cathedral was founded in 1131 on an earlier site, though the main part of the building dates from the mid-15th century. The west front with its twin towers is notable, and the painted wooden heraldic nave ceiling is dated 1520. The nave is in use as a parish church.

St. Mary's Cathedral

20 Huntly Street. Jan-Dec. Daily, 08.30-16.00 (winter), 08.30-17.00 (summer). Bookshop.

Dedicated in 1860 as a church for all the Catholics in Aberdeen, the architecture of St. Mary's is Gothic in style, with a single elegant spire. The High Altar and four Side Altars are embellished with tapestries and paintings by contemporary Scottish artists, depicting the church's involvement in the community. Stained West Window depicts the fifteen mysteries of the Rosary. Fine 19th century organ. Entrance includes a modern engraved glass window by David Gulland, depicting the martyr St. John Ogilvie.

Satrosphere, The Discovery Place

West end of Union Street in Justice Mill Lane. Open all year. Mon-Sat 10.00-16.00, Sun 13.30-17.00, closed Tues during school term. Entrance charge. Small cafe and seating area. Shop selling science-based toys and gifts. Parking available. Tel: (01224) 213232.

'Hands-on' Science & Technology Centre with between 70-100 do-it-yourself experiments, exploring sound, light, energy and the environment. Special events every 2/3 months.

Small cafe and seating area. Shop selling science-based toys and gifts.

University Zoology Museum
Along King Street, left at roundabout, situated at corner of Tillydrone Avenue and St. Machar's Drive. All year (except Christmas and New Year), Mon-Fri 09.00-17.00. Free. Parking available. Tel: (01224) 272850.
A general collection of exhibits on the animal kingdom, with particular emphasis on British birds and insects. The Botany Department gardens are adjacent. Disabled visitors welcome, but prior notice required.

NORTH EAST

Aden Country Park
On A950 between Old Deer and Mintlaw, 30m N of Aberdeen. Jan-Dec. Daily, 07.00-22.00. Wildlife Centre, May-Sept, weekends only 14.00-17.00. Free. Tearoom. Parking available. Tel: (01771) 22857.
Country Park of 230 acres containing woodland walks, picnic areas, caravan site etc. Ranger service and exhibitions, picnic areas, adventure playground, numerous walks and features. Restaurant, shop and tourist information centre. It is home of the award-winning North East of Scotland Agricultural Heritage Centre.

Alford Heritage Centre
Mart Road, Alford. 25 miles W of Aberdeen on A944. Apr-Sep, Mon-Sat 10.00-17.00, Sun 13.00-17.00. Entrance charge. Parking available. Refreshments. Tel: (0197 55) 62906.
Extensive exhibition of agricultural and rural life, mounted by Alford and Donside Heritage Association.

Alford Valley Railway
Alford Station. Apr, May, Sept, weekends only. June, July, Aug, daily. First train 11.00, last train 16.30. Parking available. Tel: (019755) 62326.
Narrow gauge railway running from Alford Station and Museum to Haughton Country Park, approx. 1 mile and Haughton Country Park to Murray Park (1 mile). Terminus near Alford Transport Museum.

Ardclach Bell Tower
Off A939, 8.5 miles SE of Nairn. Open all reasonable times. Free, apply keykeeper. (HS). Tel: 0131-244 3101.
A two-storey tower of 1655 whose bell summoned worshippers to the church and warned the neighbourhood in case of alarm.

Auchindoun Castle
In Glen Fiddich, 3m SE of Dufftown, 0.5m off A941. All times: viewed from the outside only. Free. (HS). Tel: 0131-244 3101.
A massive ruin on the summit of an isolated hill, enclosed by prehistoric earthworks. The corner stones were removed to Balvenie. In Queen Mary's wars the castle was the stronghold of the redoubtable 'Edom o'Gordon' who burned Corgarff. Jacobite leaders held a council of war there after Dundee's death at Killiecrankie.

Balmedie Country Park
Balmedie, 8 miles N of Aberdeen. Country park open Jan-Dec, daily. Visitor Centre: Apr-Sep, daily, Oct-Mar, Mon-Fri only 09.00-17.00. Free. Only Park barbecues may be used, book in advance through Ranger Service. Parking available. Tel: (01358) 42396.
Country park on the Don-Ythan coastline, a section of the attractive North-East coast with its long stretches of unbroken mobile dunes. Two large car parks, three barbecue sites, play areas, picnic sites and easy access to the beach using boardwalks. Ranger service, based in Visitor Centre, provides information on the physical, social and natural history of the area.

Balmoral Castle
On A93, 8m W of Ballater. Grounds and exhibition of paintings and works of art in the Ballroom of the castle. May-Jun-Jul daily except Sun 10.00-17.00. Donations from entry fee to charities. Tel: (013397) 42334.
The family holiday home of the Royal Family for over a century. The earliest reference to it, as Bouchmorale, was in 1484. Queen Victoria visited the earlier castle in 1848; Prince Albert bought the estate in 1852; the castle was rebuilt by William Smith of Aberdeen with modifications by Prince Albert and was first occupied in 1855. Souvenir shops, refreshment room, country walks and pony-trekking.

Balvenie Castle
At Dufftown, A941, 16m SSE of Elgin. Apr.-Sept., standard opening; closed Oct.-Mar. Parking available. (HS). Tel: 0131-244 3101.
Picturesque ruins of 13th century moated stronghold originally owned by the Comyns. Visited by Edward I in 1304 and by Mary Queen of Scots in 1562. Occupied by Cumberland in 1746. The corner stones came from Auchindoun.

Banchory Museum
Bridge Street, Banchory. Free. Contact: North East Scotland Museums Service for details of hours. Tel: (01779) 77778.

Museum (opened 1993) in library complex, features local history and natural history. Large collection of Royal commemorative china, items connected with noted fiddler Scott Skinner. Highland dress display and fine silverware by Robb of Ballater.

Banff Museum

On A98 at Banff. Jun-Sep, 14.00-17.15 (not Thu). Free. Tel: (01779) 77778.

Displays of Banff silver, arms and armour, local history and relics of James Ferguson, the 18th century astronomer. Ground floor, accessible to wheelchairs, has award-winning natural history display.

Baxter's Visitor Centre

1m W of Fochabers on main Aberdeen-Inverness road (A96). Jan-Dec. Mon-Fri 09.30-16.30 (Fri-last tour 14.00). Also Sat and Sun from mid Apr-Christmas, 11.00-16.00. Coaches please book in advance for afternoons July-Aug. Tel: (01343) 820393, ext 241.

Slide show with commentary, Old Baxter Shop, replica of the original George Baxter and Sons establishment where Baxters of Speyside were formed. George Baxter cellar, shop and tearoom. Highland cattle nearby.

Boath Doocot

Off A96 at Auldearn, 2m E of Nairn. Donation box (NTS). Tel: (01463) 232034.

A 17th century doocot (dovecote) on the site of an ancient castle where Montrose flew the standard of Charles I when he defeated the Covenanters in 1645. The plan of the battle is on display.

Borve Brew House

Ruthven, 6 miles W of Huntly. Jan-Dec. Daily, 13.00-20.00. Free. Car parking only. Refreshments. Tel: (0146 687) 343.

Guided tours and displays of small family specialist brewery.

Braeloine Centre

Glen Tanar, 3 miles SW of Aboyne on B976. Apr-Sept. Daily, 10.00-17.00. Donations to Glen Tanar Charitable Trust. Parking available. Tel: (0133 98) 86072.

Centre contains a display of natural and cultural history of Glen Tanar. Waymarked walks from centre to points of interest, viewpoints, picnic areas. Hills, woods, riverside. Glen Tanar Charitable Trust Ranger service will provide guided walks by arrangement.

Braemar Castle

A93, at Braemar. May-mid Oct, daily, exc Fri,

10.00-18.00. Entrance charge. Parking available. Tel: (013397) 41219.

This turreted stronghold, built in 1628 by the Earl of Mar, was burnt by Farquharson of Inverey in 1689. It was rebuilt about 1748 and garrisoned by Hanoverian troops. There is a round central tower, a spiral stair, barrel-vaulted ceilings and an underground pit prison. Fully furnished family residence. Interesting historical relics. Free car and bus park.

Braemar Highland Heritage Centre

Mar Road, Braemar. Jan-Dec. Daily 10.00-18.00. Extended hours Jul-Sept. Entrance charge. Parking available. Shop. Tel: (0133 97) 41944.

Static displays and specially-commissioned film telling the story of Braemar through three themes - a journey over hills explaining the history of the land, a journey through time and the history of the Braemar Royal Highland Gathering, and the building of Balmoral Castle and Royal links with the area.

Brodie Castle and Gardens

Off A96, 4.5m W of Forres. Apr-Oct. Mon-Sat 11.00-18.00. Sun 14.00-18.00. Last admission 17.15. Entrance charge. Shop. Small tearoom. Entry to grounds only by donation. Parking available. (NTS). Tel: (0130 94) 371.

The castle, associated with the Brodie family for 500 years, was largely rebuilt after the earlier structure was burned in 1645; it is based on a 16th century 'Z' plan, with additions made in the 17th and 19th centuries. The house contains fine French furniture, English, Continental and Chinese porcelain, and a major collection of paintings. A woodland walk has been laid out in the gardens by the edge of a 4-acre pond. Picnic area, adventure playground, car park, shop and small tearoom.

Buckie Maritime Museum

Cluny Place. All year, Mon.-Fri. 10.00-20.00, Sat. 10.00-12.00. Free. Parking available. Sales point. Tel: (01309) 673701.

Displays on fishing methods, coopering, lifeboats, navigation and local history. The Peter Anson Gallery houses watercolours of the development of fishing in Scotland. Sales point.

Bullars of Buchan

Off A975, 7m S of Peterhead. Parking available. Tel: (01261) 812789 (Tourist Information).

A vast chasm in the cliffs, 200 feet deep, *which no man can see with indifference* said Dr Johnson in 1773. A haunt of innumerable seabirds.

Burns Family Tombstones and Cairn
Off A94, 8m SW of Stonehaven at Glenbervie Church. All times. Free.
The Burnes (Burns) family tombstones in the churchyard were restored in 1968 and a Burns memorial cairn is nearby.

Carnegie Museum
The Square, Inverurie. Jan-Dec. Mon, Tues, Thur, Fri 14.00-17.00, Sat 10.00-13.00. Free. Shop. Tel: (01779) 77778 (NE Scotland Museums Service).
Permanent display of local archaeology, with thematic exhibitions three times a year. Just outside the town on B993 is the Bass, a 60 foot high motte.

Cashmere Visitor Centre/Johnstons of Elgin
Turn off A96, follow signs for Elgin Cathedral, cross River Lossie, entrance 150 yards on right. Mill Shop: Mon-Sat 09.00-17.30. Mill tours: Mon-Thur 10.00-16.30. Free. Parking available. Shop. Tel: (01343) 549319.
Cashmere from China and lambswool are dyed, spun and woven by Johnstons. Established in 1798 at Newmill, Elgin, this is the only British mill where raw natural materials are converted into the final product. Mill shop.

Castle Fraser
Sauchen, Inverurie. Off A944, 4m N of Dunecht and 16m W of Aberdeen. Weekends in April and October 14.00-17.00; May, Jun, Sept, daily 14.00-18.00; Jul, Aug 11.00-18.00. Grounds open all year 09.30-sunset. Entrance charge. Parking available. Shop. Tearoom. (NTS). Tel: (0133 03) 463.
Castle Fraser begun about 1575. It belongs to the same great period of native architectural achievements as Crathes and Craigievar Castles, and is the largest and grandest of the Castles of Mar. Two notable families of master masons, Bel and Leiper, were involved in its construction, completed in 1636. Noted for its great hall. Garden and picnic area and tearoom.

Cloverleaf Fibre Stud
8m N of Huntly. Take A97, then take turning to Netherdale on right. The farm is 300 yds from junction. Jan-Dec. Guided tours at 11.00, 13.00 and 15.00; other times by arrangement. Parking available. Tel: (01466) 780879.
Working farm breeding llamas, alpacas, guanacos, reindeer, goats bearing cashmere, cashgora and mohair. Rare breeds of sheep. Garments for sale on display together with spinning and knitting fibres obtained from the animals.

Corgarff Castle
Off A939, 15m NW of Ballater. Opening standard, key-keeper in winter. Entrance charge. Parking available. (HS). Tel: 0131-244 3101.
A 16th century tower house, converted into a garrison post and enclosed within a star-shaped loopholed wall in 1748. The castle was burned in 1571 by Edom o' Gordon and the wife, family and household of Alexander Forbes, the owner, perished in the flames.

Craigellachie Bridge
Near A941, just N of Craigellachie, 12m SSE of Elgin. Parking available.
One of Thomas Telford's most beautiful bridges. Opened in 1814, it carried the main road till 1973 when a new bridge was built alongside. It has a 152 ft. main span of iron, cast in Wales, and two ornamental stone towers at each end.

Craigston Castle
Turriff-Fraserburgh road, 8m SE of Banff. Can be seen from the road. Open by appointment only, June-Sept. Entrance charge. Parking available. Tel: (018885) 228.
Seat of the Urquhart family since its building 1604-07. Can be seen from the Turriff to Fraserburgh road. Adjacent woodlands of interesting species etc. Parking.

Crathes Castle and Gardens
Off A93, 3m E of Banchory. Castle, Visitor Centre, Shop and Restaurant. Apr-Oct, daily 11.00-18.00. Garden and grounds all year 09.30 to sunset. Entrance charges. Trust shop, plant sales, restaurant, wayfaring course, adventure playground, picnic area, dog walks. Parking available. Ranger service. Tel: (0133 044) 525.
The double square tower of the castle dates from 1533 and the building, an outstanding example of a Scottish tower house, was completed in 1660. The notable interior includes the fascinating painted ceilings, dating from 1599, in the Chamber of the Nine Nobles, the Chamber of the Nine Muses and the Green Lady's Room. The Queen Anne and Victoria wings were destroyed by fire in 1966. The Queen Anne wing only was rebuilt and opened in 1972. Yew hedges dating from 1702 enclose a series of small gardens with fine collections of trees and shrubs. Nature trails designed for wheelchair users. Shop, licensed restaurant and snack bar; formal gardens, grounds with 7.5 miles of wayfaring trails, visitor centre with exhibition rooms and field study centre. Ample parking, cars and coaches.

Crathie Church

Crathie, 8m W of Ballater. 1 Apr.-31 Oct., daily 09.30-17.30, Sun 14.00-17.00 (services held at 11.30, Sun). Free.

This small church, built in 1895, is attended by the Royal Family when in residence at Balmoral.

Cullen Old Church

Signposted in Cullen. Apr-Sept, daily 14.00-16.00. Free. Parking available. Tel: (01542) 40757.

12th-century parish church with 16th and 17th century additions. Although essentially 14th century, this church with its fine sacrament house still incorporates some 12th-century work.

Dallas Dhu Distillery

Off the A940, 2m S of Forres. Opening standard exc closed Thur pm and all day Fri from Oct-Mar. Entrance charge. Parking available. Shop. (HS). Tel: 0131-244 3101.

Built at the end of the 19th century, this picturesque little distillery is a perfectly preserved time-capsule of the distiller's craft and a monument to Scotland's most famous product. Visitors may take guided tours or explore at leisure. Multi-lingual video on the history of Scotch whisky, a taste of the 'water of life', exhibition. Shop offering nearly 200 different whiskies. Picnic site.

Delgatie Castle

Off A947, 2m E of Turriff. Apr-Oct. Daily 14.00-17.00. Entrance charge. Tel: (01888) 62750.

Tower house, home of the Hays of Delgatie, dating back to the 11th century with additions up to the 17th century. Its contents include pictures and arms; the notable painted ceilings were installed c. 1590. Mary, Queen of Scots stayed here for three days in 1562; a portrait hangs in the room she used. Turnpike stair of 97 steps.

Deskford Church

Off B9108, 4m S of Cullen. Open all reasonable times. Free. (HS). Tel: 0131-244 3101.

This ruined building includes a rich carving which bears an inscription telling that *this present lovable work of sacrament house* was provided by Alexander Ogilvy of Deskford in 1551.

Drum Castle

Drumoak, by Banchory. Off A93, 10m W of Aberdeen. Apr & Oct, Sat & Sun 14.00-17.00. May-Sep, daily 14.00-18.00. Garden of Historic Roses, May-Oct, daily 10.00-18.00. Grounds

open all year, 09.30-sunset. Entrance charge to Castle. Play and picnic area. Tearoom. Publications. Parking available. (NTS). Tel: (01330) 811204.

A massive granite tower built towards the end of the 13th century adjoins a mansion of 1619. The Royal Forest of Drum was conferred in 1323 by Robert the Bruce on his armour-bearer and clerk-register, William de Irwin. The family connection remained unbroken until the death of Mr H Q Forbes Irvine in 1975. The house stands on a 400 acre estate with lawns, rare trees and shrubs, and inside are antique furniture and silver, family portraits and relics. Coffee room, adventure playground and wayfaring course.

Drummuir Castle

Just off B9014 between Keith and Dufftown. May-Sept, Sun 14.00-16.00. Parking available. Tel: (0154 281) 225.

Victorian castle with magnificent Lantern Tower. Recently restored home of the Duff family. Tours provided by owners. Garden and grounds.

Duff House

At Banff. Under restoration. No access at present. Parking available. (HS). Tel: 0131-244 3101.

Although incomplete, William Adam's splendid and richly detailed mansion is among the finest works of Georgian Baroque architecture in Britain. There is an interpretative exhibition.

Dufftown Museum

The Clock Tower, The Square, Dufftown. Apr, May, Oct, Mon-Sat 10.00-17.30; June, Sept, Mon-Sat 09.30-18.00, Sun 14.00-18.00; July, Aug, Mon-Sat 09.30-18.30, Sun 10.00-12.30, 13.30-18.00. Free. Tel: (01309) 673701.

Displays on local and social history themes. Tourist Information Office.

Duffus Castle

Off B9012, 5m NW of Elgin. Opening standard. Free. (HS). Tel: 0131-244 3101.

Massive ruins of a fine motte and bailey castle, surrounded by a moat still entire and water-filled. A fine 14th century tower crowns the Norman motte. The original seat of the de Moravia family, the Murrays, now represented by the Dukedoms of Atholl and Sutherland.

Dunnottar Castle

Off A92, S of Stonehaven. Mid Mar-Oct, Mon-Sat 09.00-18.00. Sun 14.00-17.00. Nov-mid Mar, Mon-Fri 09.00-Dusk. Parking available. Tel: (01569) 62173.

An impressive ruined fortress on a rocky cliff 160 feet above the sea, a stronghold of the Earls Marischal of Scotland from the 14th century. Montrose besieged it in 1645. During the Commonwealth wars, the Scottish regalia were hidden here for safety. Cromwell's troops occupied the castle but in 1652 this treasure was smuggled out by the wife of the minister at Kinneff, 7 miles south, and hidden under the pulpit in his church.

Elgin Cathedral
North College Street, Elgin. Opening standard exc Oct-Mar closed Thurs pm and all day Friday. Entrance charge. (HS). Tel: 0131–244 3101.
When entire, this was perhaps the most beautiful of Scottish cathedrals, known as the lantern of the North. It was founded in 1224, but in 1390 it was burned by the Wolf of Badenoch. It did not fall into ruin until after the reformation. Much 13th-century work still remains; the nave and chapter house are 15th-century. There is a 6th-century Pictish slab in the choir.

Elgin Museum
High Street, Elgin. Apr-Sept, Mon-Fri (exc. Wed) 10.00-17.00, Sat 11.00-16.00, Sun 14.00-17.00. Entrance charge. Tel: (01343) 543675.
An award-winning museum housing a world famous collection of Old Red Sandstone, Permian and Triassic fossils. Also exhibited are items ranging from prehistoric to modern times and natural history specimens of the area.

Falconer Museum
Tolbooth Street, Forres. 12m W of Elgin. May, June, Sept, Mon-Sat 09.30-18.00, Sun 14.00-17.00; July, Aug, Mon-Sat 09.30-18.30, Sun 12.00-17.30; Nov-Apr, Mon-Fri 10.00-12.30; 13.30-16.30. Free. Shop. Tel: (01309) 673701.
Displays on local history, natural history, fossils and temporary exhibitions. New display features the Corries folk duo.

Fasque
Approx. 0.5 mile N of Fettercairn on the Edzell-Banchory road (B974). May-Sep, daily (not Fri) 13.30-17.30. Entrance charge. Parking available. Small shop. Refreshments by arrangement. Tel: (0156 14) 569.
Bought by Sir John Gladstone in 1829, Fasque was home to William Gladstone, four times Prime Minister to Queen Victoria, for much of his life. Today, the sixth generation of the family live in the house. Downstairs very little has changed - the kitchen, sculleries, washroom, knives hall, bakery and buttery contain a wealth of domestic articles.

Magnificent cantilever staircase leads to state rooms, vast drawing room, library and bedrooms. Red deer roam in the park in front of the house. The family church in the grounds, St. Andrews, welcomes visitors.

Fettercairn Arch
In Fettercairn. On B9120, 4m W of Laurencekirk. All times. Free.
Stone arch built to commemorate the visit by Queen Victoria and the Prince Consort in 1861.

Fettercairn Distillery Visitors' Centre
5m W of the A94 Perth to Aberdeen road at Fettercairn. 0.5m W of Fettercairn square. Mon-Sat 10.00-16.30 (last tour 16.00). Free. Parking available. Gift shop. Tel: (0156 14) 205.
Fettercairn is one of the oldest licensed distilleries in Scotland. Tours describe the processes involved in distilling malt whisky and the lives of the people in the Mearns. Audio-visual presentation.

Findhorn Foundation
From Forres take B9011 to Kinloss and Findhorn for 1 mile, turn left immediately after Esso Seapark garage to Findhorn and just after Kinloss Air Base on right is Findhorn Foundation. Sign also says Findhorn Bay Caravan Park. Visitor Centre open all year, afternoons only in winter. Free. Parking available. Green Room Cafe open all day in summer, pm only in winter. Apothecary snack bar. Tel: (01309) 690311.
The Findhorn Foundation Community was founded in 1962 and has grown into an established community of resident members based on the spiritual beliefs of living in co-operation with nature and the planet. There are energy efficient buildings and a 75kw wind generator. There are weaving and pottery studios, a performing arts centre, and gardens at the Park and at Cullerne.

Fochabers Folk Museum
Fochabers. All year. Winter, daily 09.30-13.00, 14.00-17.00. Summer, daily 09.30-13.00, 14.00-18.00. Parking available. Tel: (01343) 820362.
An interesting conversion of an old church housing a large collection of horse-drawn carts on the top floor, and on the ground floor a varied collection of local items, giving the history of Fochabers over the past 200 years.

Foggieley Sheepskin Rugs
Craigievar, Alford on B9119 Aberdeen-Tarland Road. Jan-Dec. Mon-Fri 09.00-18.00. Sat & Sun 10.00-17.00. Free. Parking available. Shop. Tel: (0133 98) 83317.

Tannery workshop where skins are taken from their raw state to finished rugs. Shop sells rugs, leather and sheepskin goods and clothing.

Fordyce Joiner's Workshop and Visitor Centre
1.5 miles off A98, W of Portsoy. Easter-Oct. Daily, 10.00-17.00. Garden open all reasonable times. Free. Parking available.
This attraction describes the trade of the country joiner/carpenter over the last century and a half, through video, photographic, tool and machinery displays. Wood craftsmen at work in the former workshop. As part of the development, a Victorian garden has been laid out close to the Fordyce Burn. Fordyce, one of Scotland's best conserved small villages and largely traffic-free, is built around a 16th century castle and an early church containing splendid canopied tombs.

Forvie Nature Reserve/Visitor Centre
Off A974, 4m N of Newburgh turn at crossroads to Collieston, 1m turn right to Visitor Centre. Weekends all year, 10.00-17.00; weekdays, May-Aug 10.00-17.00. Free. Prior booking for group visits. Parking available. Tel: (0136 887) 330.
The nature reserve is an area of dunes, moorland and cliffs on an estuary. The visitor centre has an exhibition and audio-visual programme. There is a wildlife garden, a pond and a tree nursery.

Fowlsheugh Nature Reserve
Access along cliff-top path north from small car park at Crawton, signposted from A92, 3m S of Stonehaven. All times. (RSPB). Tel: 0131-557 3136.
Large and spectacular seabird colony, best seen April-July. Small visitor centre in car park is open Apr-Aug, with information warden.

Fyvie Castle
Off A947, 8m SE of Turriff and 25m NW of Aberdeen. Easter, weekends Apr & Oct, 14.00-17.00. May, daily 14.00-18.00. Jun-Aug, daily 11.00-18.00. Sept, daily 14.00-18.00. Grounds open all year, 09.30-sunset. Entrance charges. Parking available. Exhibition. Shop. Tearoom. (NTS). Tel: (0165 1) 891266.
The five towers of Fyvie Castle enshrine five centuries of Scottish history, each being built by the five families who owned the castle. The oldest part dates from the 13th century and it is now one of the grandest examples of Scottish baronial architecture. Apart from the great wheel stair, the finest in Scotland, and the 17th century morning room, with its contemporary panelling and plaster ceiling, the interior as created by the 1st Lord Leith of Fyvie reflects the opulence of the Edwardian era. There is an exceptionally important collection of portraits including works by Batoni, Raeburn, Ramsay, Gainsborough, Opie and Hoppner. In addition, there are arms and armour and 16th century tapestries. Tearoom, grounds including loch.

Fyvie Church
Off A947, 7m NW of Oldmeldrum. Open by arrangement. Parking available. Free. Tel: (0165 16) 230 or 335.
An attractive church with notable stained glass by Tiffany, Celtic stones and 17th-century panelling inside. 'Tifty's Annie' of local ballad fame is buried in the churchyard, and nearby a cross marks the site of a 12th-century monastery.

Glendronach Distillery
On B9001, between Huntly and Aberchirder, 19m N of Inverurie. All year, Mon-Fri 10.00 or 14.00 (by arrangement only). Free. Tel: (0146682) 202 (08.30-16.30).
Visitor Centre and guided tour around malt whisky distillery dating from 1826.

Glenfarclas Distillery
Off A95, 17m WSW of Keith and 17m NE of Grantown-on-Spey. Jan-Dec, exc. Xmas and New Year. Oct-May, Mon-Fri 09.00-16.30. June-Sept, also Sat 10.00-16.00, Sun 13.00-16.00. Other times by arrangement. Gift shop. Tel: (0180 72) 257/245.
Tours of a well-known malt whisky distillery, visual exhibition and museum of old illicit distilling equipment in Reception Centre.

Glenfiddich Distillery
Just N of Dufftown on A941, 16m S of Elgin. All year, weekdays 09.30-16.30 (except between Xmas and New Year). Also Easter-mid Oct, Sat 09.30-16.30, Sun 12.00-16.30. Free. Tel: (01340) 20373.
After an audio-visual programme available in six languages, visitors are shown around the distillery and bottling hall and are then offered a complimentary dram. Picnic area, gift shop at car park.

The Glenlivet Distillery Visitor Centre
B9008, 10m N of Tomintoul. Easter-end Oct, Mon-Sat 10.00-16.00 (July and Aug 19.00). Free. Coach parties by arrangement. Tel: (018073) 427 (during season) and (015422) 6294 (during winter).
Guided tours of distillery. Exhibits of ancient whisky tools and artefacts and life-size reproduction of Landseer's painting 'The Highland Whisky Still'. Free whisky sample

Children under 8 not admitted to production areas but welcome to Reception Centre.

Glenlivet Estate

Forest Office, Main Street, Tomintoul. Information Centre open July and Aug, 10.00-12.30, other times by arrangement depending on availability of Estate Ranger. Information also from Tomintoul Tourist Information Centre, The Square. Access to estate at all reasonable times. Free. Charge for Ranger-led Landrover tours. Tel: (0180 74) 283 or TIC (0180 74) 285.

Part of the Crown Estate, nearly 90 square miles of sheltered glens, forests and heather moors in the foothills of the NE Cairngorms. Over 40 miles of waymarked trails including the Speyside Way provide access for walking, mountain biking, pony trekking, Nordic skiing and other outdoor activities. An interpretative centre provides information about walks, history, wildlife and land use, and the Estate Ranger is available for advice on routes and places of interest. Landrover tours, slide talks, free Estate map and guide.

Glenmuick and Lochnagar

9 miles S of Ballater along minor road off B976. Visitor Centre open Easter-Oct. Parking available.

Superb mountain and loch scenery, including one of Scotland's best-known peaks. Upland plants and animals, including red deer. Well-developed network of walks give access to remote mountain scenery - around the loch and, for more experienced walkers, on the surrounding hills.

Glenshee Chairlift

Off A93, 10m S of Braemar. Xmas-mid Oct. Daily, 09.00-17.00. Charge for chairlift. Parking available. Shop. Licensed restaurant. Tel: (0133 97) 41320.

Ascends the Cairnwell mountain (3,059 feet) from the summit of the highest main road pass in Britain (2,199 feet). Restaurant.

Grampian Transport Museum

At Alford, 25m W of Aberdeen on A944. Apr-Nov, daily 10.00-17.00. Entrance charge. Parking available. Gift shop. Tel: (019755) 62292.

A large independent transport museum, opened in April 1983. Extensive collection of road vehicles, including horse drawn, steam, commercial and vintage motor cars. Pedal cycles and motorcycles also well represented. Highland rail transport is described in the railway museum in Alford's former railway station.

Grassic Gibbon Centre

Arbuthnott, Laurencekirk. On B967, 10 miles S of Stonehaven. Easter-Oct. Daily, 10.00-16.30. Entrance charge. Parking available. Gift shop. Coffee shop. Tel: (01561) 61668.

Visitor centre dedicated to the life and times of Lewis Grassic Gibbon (James Leslie Mitchell), featuring an exhibition with audio-visual display. Children's play area outside. Disabled access and toilet.

Russell Gurney Weavers

Braecroft, Muiresk. 2.5 miles from Turriff, off B9024. Jan-Dec. Mon-Sat 09.30-17.30. Free. Car parking only. Shop. Tel: (01888) 63544.

Small business involved in handweaving clothing fabrics in natural fibres, plus a range of made-up articles such as ties, scarves, stoles and shawls. The production processes can be demonstrated to visitors. Handweaving courses.

Haddo Country Park

B999 Aberdeen-Pitmedden road, signposted to right between Pitmedden and Tarves. Discovery Room open daily, 11.00-18.00 during summer season and at various other times. Free. Parking available. Tel: (01651) 851489.

180 acres, including woodland walks, lake, ponds, bird hides, picnic areas, adventure playground and Discovery Room. Ranger service.

Haddo House

Off B999, 4m N of Pitmedden, 19m N of Aberdeen. May-Sept, daily 14.00-18.00. June-Aug, daily 11.00-18.00. Apr and Oct, weekends 14.00-17.00. Grounds open all year 09.30-Sunset. Entrance charges. Parking available. Trust shop. Restaurant. (NTS). Tel: (016515) 440.

Designed in 1731 by William Adam, a pupil of Sir William Bruce and father of the Adam brothers, for William, second Earl of Aberdeen, Haddo House replaced the old House of Kellie, home of the Gordons of Methlick for centuries. Much of the interior is 'Adam Revival' carried out about 1880 for John, seventh Earl and first Marquess of Aberdeen and his Countess, Ishbel. Garden, Trust shop and tearoom.

Haughton Country Park

25m W of Aberdeen on A944, 0.5m N of the village of Alford. All year. Free. Parking available. Tel: (019755) 62453 or 62107.

Country Park with visitor centre and caravan site.

Huntly Castle

Castle Street, Huntly. Opening standard, exc

Oct-Mar, closed Thurs pm and all day Fri. Entrance charge. (HS). Tel: 0131–244 3101.

An imposing ruin which replaced mediaeval Strathbogie Castle which, until 1544, was the seat of the Gay Gordons, the Marquesses of Huntly, the most powerful family in the north until the mid-16th century. There are elaborate heraldic adornments on the castle walls. The castle, now stands in a wooded park, was destroyed by Moray in 1452, rebuilt, then rebuilt again in 1551-54, burned 40 years later and again rebuilt in 1602.

International League for the Protection of Horses

Belwade Farm, between Kincardine O'Neil and Aboyne on A93. Jan-Dec. Wed, Sat, Sun 14.00-16.00. Free, donations welcome. Parking available. Gift shop. Tel: (0133 98) 87186.

Scottish rest and rehabilitation centre for the International League for the Protection of Horses, which is the largest equine welfare organisation in the world.

Kildrummy Castle

A97, 10m W of Alford. Opening standard. Weekends only in winter. (HS). Tel: 0131-244 3101.

The most extensive example in Scotland of a 13th century castle. The four round towers, hall and chapel remains belong in substance to the original. The great gatehouse and other work is later, to the 16th century. It was the seat of the Earls of Mar, and played an important part in Scottish history until 1715 when it was dismantled.

Kildrummy Castle Gardens Trust

A97, off A944, 10m W of Alford, Aberdeenshire. Apr-Oct, daily 10.00-17.00. Children must be accompanied. Parking available. Tel: (0197 55) 71277 or 71203.

The shrub and alpine garden in the ancient quarry are of interest to botanists for their great variety. The water gardens lie below the ruined castle. Specimen trees are planted below it in the Back Den. Play area, video room, woodland walk. Plants for sale. Interesting old stones displayed. Museum opens on request. Dogs must be kept on leash.

Kindrochit Castle

Balnellan Road, Braemar. Free. All reasonable times. Parking available.

Ruins of ancient important fortification. Legend indicates that Malcolm Canmore built the first castle of Kindrochit in the 11th century. The existing remains stand above the Clunie and consist of walls and grass-grown embankments.

Kinkell Church

On the E bank of the Don, 2m S of Inverurie, off B993. All reasonable times. Free. (HS). Tel: 0131-244 3101.

The ruins of an early 16th century parish church with some ornate details including a rich sacrament house of unusual design, dated 1524.

Kinneff Old Church

Off unclassified road, E of A92, 2m N of Inverbervie. All reasonable times. Free. Parking available. (Kinneff Old Church Preservation Trust).

Part of this historic church formed the original building in which the Crown Jewels of Scotland were hidden for nine years after being smuggled from Dunnottar Castle through Cromwell's besieging army in 1651. In the present church, which dates from 1738, are the recently restored memorials to the parish minister, Rev. James Grainger, who concealed the regalia under the flagstones of the church; and to the governor of the castle, Sir George Ogilvy of Barras.

Lecht Ski Centre

Off A939, 7m SE of Tomintoul. Jan-Dec. Daily 08.30-17.30. Charge. Parking available. Licensed cafeteria. Tel: (0197 56) 51440.

Ski tows operating to slopes on both sides of the Lecht Road, famous for its snowfalls. Ski hire, ski school. Dry ski slope.

Leith Hall

B9002, 7m S of Huntly. (House) May-Sept, daily 14.00-18.00; Oct, Sat & Sun 14.00-17.00. (Grounds) all year 09.30-sunset. Entrance charges for house. Gardens and grounds by donation. Parking available. Tearoom (NTS). Tel: (014643) 216.

The mansion house of Leith Hall is at the centre of a 263-acre estate which was the home of the head of the Leith and Leith-Hay family from 1650. The house contains personal possessions of successive lairds, most of whom followed a tradition of military service. The grounds contain varied farm and woodlands. There are two ponds, a bird observation hide and three countryside walks, one leading to a hilltop viewpoint. Unique 18th century stables; Soay sheep; ice house. Extensive and interesting informal garden of borders, shrubs and rock garden. Picnic area and tearoom.

Loanhead Stone Circle

0.25m NW of Daviot, 5m NW of Inverurie, off B9001. All reasonable times. Free. (HS). Tel: 0131-244 3101.

The best known example of a widespread group of recumbent stone circles in east Scotland.

Lochindorb

Unclassified road off A939, 10m NW of Grantown-on-Spey.

On an island in this lonely loch stand the ruins of a 13th-century castle, once a seat of the Comyns. It was occupied in person by Edward I in 1303 and greatly strengthened. In 1336 Edward III raised the siege in which the Countess of Atholl was beleagured by the Regent Moray's troops. In 1371 the castle became the stronghold of the 'Wolf of Badenoch', the vicious Earl of Buchan who terrorised the area. It was dismantled in 1456.

Lossiemouth Fisheries and Community Museum

Situated at the harbour, East Basin, Lossiemouth. Apr-Sept, Mon-Sat 11.00-17.00. Entrance charges. Parking available. Tel: (01343) 813772.

Permanent features include Memorial Room for lost/drowned, killed in active service, fishermen and study of the late J. Ramsay McDonald, Prime Minister.

McEwan Gallery

On A939, 1m W of Ballater. Open all year, exc. Xmas and New Year, daily 10.00-18.00. Free. Parking available. Tel: (013397) 55429.

An unusual house built by the Swiss artist Rudolphe Christen in 1902, containing works of art, mainly of the Scottish school. Also natural history and sporting books. Occasional special exhibitions are held. Full advisory and restoration services.

Marnoch Old Church

Situated off the A97 Banff-Huntly Road. Free. Parking available. Access obtainable by telephoning (014665) 885/276.

The forced induction of an unwanted minister here in 1841 was a flashpoint leading to the Disruption of the Kirk in 1843 and the formation of the Free Church. Erected 1792. Standing stone nearby.

Millbuies Lochs

Longmorn, 5 miles S of Elgin on A941 to Rothes. Jan-Dec (fishing Mar-Oct). Daily. Free. Parking available. Tel: (01343) 86234.

The lochs are in a wooded setting with numerous walks, where wildlife and flora can be seen. Four boats are available for anglers.

Mill of Towie

Auchindachy, 3 miles SW of Keith on B9014. Mill: Easter-Xmas, Mon-Sat 10.00, Sun 11.00-16.00. Grain Store: May-Oct Mon-Sat exc Tues, 10.30-17.00. Sun 10.30-18.30. Entrance charges.

Parking available. Craft shop. Restaurant/tearoom. Tel: (0154 281) 307.

Nestling in the hills beside the River Isla, the Mill of Towie has been restored to full working order. Tours of the 19th-century oatmeal mill by the miller. Picnic and play area beside the river.

Monymusk Arts Centre

Monymusk 18 miles W of Aberdeen on A944 Alford road. May-Sep (crafts), Sept-Feb (music). Daily 10.00-16.00. Charge for performances. Parking available. Gift shop. Tearoom.

Musical recitals, arts and crafts exhibitions, a museum of local history and topography all have a place in this building, originally an 18th century lapidary mill. In 1801 the Episcopal congregation at Blairdaff moved to Monymusk and converted the mill into a church. During World War II the church was boarded up and used to store furniture for the next fifty years, but has now been restored by the Monymusk Arts Trust. The church organ is the subject of a restoration project.

Monymusk Walled Garden

Home Farm, Monymusk, 20 miles from Aberdeen on B993. Mar-Oct: Tues-Sat 10.00-17.00, Sun 14.00-17.00. Nov-Mar: Tues, Sat 10.00-17.00, Sun 14.00-17.00. Nov-Mar: Tues, Thur, Sat 10.00-15.00. Also open Mons in Apr, May, Sept, Oct. Parking available. Tel: (0146 77) 543.

In 1796, Monymusk Walled Garden was 'a gloire to the parrish and delighte to the beholder'. Currently under restoration, it is now a nursery garden specialising in herbaceous plants and including unusual varieties. Trees, shrubs, climbers, seeds and bulbs available. Walks, gardening courses throughout the year. Period plants and display borders.

Moray Motor Museum

Bridge Street, Elgin. 0.5m off main Inverness/Aberdeen road. April-Oct. Daily. 11.00-17.00. Entrance charge. Parking available. Small shop. Restaurant. Tel: (01343) 542660.

Unique collection of over 40 cars and motor cycles housed in an old mill building.

Mortlach Church

Dufftown. Easter-Oct, daily 10.00-16.00 (except during services). Donations appreciated. Tel: (01340) 20380.

Founded c 566 AD by St. Moluag. Part of present building dates from 11th/12th centuries. In 1016 it was lengthened by 3 spears length on the command of King Malcolm after his victory over the Danes. Believed to be one of the oldest churches in continual use for public worshop. Sculptured stones in vestibule and very fine stained glass. Battle stone in churchyard; old watch tower.

Nairn Fishertown Museum
Laing Hall, King Street. May-Sept, Mon-Sat 14.30-16.30; Mon, Wed & Fri 18.30-20.30. Parking available. Tel: (01667) 53331.
A collection of photographs and articles connected with the Moray Firth and herring fishing industries during the steam drifter era. Exhibits on domestic life of the fishertown. Model boats.

Nairn Leisure Park
Marine Road, Nairn. Swimming, steam room, adventure park; Jan-Dec, Mon-Fri 08.00-21.00, Sat & Sun 09.00-17.00. Outdoor games complex open Easter-Sept, daily 11.00-18.00 (21.00 in July & Aug). Activity charges. Parking available. Refreshments. Tel: (01667) 53061.
Set beside town beach, on the Moray Firth, Nairn Leisure Park has indoor and outdoor sporting and games facilities, including swimming pool and steam room with picnic patio, aerial runway, adventure play trails, trim trail, adventure fort, outdoor board games, woodland suspension bridge, toddlers' playground and more.

Nairn Literary Institute Museum
Viewfield House, Nairn. June-Sept. Mon-Sat 14.30-16.30. Free, donations welcome. Parking available.
The museum is housed in a three-storey building dating from around 1803, and has a collection of ethnographic material, natural history and artefacts illustrating social and local history. The museum was founded in 1858 by a local doctor, Dr. Grigor, and remains, with the Institute, a private charitable trust.

Nelson Tower
Grant Park, Forres. May-Sept. Tues-Sun 14.00-16.00. Free. Parking available. Sales point. Tel: (01309) 673701.
The tower has displays on the life of admiral Nelson, the Forres Trafalgar Club, and views of old Forres. Viewpoint looks over the Moray Firth.

North East Falconry Visitor Centre
Broadland, Cairnie, 3 miles from Huntly. Signposted off A96 and A920. Apr-Oct, daily, 10.00-18.00. Nov-Mar, Sat & Sun 10.00-dusk. Entrance charges. Parking available. Gift shop. Tearoom. Tel: (01466) 87344.
Flying displays of owls, hawks and falcons at

11.00 and 14.00. Coffees, teas and soft drinks available.

North East of Scotland Agricultural Heritage Centre (Aden Country Park)
On A950 between Old Deer and Mintlaw, 30m N of Aberdeen. May-Sept, daily 11.00-17.00. Apr, Oct, Sat & Sun 12.00-17.00. Parking available. Tel: (01771) 22857.
Housed in the carefully restored Aden Home Farm, the Centre imaginatively interprets 20th-century estate life with audio-visual programme, horseman's house and costume guide. Additionally, NE farming life and innovation over 200 years are highlighted in the award-winning (2nd Prize Scottish Museum of the Year Awards 1988 and Certificate of Distinction in the British Tourist Authorities "Come to Britain" Awards 1988) "Weel Vrocht Grun" exhibition by use of special dioramas, atmospheric soundtrack and video film.

Northfield Farm Museum
10m W of Fraserburgh. From A98 follows signs for New Aberdour. From B9031 follow New Pitsligo signs. June-Sept. Daily, 11.00-17.30. Entrance charge. Parking available. Tel: (017717) 504.
A large collection of farm equipment including tractors, implements, stationary engines, household bric-a-brac from the 1870's.

Oatmeal Mill
Montgarrie Mills, 1 mile N of Alford. Apr-Oct. By arrangement only. Tues & Thur at 14.00 and 15.30. Entrance charge. Parking available. Tel: (0197 55) 62209.
A family-owned working watermill which has been in continuous production since at least the 1870s, milling oatmeal in the traditional way. Visitors are accommodated while work is in progress, and must prebook.

Old Mills
W end of Elgin off the A96. Apr-Sept, Tue-Sun 09.00-17.00. Entrance charge. Parking available. Tel: (01309) 673701.
The oldest and only remaining meal mill on the River Lossie. Its history can be traced back to a Royal Charter of 1230 granting its rights to the monks of Pluscarden Priory. Visitor Centre, coffee shop, craft centre and picnic area.

Old Semeil Herb Garden
Just off the A944 Aberdeen-Corgarff road. Easter-Sept. April, weekends only. May-Aug, daily exc. Thurs. Sept, Mon-Sat, exc Thurs. 10.00-17.00. Free. Parking available. Gift shop, plant sales. Tel: (019756) 51343.

Specialist Herb Plant Nursery. Plant sales, display herb garden, garden pottery, books, seeds, gifts, unusual plants, etc. The Garden Room (seating 24) for teas, home baking.

Pitsligo Castle
by Rosehearty, 3m W of Fraserburgh. All times. Free.
Ruined castle dating from 1424 which passed through various families to the 4th and last Lord Pitsligo who is remembered for his generosity to the poor and for his successful attempts to evade arrest after the '45 Jacobite Rebellion.

Pluscarden Abbey
From B9010 at Elgin take unclassified road to Pluscarden, 6m SW. All year daily 05.00-20.30. Free. Tel: (0134 389) 257/388 (09.00-11.00 and 14.30-17.00).
Originally a Valliscaulian house, the monastery was founded in 1230. In 1390 the Church was burned, probably by the Wolf of Badenoch who burned Elgin about the same time. It became a dependent priory of the Benedictines' Abbey of Dunfermline in 1454 until the suppression of monastic life in Scotland in 1560. Thereafter the buildings fell into ruins until 1948 when a group of Benedictine monks from Prinknash Abbey, Gloucester, returned to restore it. Monastic church services open to the public.

Randolph's Leap
Off B9007, 7m SW of Forres. Parking available.
The River Findhorn winds through a deep gorge in the sandstone, and from a path above are impressive views of the clear brown water swirling over rocks or in still dark pools. Randolph's Leap is the most striking part of this valley.

Revack Estate
Grantown-on-Spey. 14 miles north east of Aviemore on the B970. Tel: (01479) 872234.
Open all year 10am-6pm (last entry 5pm). Visit a true Highland estate with beautifully laid out gardens, famous orchid houses, woodland walks and trails. Plus Adventure Playground, Gift Shop, Plant Sales, Licensed Restaurant/ Coffee Shop.

Rob Roy's Statue
Peterculter by A93. All times. Free.
Statue of Rob Roy standing above the Leuchar Burn can be seen from the bridge on the main road.

Royal Lochnagar Distillery Visitor Centre
Just off B976. Turn off A93 at Crathie, nr. Ballater. Jan-Dec exc. Xmas and New Year. Mon-Fri 10.00-17.00. Also Sat 11.00-16.00 (Easter-Oct). Parking available. Gift shop. Coffee shop. Tel: (0133 97) 42273.
The distillery, which was granted a Royal Warrant of Appointment by Queen Victoria in 1848, is set in beautiful scenery close to Balmoral Castle. New visitor centre features the distillery's associations with Queen Victoria. Tours and tasting. Home of Royal Lochnagar Special Reserve Single Malt Whisky.

St. Mary's Church, Auchindoir
3m N of Kildrummy. All reasonable times. Free. (HS). Tel: 0131-244 3101.
Ruins of one of the finest medieval parish churches remaining in Scotland.

St. Mary's Parish Church, Monymusk
Village Square, Monymusk, 18 miles from Aberdeen. Apr-Oct. Daylight hours. Free. Parking available.
The only Norman church in north-east Scotland, St. Mary's has been in constant use since it was built in the 12th century. The site was visited by St. Columba. Modern church music was introduced to Scotland here in the 17th century, and John Wesley preached here twice.

St. Ninian's Chapel, Tynet
Tynet, 3m E of Fochabers on A98. All year, dawn-dusk. Free. Parking available. The Church is in use weekly and is open daily. Visitors are requested to respect its character as a place of worship. The access road is single-track and is unsuitable for coaches. Tel: (01452) 32196.
Built about 1755 by the Laird of Tynet, ostensibly for his own use as a sheepcote but in reality as a Mass centre for the Catholics of the neighbourhood. It has undergone many extensions and alterations since, the latest being in the 1950s under the direction of Ian G. Lindsay, RSA. St. Ninian's has the distinction of being the oldest post-Reformation Catholic church still in use. Mass 17.30 Saturday, all year.

Scottish Sculpture Workshop and Sculpture Walk
Main Street, Lumsden, between Alford and Huntly. Jan-Dec. Mon-Fri 10.00-16.00 or by arrangement. Free. Parking available. Tel: (0146 46) 372.
Founded in 1979, and led since then by

Frederick Bushe, a sculptor of international standing, the workshop is a fusion of local culture and international influences, bringing sculptors from all over the world to work in wood, ceramic, constructed and cast metal, granite and other stone. The workshop aims to place sculpture in the community, and the results are to be seen all over Scotland.

Seamen's Memorial
Buckie. Key at 6 New Street. Free. Parking available. Tel: (01542) 32426.
A small chapel with beautiful stained glass windows dedicated to local fishermen who lost their lives at sea since 1946. Opened by HM The Queen in 1982.

Speyside Cooperage Visitor Centre
Situated on the A941. 3 miles N of Glenfiddich Distillery. Open all year, exc Xmas and New Year. Mon-Fri 09.30-16.30, all year. Easter-Sept also open on Sats 09.30-16.30. Tel: (01340) 871108.
The only working Cooperage in Britain with a Visitor Centre. Facilities include an exhibition entitled: "From the Acorn to the Cask". A viewing gallery over 2 workshops and a gift shop which specialises in wooden goods.

Speyside Heather Garden Centre
From Aviemore take B9152 (old A9) approx 4.5 miles N until you turn right onto A95 Elgin/ Grantown-on-Spey road. Continue on A95 for approx 4m. Watch for 'Thistle' signs to Heather Centre. Turn left on Skye of Curr road. Heather Centre is 200 yds up on right-hand side. Closed Jan, except by appointment. Mar-Oct, Mon-Sat 09.00-17.00/18.00 (Sun 10.00-17.00/18.00); Nov-Feb, Mon-Sat 09.00-17.00 (closed Sun). Garden and Craft Shop - Free. Parking available. Tel: (0147 985) 359.
Centre consists of Heather Heritage Centre which houses an exhibition on historical uses of heather, eg thatching, weaving ropes doormats, baskets; its uses in medicine, drinks, dyeing wool, etc. Heather Craft Shop. Tearoom. Plant sales and gift shop. Ornamental garden and landscaped show garden displaying approx. 300 varieties of heathers.

Statesman Cruises
Kylesku Bridge, A894 over Loch a' Cairn Bhan. March-Oct. Daily, 11.00 and 14.00. Charge for cruise. Parking available. Tel: (0157 14) 446.
Boat cruises up Loch Glencoul to Eas Coul Aulin, Britain's highest waterfall, most of which can be seen from the boat. During the cruise, in sheltered waters, seals may be seen, also golden eagles, herons, ravens, guillemot, peregrine falcon, red and black throated divers, greylag geese, terns and shag.

Stonehaven Tolbooth Museum
At quay at Stonehaven. Jun-Sep, daily (except Tue) 14.00-17.00, plus Mon, Thu, Fri and Sat 10.00-12.00. Free. Tel: (01779) 77778.
This 16th-century former storehouse of the Earls Marischal was later used as a prison. In 1748-49 Episcopal ministers lodged inside and baptised children through the windows. The museum displays local history, archaeology and particularly fishing.

Strathisla Distillery
Keith. Easter-Sept. Mon-Fri 09.00-16.30. Free. Tel: (0154 22) 7471.
A typical small old-fashioned distillery, one of the oldest established in Scotland, dating from 1786. Reception Centre with video presentation.

Sueno's Stone
At E end of Forres. All times. Free. (HS). Tel: 0131-244 3101.
One of the most remarkable early sculptured monuments in Scotland, 20 feet high with elaborate carving.

Tarves Medieval Tomb
4m NE of Oldmeldrum, in the kirkyard of Tarves. All reasonable times. Free. (HS). Tel: 0131-244 3101.
A fine altar-tomb of William Forbes, the laird who enlarged Tolquhon Castle. It shows an interesting mixture of Gothic and Renaissance styles.

Tolquhon Castle
Off B999, 7m ENE of Oldmeldrum. Apr-Sept, opening standard. Oct-Mar, weekends only. Entrance charge. (HS). Tel: 0131-244 3101.
Once a seat of the Forbes Family, an early 15th century rectangular tower, with a large quadrangular mansion of 1584-89. Two round towers, a fine carved panel over the door, and the courtyard are features.

Tomintoul Museum
The Square, Tomintoul. Apr, May, Oct, Mon-Sat 10.00-17.30, Sun 14.00-17.30; June, Sept, Mon-Sat 09.30-18.00, Sun 14.00-18.00; July, Aug, Mon-Sat 09.30-19.00, Sun 10.00-13.00, 14.00-19.00. Free. Tel: (01309) 673701.
At 1160 feet Tomintoul is the highest village in the Highlands. Museum has displays on local history, folklife, a reconstructed farm kitchen, wildlife, climate, landscape and geology. Tourist Information Centre.

Tomnaverie Stone Circle
3m NW of Aboyne. All reasonable times. Free. (HS). Tel: 0131-244 3101.

The remains of a recumbent stone circle probably 1800-1600 BC. Unexcavated.

Tugnet Ice House

Spey Bay, 5m W of Buckie. May-Sep, daily 10.00-16.00. Free. Parking available. Sales point. Tel: (01309) 673701.

Permanent exhibition telling the story of the River Spey, its salmon fishing and wildlife, established in a historic ice house building, possibly the largest in Scotland, dated 1830. Picnic site.

Ugie Salmon Fish House

At the mouth of the River Ugie across from the golf course in Peterhead. Mon-Fri 09.00-12.00 and 14.00-17.00; Sat 09.00-12.00. Free. Parking available. Tel: (01779) 76209.

The oldest Salmon Fish House in Scotland dating from 1585. Built for George Keith, 5th Earl Marischal of Scotland. Fresh and smoked salmon always available.

The Village Store

In centre of Aberlour on main street. Jan-Dec, Mon-Sat 10.00-18.00. Sun 14.00-17.30. Closed Xmas and New Year. Free. Parking available. Tel: (01340) 871243.

This old village general store has all the original fittings, records and stock dating back to the 1920's. A fascinating insight into shopping history. Scottish crafts, cards, preserves and sweets on sale.

THE NORTHERN HIGHLANDS

Achiltibuie Hydroponicum

Achiltibuie, 26 miles NW of Ullapool. Easter-Sept. Daily tours at 10.00, 12.00, 14.00, 17.00. Entrance charge. Parking available. Shop. Refreshments. Tel: (0185 482) 202.

Guided tours tell the story of Robert Irvine's 'Garden of the Future' - a garden without soil. Strawberries hang overhead, bananas, figs, grapes, lemons, flowers, herbs and vegetables all grow happily in this remote corner of Scotland. Tours last approximately 45 minutes. Hydroponic growing kits and souvenirs available.

Achiltibuie Smokehouse

Altandhu, 5 miles west of Achiltibuie, NW of Ullapool. Jan-Dec, Mon-Sat 09.30-17.00. Parking available. Shop selling Summer Isles Foods. Tel: (0185 482) 353.

Operating salmon/kipper smokehouse with viewing gallery, so that visitors can learn about salmon filleting, salmon/kipper smoking, slicing and packing.

Aigas Dam Fish Lift

Aigas Power Station, 3 miles W of Beauly on A831 to Cannich. June-Oct exc. public hols. Mon-Fri 10.00-11.00, 14.45-15.45. Free. Car parking only. Tel: (01463) 782412.

Hydro Electric's Aigas Power Station and Dam are situated on the River Beauly. This river is known for migratory salmon which return from the Atlantic Ocean to spawn in the autumn. The Borland type fish lift is a feature of Aigas Dam that allow migratory fish free access to the upper river. This one is fitted with a viewing chamber, so that the salmon can be seen effortlessly rising from the lower portion of the river to the upper reservoir to reach the spawning grounds.

Ardvreck Castle

A837, 11m E of Lochinver, on Loch Assynt. All reasonable times. Free.

Built in 1490 by the MacLeods, who in the mid-13th century obtained Assynt by marriage; the three-storeyed ruins stand on the shores of Loch Assynt. After his defeat at Culrain, near Bonar Bridge, in 1650, the Marquess of Montrose fled to Assynt but was soon captured and confined here before being sent to Edinburgh and executed.

Badnaban Cruises

Badnaban, 2.5 miles S of Lochinver, just off the coastal road to Achiltibuie/Ullapool. Jan-Dec (weather permitting). May-June best time for seabirds nesting. Sailings at 10.00, 13.00, 15.00. Charge. Car parking available. Passengers may embark/disembark at Lochinver Pier by previous arrangement. Tel: (0157 14) 358.

Small boat (up to 8 passengers) cruises to seal colonies and seabird nesting sites on islands in Enard Bay, views of Assynt peaks from an unusual angle. All sailings depend on weather and tides, and are at skipper's discretion.

Beauly Priory

At Beauly, A9, 12m W of Inverness. Open all reasonable hours. Free. Parking available. (HS). Tel: 0131—244 3101.

Ruins of a Valliscaulian Priory founded in about 1230. Notable windows and window-arcading.

Beinn Eighe National Nature Reserve

W of A896/A832 junction at Kinlochewe. Tel: (0144 584) 258.

The first National Nature Reserve in Britain, of great geological and natural history interest. Car park and nature trails on A832 NW of Kinlochewe. Aultroy Cottage Visitor Centre on A832, 1m nearer Kinlochewe. Car park, toilets.

Caithness Glass

Airport Industrial Estate, Wick. All year. Mon-

Sat 09.00-17.00, Sun 11.00-17.00 (Winter, closed Sun). Free. Restaurant and factory shop. Tel: (01955) 2286.

See hand-made glass blowing from the raw materials stage through all the processes to the finished article. Cafe and factory shop. Ample car/coach parking.

Cape Wrath
12m NW of Durness. Ferry: Tel: (01971) 511376. Minibus: Tel: (01971) 511287 or 511343.

The most northerly point of Scotland's north-west seaboard. A passenger ferry (summer only) connects with a minibus service to the cape.

Castle Stuart
5m E of Inverness on B9039. Jan-Dec, 10.00-17.00 in summer, 10.00-16.00 winter. Entrance charge. Gift shop. Parking available. Tel: (01463) 790 745.

Built in 1625 by James Stuart, 3rd Earl of Moray, on land bestowed by Mary Queen of Scots to her half-brother James, Regent and 1st Earl of Moray. Small, attractive garden. Gift shop.

Castles Girnigoe and Sinclair
3m N of Wick. Take road to Staxigoe and follow signs to castle. All times. Free. Care to be taken in wet weather. Parking available.

Two adjacent castles on a cliff-edge above Sinclair's Bay, one time strongholds of the Sinclairs, Earls of Caithness. Girnigoe is the older, dating from the end of the 15th century; Sinclair was built 1606-07. Both were deserted c. 1679 and 20 years later were reported in ruins.

Cawdor Castle
At Cawdor on B9090, 5m SW of Nairn. May-first Sun in Oct. Daily 10.00-17.30, last admission 17.00. Entrance charge. Gift shop, book shop, wool shop. Parking available. Restaurant, snack bar, picnic area. Tel: (016677) 615.

The old central tower of 1372, fortified in 1454 (a family home for over 600 years), is surrounded by 16th-century buildings, remodelled during the following century. Notable gardens surround the castle. Shakespeare's Macbeth was Thane of Cawdor, and the castle is one of the traditional settings for the murder of Duncan. Licensed restaurant, snack bar and picnic area in grounds; beautiful gardens and extensive nature trails; 9-hole pitch and putt golf course and putting green.

Choraidh Croft
10 miles E of Durness on A838, halfway along W shore of Loch Eriboll. May-Oct. Daily 10.00-20.30. Entrance charge, accompanied children free. Parking available. Crafts and wool for sale. Tearoom. Tel: (01971) 511235.

Working croft with rare breeds of domestic farm animals, aquariums and pond containing sea life. Exhibition of crofting life past and present. Pets' corner, croft walk taking in animal enclosures and pointing out features of interest on the croft and in the surrounding countryside.

Clan Gunn Heritage Centre and Museum
Latheron, 16m SW of Wick. June-Sept, Mon-Sat 11.00-17.00. Also Sun, July and Aug, 14.00-17.00. Entrance charge. Parking available. Gift shop. Tel: (0159 32) 325.

Clan Gunn Heritage Centre at Latheron Old Parish Church shows the dramatic story of this ancient Scottish clan from its Norse origins to the present. Links with America - before Columbus - are traced by way of the effigy of a 14th century knight on a rock ledge in Massachusetts.

Clynelish Distillery
Just off A9 at northern outskirts of Brora. Jan-Dec, exc. Xmas and New Year. Mon-Fri 09.30-16.30. Parking available. Shop. Tel: (01408) 621444.

The first Clynelish Distillery was built in 1819, as part of a scheme of economic improvement by the Marquess of Stafford, husband of the heiress to the Sutherland estates. These were early days for purpose-built distilleries, but the aim was to reduce illicit distilling by giving local farmers a legitimate market for their barley. The whisky is now produced at a new distillery with six stills, which was built alongside the original premises in 1967.

Corrieshalloch Gorge
A835 at Braemore, 12m SSE of Ullapool. All times. Free. Parking available. (NTS). Tel: (01463) 232084.

This spectacular gorge, 1m long and 200 feet deep, contains the Falls of Measach which plunge 150 feet. Suspension bridge viewpont.

Craig Highland Farm
2 miles E of Plockton on shore road to Stromeferry. Mar-Oct, 10.00-dusk. Entrance charge. Car parking only. Tel: (0159 984) 205.

Rare breeds farm on the shores of Loch Carron, dedicated to the conservation of domestic farm animals, poultry and waterfowl. Visitors meet and may feed animals including pigs, sheep, rabbits, pheasants, goats, pony, llama. Much stock is now critically rare, especially ancient breeds of Highland sheep, some of which are now fewer than 100 in number. Site overlooks seals, a heronry, pine woodland towards the Applecross hills over the loch. Private shore and coral strand.

Croick Parliamentary Church
On unclassified road up Strathcarron, 10m W of Ardgay. All reasonable times. Communion service on last Sun in July. Free.
Designed by Thomas Telford, Croick Church is one of the 32 'parliamentary' churches built in the Highlands and Islands during the 1820s. During the Clearance of Glencalvie in May 1845, crofters evicted sheltered briefly in the churchyard and left sad messages that can still be seen, scratched on the church's east window.

Cromarty Courthouse
Church Street, Cromarty. 25 miles N of Inverness by A9 then A832. Apr-Oct 10.00-18.00. Nov-Mar 12.00-16.00. Entrance charge. Parking available. Shop. Tel: (0138 17) 418.
Cromarty County Courthouse, built in 1773, has been converted into an award-winning museum with animated figures such as Sir Thomas Urquhart, one of Scotland's great eccentrics. A trial has been reconstructed in the courtroom. Folk tales of the area are told, and the story of Cromarty's remarkable growth in the 18th century. Also available, a personal tape tour of the old town. "narrated" by Hugh Miller, Cromarty's most famous son.

Dornoch Cathedral
In Dornoch. All year. 09.00-dusk. Free.
Founded in 1224 by Gilbert, Archdeacon of Moray and Bishop of Caithness. this little cathedral was partially destroyed by fire in 1570, restored in the 17th century, in 1835-37, and again in 1924. The fine 13th-century stonework is still to be seen.

Dornoch Craft Centre
Town Jail. All year. Summer, Mon-Sat 09.30-17.00, Sun 12.00-17.00; Winter, Mon-Fri 09.30-17.00. Free. Tel: (01862) 810555.
Weaving of tartans on Saurgr power looms, kilt making and soft toy making. Small exhibition in Jail cells. Coffee room (Apr-Sep).

Dounreay Exhibition Centre
Dounreay, 10m W of Thurso, signposted off A836. Mid May-mid Sept. Exhibition open Tues-Sun (not Mon), 10.00-16.00. Tours: Tues-Sun, 11.45, 13.00, 1415. Please book in advance. Over 12s only. Free. Parking available. Tel: (01847) 802121, ext. 2702.

In operation since 1959, Dounreay Fast Reactor has been supplying grid electricity since the earliest days of the British nuclear industry. The site now provides and international research and development facility. The Dounreay Exhibition Centre has two floors of information, models, videos and hands-on exhibits, suitable for all ages. Tours of the Prototype Fast Reactor, available to visitors over 12 years old, leave the centre each day.

Duirinish Gardens and Nursery
4 miles from Kyle of Lochalsh. Follow signs for Plockton and turn right at Duirinish. Lodge is on left hand side at the top of the hill. Open Mar-Nov, Mon-Sat, dawn-dusk. Nursery on site - plants for sale. Voluntary contributions go to charity. Limited car parking. Tel: (0159 984) 268.
Duirinish Lodge has a wild woodland garden which hosts a wide variety of trees, rhododendrons, azaleas and heathers, as well as a small shrubbery. There are excellent views of Applecross and the Isles of Skye and Raasay.

Duncansby Head
The NE point of mainland Scotland, 18m N of Wick. All times. Free.
The lighthouse on Duncansby Head commands a fine view of Orkney, the Pentland Skerries and the headlands of the east coast. A little to the south are the three Duncansby Stacks, huge stone 'needles' in the sea. The sandstone cliffs are severed by great deep gashes (geos) running into the land. One of these is bridged by a natural arch.

Dun Donaigil Broch
20m N of Lairg. A836, then on Loch Hope road. All times. Free. (HS). Tel: 0131—244 3101.
Notable example of a prehistoric broch.

Dunnet Head
B855, 12m NE of Thurso. Parking available.
This bold promontory of sandstone rising to 417 feet is the northernmost point of the Scottish mainland with magnificent views across the Pentland Firth to Orkney and a great part of the north coast to Ben Loyal and Ben Hope. The windows of the lighthouse are sometimes broken by stones hurled up by the winter seas.

Dunrobin Castle and Gardens
Off A9, 12.5m NNE of Dornoch. May, Mon-Thurs 10.30-12.30. 1-15 Oct, Mon-Sat 10.30-16.30, Sun 13.00-16.30. Last admission 16.00. June-Sept, Mon-Sat 10.30-17.30, Sun 13.00-17.30. Last admission 17.00. Other times by arrangement. Gardens open all year round.

Parking available. Gift shop. Tearoom. Tel: (01408) 633177.

Magnificently set in a great park and formal gardens, overlooking the sea. Dunrobin Castle was originally a square keep built about 1275 by Robert, Earl of Sutherland, from whom it got its name Dun Robin. For centuries this has been the seat of the Earls and Dukes of Sutherland. The present outward appearance results from extensive changes made 1845-50. Fine paintings, furniture and a steam-powered fire engine are among the miscellany of items to be seen. Beach and tearoom.

Eagle Stone

By A834 on the east side of village of Strathpeffer. All reasonable times. Free.

A Pictish stone which has two symbols etched into its surface. One is the shape of a horseshoe and the other is of an eagle. Several theories as to the stone's origin exist - one of which is that it is a marriage stone.

Eas Coul Aulin Falls

At the head of Loch Glencoul, 3m W of A894. Contact Mr. Watson, Tel: (015714) 446.

The tallest waterfall in Britain, dropping 658 feet (200 metres). There are occasional cruises to the waterfall.

Falls of Glomach

NE off A87, 18m E of Kyle of Lochalsh. (NTS).

One of the highest falls in Britain, 370 feet, set in a steep narrow cleft in remote country. The best approach is from the Dorusdain car park (Forestry Commission), 2.5 miles off the north section of the loop in the old A87. Path 5 miles: allow 5 hours for round trip. Stout footwear, protective clothing, food and compass essential.

Falls of Shin

A836, 5m N of Bonar Bridge.

Spectacular falls through rocky gorge; famous for salmon leap.

Fearn Abbey

Take A9 N from Alness for 12m, turn right onto B9165.

The Abbey was founded in the 13th century. It was converted into a parish church, but in 1742 the roof fell in during a service killing 42 people, a disaster prophesied by the Brahan Seer. The restored church (the nave and choir of the Abbey) is still a parish church, but the North and South Chapels are still roofless.

Fortrose Cathedral

At Fortrose, 8m SSW of Cromarty. Opening standard. Free. (HS). Tel: 0131—244 3101.

The surviving portions of this 14th-century cathedral include the south aisle with its vaulting and much fine detail.

Fossil Visitor Centre

Village Hall, Spittal, 10 miles S of Thurso on A895. June-Sept. Tue-Sat 10.00-16.00. Entrance charge. Entrance to hall is free. Parking available. Gift shop. Tearoom. Tel: (June-Sept) (0184 784) 266.

Spittal village hall has exhibitions of local history, the Flows, and the wildlife of the area. The Fossil Centre has displays of fossils, geology and the flagstone industry.

Fyrish Monument

Above village of Evanton on Fyrish Hill, off A9. All times. Free.

Curious monument erected in 1782 by Sir Hector Munro who rose from the ranks and distinguished himself at the relief of Seringapatam. The monument is a replica of the Indian gateway and was built to provide work at a time of poverty and unemployment in the Evanton area.

Gairloch Heritage Museum

In Gairloch, on A832. Easter-end Sep, Mon-Sat 10.00-17.00. Tel: (01445) 2287.

Award-winning museum with displays of all aspects of the past life in the West Highland area from prehistoric times to the present day. Licensed restaurant attached.

Glen Ord Distillery

On the outskirts of Muir of Ord, just off A832, 15 miles W of Inverness. Jan-Dec, exc Xmas and New Year. Mon-Fri 09.30-12.00. Parking available. Gift shop. Tel: (01463) 870421.

Licensed in 1838, Glen Ord is in an area with an ancient tradition of distilling - last survivor of no less than nine distilleries which operated around Muir of Ord in Victorian days. Guided tours show the main processes of distilling, and visitors can taste the Glen Ord single malt whisky produced in the distillery's six stills.

Grey Cairns of Camster

6m N of Lybster on Watten Road, off A9. All reasonable times. Free. (HS). Tel: 0131—244 3101.

Two megalithic cairns: a round cairn and a long cairn containing chambers, probably 4th millenium BC.

Groam House Museum and Pictish Centre

High Street, Rosemarkie. 1 May-1 Oct, Mon-Sat 11.00-17.00, Sun 14.30-16.30. Tel: (01381) 20961.

This small museum, now a Pictish Centre for Ross and Cromarty, contains a splendid Pictish symbol stone, c. 750 AD. and other fragments, all found in Rosemarkie. Also hangings and representations of other Pictish stones with video programmes on the Picts and the Brahan Seer with a selection of photos and a shop.

Neil M. Gunn Memorial Viewpoint
Heights of Brae, Strathpeffer. All reasonable times. Free. Parking available.
Memorial viewpoint for the author Neil M. Gunn who lived nearby.

Handa Island Nature Reserve
Handa Island, 3m NW of Scourie. Small open ferry from Tarbet, or boat trips. Easter-Sept by Scourie Boats, contact: Ken Nash, Rangoon, Scourie. Tel: (01971) 502011. Charges for boats and for entrance to Handa Island Visitor Centre (open April-early Sept).
An island seabird sanctuary with vast numbers of fulmars, shags, gulls, kittiwakes and auks. Arctic and great skuas on moorland. Shelter for visitors with displays.

Hidden Hills
At Kintradwell, 2 miles N of Brora, and Borrobol, 13 miles W of Helmsdale. May-Aug. Charge for tours, including lunch. Car parking only. Tel: (0143 13) 264 (Borrobol) or (01408) 621422 (Kintradwell). Bookings also through Helmsdale TIC (0143 12) 640.
Two private estates offering a fascinating and complex environment for birdlife, flora and fauna. Three different guided wildlife tours are led by a local expert who introduces mammals, birds and land use in places far from public highways. Historic monuments dating back three centuries are also explained. Red deer are approached and seen in large parties. Extensive botany. Springtime bird list runs to around 130 species. Walks can be energetic or less demanding, depending on tour.

Highland and Rare Breeds Farm
Avalon, Elphin, 14 miles N of Ullapool on A835. May-Sept. Daily, 10.00-17.00. Entrance charge. Parking available. Theme shop. Refreshments. Tel: (0185 486) 204.
The Scottish Farm Animal Centre has 40 breeds, ancient and modern, in 15 acres of farmland, river and mountain scenery. Highland cattle, Soay and Hebridean sheep, goats and outdoor pigs, poultry and rabbits live on this croft, adapted for education and conservation. This working organic farm also has an exhibition of farm tools, some farmwork demonstrations, guided tours and information sheets.

Inverewe Gardens
On A832, 6m NE of Gairloch. (Gardens) all year, daily 09.30-sunset. (Visitor Centre and Shop) Apr-late May, early Sept-mid Oct, Mon-Sat 10.00-17.30, Sun 14.00-17.30. Late May-early Sept, Mon-Sat 09.30-17.30, Sun 12.00-17.30. Restaurant closes 16.30. Entrance charges. Parking available. Trust shop. Restaurant. Tel: (0144 586) 200.
Plants from many countries flourish in this garden created by Osgood MacKenzie over 120 years ago, giving an almost continuous display of colour throughout the year. Eucalyptus, rhododendrons, and many Chilean and South American plants are represented in great variety, together with Himalayan lilies and giant forget-me-nots from the South Pacific. Garden for disabled, shop, restaurant, caravan and camp site, petrol, plants sales. Groups of disabled visitors welcome.

Kingspark Llama Farm
Berriedale, on A9 N of Helmsdale. Jan-Dec. Daily, dawn-dusk. Entrance charge. Parking available. Gift shop. Tel: (0159 35) 202.
A breeding llama farm where visitors can mix freely with geldings, females (some with babies), and the stud male 'T.C.'. A llama walk along Dunbeath Strath can be booked. Within the park, raccoons, goats, pheasants, peacocks, a variety of birds, and chipmunks.

Laxford Cruises
Fanagmore, 3 miles N of Scourie. Signposted. Easter-mid Sept. 10.00-16.00. Charge for cruises. Parking available. Tel: (01971) 502409.
Pleasure cruises around Loch Laxford, seeing many different species of birds; also seals, occasional sightings of otters, dolphins, porpoises and whales.

Leckmelm Shrubbery and Arboretum
3 miles S of Ullapool on A835. Apr-Sept, daily 10.00-18.00. Honesty box. Parking available. Tel: (01854) 612356.
Delightful 10-acre arboretum and 2.5 acre walled garden on the shores of Loch Broom, laid out in the 1870s and under restoration since 1985. Some rare and unusual trees and a wide range of rhododenrons and azaleas.

Lhaidhay Croft Museum
On A9, 1m N of Dunbeath. Easter-mid Oct, daily 10.00-18.00. Entrance charge. Parking available. Tearoom. Picnic area. Tel: (015933) 244.
An early 18th-century croft complex with stable, dwelling house and byre under one thatched roof with adjoining barn. Completely

furnished in the fashion of its time. The barn has a notable crux roof. Picnic area.

Lochbroom Museum
Quay Street, Ullapool. Jun-Aug, Mon-Sat 09.00-22.00. Sept-May, Mon-Sat 09.00-18.00. Tel: (01854) 612356.
A tiny museum of character, established for 50 years, and telling the story of Ullapool and the Loch Broom area. Fine rock collection illustrates the land formation of the area. Artefacts from ancient times to World War II, and relics associated with famous people from the Duke of Wellington to Sir Harry Lauder.

Lyth Arts Centre
Signposted 4 miles off A9 between Wick and John O'Groats. Jul-Aug, daily 10.00-18.00. Entrance charge, free for children, students, OAP, unemployed. Parking available. Snack bar. Tel: (0195 584) 270 (Apr-Sept)/0131-226 6424 (Oct-Mar).
Up to ten new exhibitions of contemporary fine art shown simultaneously each season, ranging from local landscape to the work of established British and foreign artists. Regular performances by touring drama, music and dance companies.

Sir Hector MacDonald's Memorial
Mitchell Hill, Dingwall. All times. Free.
An impressive monument erected to the memory of General Sir Hector MacDonald, who was born near Dingwall in the parish of Ferintosh in 1853.

Mallaig Marine World
The Harbour, Mallaig, 45 miles N of Fort William on A830. Jun-Sept, daily, 09.00-21.00, Oct-May 09.00-17.00. Entrance charges. Parking available. Gift shop. Tel: (01687) 2292.
Marine aquarium and exhibition featuring local marine species. Fishing displays on the work of the Mallaig fishing fleet. Video illustrating boats at work at different fishings and in all weathers, including the work of the lifeboat. Pond garden, indoor and outdoor seating, marine scientist on hand.

Hugh Miller's Cottage
Church Street, Cromarty, 22m NE of Inverness via Kessock Bridge. Apr-Sept, Mon-Sat 10.00-13.00, 14.00-17.00; Sun 14.00-17.00. Entrance charges. (NTS). Tel: (0138 17) 245.
The birthplace of Hugh Miller (1802—56) - stonemason - became eminent geologist, naturalist, theologian and writer. The furnished thatched cottage, built c 1711 by his great grandfather, contains an exhibition and video programme on his life and work.

Northlands Viking Centre
The Old School, Auchingill, Caithness. On A9 between Wick and John O'Groats. June-Sept, daily, 10.00-16.00. Admission charge. Parking. Shop. Picnic area. Toilets.
The displays explore the chambered cairns, brochs, and Picts of pre-Viking Caithness through to the late Norse period and the excavations of the settlments at Freswick; also features the archaeological contribution made by John Nicholson. Broch nearby.

Ousdale Weaving
Ousdale, Berriedale, 7 miles N of Helmsdale on A9. Easter-Oct, daily, 09.00-17.00. Nov-Easter, Mon-Fri 09.00-17.00. Free. Parking available. Gift shop. Tearoom. Tel: (0143 12) 371.
Fabrics, shawls, serapes being produced for sale in the mill shop and for export all over the world. Explanatory boards describe the processes of weaving in a number of languages.

St. Duthus Chapel and Collegiate Church
Tain. Chapel: All reasonable times. Free. Museum: Easter-Sept 10.00-16.30. Entrance charge. Tel: (01862) 892140 or 893422.
The chapel was built between 1065 and 1256. St. Duthus died in 1065 and was buried in Ireland, but 200 years later his remains were transferred to Tain. The chapel was destroyed by fire in 1427. St. Duthus Church was built c 1360 by William, Earl and Bishop of Ross, in Decorated style, and became a notable place of pilgrimage. Folk museum and Clan Ross Centre in grounds.

St. Mary's Chapel, Crosskirk
Off A836, 6m W of Thurso. All reasonable times. Free. (HS). Tel: 0131—244 3101.
A rudely-constructed chapel with very low doors narrowing at the top in Irish style. Probably 12th century.

St. Peter's Church
Near the Harbour at Thurso. All reasonable times. Free.
Ruins situated in the attractively restored old part of Thurso. Of mediaeval or earlier origin; much of the present church dates from the 17th century.

Smoo Cave
A838, 1.5m E of Durness. All reasonable times. Free. Tel: (01971) 511259.
Three vast caves at the end of a deep cleft in the limestone cliffs. The entrance to the first resembles a Gothic arch. The second cavern, access difficult, has a waterfall. The third is inaccessible.

Strathnaver Museum

Off A836, at Farr, near Bettyhill. Apr-Oct, Mon-Sat, 10.00-17.00. Entrance charge. Parking available. Tel: (016412) 421.

The former Farr Church (18th century) now houses this museum of local history. This is historic Clan MacKay country and is associated with the Sutherland Clearances.

Summer Isles

Off Achiltibuie, Ullapool, Wester Ross. Cruises from Ullapool: Mackenzie Marine, tel: (01854) 2008. From Achiltibuie, tel: (01854) 82200. Enquire at Post Office.

An attractive group of islands, the largest of which is Tanera Mhor. Pleasure cruises give views of seals, birdlife and extraxordinary rock formations, occasionally landing on one of the islands. Suitable for fully-equipped campers, canoeing, yachting.

Sutherland Pottery

Shinness, 4.5 miles N of Lairg. Apr-Oct, daily 08.00-22.00. Free. Parking available. Pottery shop. Tearoom. Tel: (01549) 2223.

Hand-thrown and decorated pottery. Visitors can participate in pot-making, buy pots from the adjoining showroom, walk around the croft, which is still active, and see artefacts and implements preserved from the days of the present owner's parents, and earlier.

Tamdhu Distillery

Off B9102 8m W of Craigellachie at Knockando. Apr-Oct, Mon-Fri 10.00-16.00. Also Sat, June-Sept. Free. Parking available. Tel: (0134 06) 486.

Guided tour with large graphic display and views of distilling plant from viewing gallery. Visitor centre, tasting.

Thurso Heritage Museum

Town Hall, Jun-Sep, Mon-Sat 10.00-13.00, 14.00-17.00.

Exhibition of agricultural and domestic life, local trades and crafts with a room of an old Caithness cottage.

Timespan Heritage Centre

Dunrobin Street, Helmsdale. 70 miles N of Inverness on A9 to John O'Groats. Easter-Oct. Mon-Sat 10.00-17.00, Sun 14.00-17.00 (18.00 in July & Aug). Entrance charge. Parking available. Gift shop. Tel: (0143 12) 327.

Award-winning Timespan features the dramatic story of the Highlands, from Picts and Vikings, murder at Helmsdale Castle, the last burning of a witch, the Highland Clearances, the Church, the 19th-century sporting scene, the Kildonan Goldrush, through the crofting and fishing past to the present day and the North Sea oilfields. Scenes from the past are re-created with life-size sets and sound effects. Audio visual. Herb garden, beside Telford's bridge over the River Helmsdale.

Torridon

Off A896, 9m SW of Kinlochewe. Estate open all year. Countryside Centre, May-late Sept, Mon-Sat 10.00-17.00, Sun 14.00-17.00. Entrance charge. Parking available. (NTS). Tel: (0144 587) 221.

About 16,000 acres of some of Scotland's finest mountain scenery whose peaks rise over 3,000ft. Of major interest also to geologists: Liathach (3,456 ft) and Beinn Alligin (2,232 ft) are of red sandstone, some 750 million years old. The NTS Visitor Centre at the junction of A896 and Diabaig road has audio-visual presentations of wild life. Deer Museum (unmanned) and deer park open all year. Ranger led walk in season. Disabled access to visitor centre and deer museum only.

Ullapool Museum

7 & 8 West Argyle Street, Ullapool. Late Mar-early Nov. Mon-Fri, 10.00-17.00 (also 19.00-21.00, June-Sept). Entrance charge. Gift shop.

A collection of items of both local and general interest.

Wick Heritage Centre

Bank Row, Wick. Jun-Sep, Mon-Sat 10.00-17.00, or by arrangement for groups. Entrance charge. Tel: (01955) 3385.

Prize-winning exhibition of the herring fishing industry; also displays of domestic and farming life. Gardens and tearoom.

WESTERN AND CENTRAL HIGHLANDS

Abriachan Garden Nursery

North shore of Loch Ness, 9 miles west of Inverness on A82. Jan-Dec (exc. Xmas and New Year). 09.00-19.00 or dusk. Parking available. Plants for sale in nursery. Tel: (0146 386) 232.

Extensive gardens of shores of Loch Ness. Interesting and careful plantings in beds terraced up hillside. Woodland walks. St. Columba's Font (historic stone) on site.

The Aluminium Story (Kinlochleven Visitor Centre & Library)

Linnhe Road, Kinlochleven. 21 miles S of Fort William on B863 - turn off A82 at North Ballachulish. Mid Apr-mid Oct, Mon-Fri 10.00-17.00, Sat & Sun 12.00-16.30. Mid Oct-mid Apr, Tue & Thur 10.00-12.00, 13.00-17.00, Wed, Fri, Sat 10.00-12.00, 13.00-15.00. Free. Tel: (0185 54) 663.

Imaginative audio-visual display and video presentation telling the story of an industry and a community - how the combination of hilly terrain, water and human ingenuity brought aluminium smelting to Kinlochleven over 80 years ago. Outside, a giant sundial.

Ardanaiseig Gardens
E of B845, 22m E of Oban. 31 Mar-31 Oct, daily 10.00-dusk. Entrance Charge. Parking available. Tel: (018663) 333.
Rhododendrons, azaleas, rare shrubs and trees. Magnificent views across Loch Awe and of Ben Cruchan. The hotel restaurant is open for morning tea, luncheon and afternoon tea.

Ardchatten Garden
Adjoining Ardchattan Priory, 5 miles E of Connel Bridge. Apr-Nov. Daily, dawn to dusk. Entrance charge. Parking available. Refreshments/light lunches. Tel: (0163 175) 274.
A lochside garden, restructured by the present owner in 1950, and before that, by his mother in 1904. It now comprises a 2-acre wild garden to the west of Ardchattan House, with over 200 different shrubs, including shrub roses and 30 species of sorbus, with wild flowers. A formal garden in front of the house leads down to Loch Etive, with two herbaceous borders, three shrub borders, rock garden, and fine views of Mull to the west and Ben Cruachan to the east.

Ardchattan Priory
On the N side of Lower Loch Etive, 6.5m NE of Oban. Open all times. Free. (HS). Tel: 0131-244 3101
One of the Valliscaulian houses founded in Scotland in 1230, and the meeting place in 1308 of one of Bruce's Parliaments, among the last at which business was conducted in Gaelic. Burned by Cromwell's soldiers in 1654, the remains include some carved stones. The gardens of Ardchattan House, adjoining the Priory, are open Apr-Sep; admission charge. Achnaba Church, near Connel, has notable central communion pews.

Ardnamurchan Natural History and Vistor Centre
From Salen take the B8007 for 7m to Glenborrodale. The Centre is 2m further on. Apr-Oct, Mon-Sat 10.30-17.30; Sun 12.00-17.30. Admission free. Parking available. Tel: (0197 24) 254 or 263.
Designed for the Glasgow Garden Festival, this attractive Douglas fir building houses static displays of local geology and wildlife plus stone byre converted to audio-visual building for 13-minute film of local ecology. Coffee shop, books and gifts.

Ardfearn Nursery
Bunchrew, 4 miles W of Inverness on A863. Jan-Dec. Daily 09.00-17.00. Free. Parking available. Tel: (01463) 243250.
Horticultural adviser and broadcaster Jim Sutherland and his son Alasdair have created a small family nursery on the shores of the Beauly Firth. Wide variety of plants of extreme hardiness, attractive display beds containing over 1,000 species and cultivars, with easy access for all including wheelchairs. Sales area with shrubs, trees, heathers, rhododendrons, conifers and alpines.

Ardtornish Estate
Morvern, Argyll, 40 miles SW of Fort William on Sound of Mull. Mar-Oct. Estate open all day, gardens 09.00-18.00. Entrance charge for gardens. Car parking only. Shop. Tel: (01967) 421288.
Interesting Victorian Highland estate. Castle, gardens, market garden.

Arduaine Garden
20m S of Oban on the A816, joint entrance with Loch Melfort Hotel. Jan-Dec. Daily, 09.30-sunset. Entrance charge. Parking available. (NTS). Tel: (018522) 366.
Noted west coast garden of particular interest to plantsmen and garden enthusiasts.

Argyll Forest Park
W and NW from Loch Long almost to Loch Fyne: A815, B839, B828 and A83. Parking available. (FE). Tel: (0136 984) 666.
Three forests - Ardgartan, Glenbranter and Benmore - cover 60,000 acres of superb scenery. There are scores of forest walks through old estate woodlands, such as the famous waterfall walks of Puck's Glen and Lauder. The Lauder Walks, once an outstation for the rhododendron collection for the Royal Botanic Garden, are best viewed in late spring when the shrubs are in bloom. Guided walks in summer. Guidebook available in local shops.

Argyll Wildlife Park
Dalchenna, Inveraray, Argyll. On A83, 2 miles from Inveraray. Open all year 09.30-18.00/dusk. Entrance charge. Tearoom. Tel: (01499) 2264.
60 acre site, with one of Europe's largest collection of wildfowl, a large owl collection, with an emphasis on Scottish wildlife.

Auchindrain Old Highland Township
On A83, 5.5m SW of Inveraray. Apr-Sept. Daily, 10.00-17.00 (exc. Sat in Apr, May, Sept). Entrance charge. Parking available. Shop. Refreshments. Tel: (0149 95) 235.
Auchindrain is an original West Highland

township, or village of great antiquity and the only communal tenancy township in Scotland to have survived on its centuries old site much in its original form. The township buildings which have been restored and preserved are furnished and equipped in the style of various periods to give the visitor a living experience of what life was really like for the Highlander in past centuries. Visitor centre; shop; refreshments; picnic area; car park and toilets.

Aviemore Mountain Resort
Off A9, 32m S of Inverness. All year. Daily. Admission free (charge for facilities). Parking facilities. Tel: (01479) 810624.
Leisure, sport and conference centre with wide range of recreational and entertainment facilities, including: cinema/theatre, swimming pool, ice rink, saunas, artificial ski slope, go-karts, discos, restaurants, and many more.

Barguillean Garden
Glen Lonan, 3m W of Taynuilt. Jan-Dec. Daily 09.00-dusk. Entrance charge, children free. Parking available. Refreshments for groups by arrangement. Tel: (0186 62) 254.
Eleven acres of lochside woodland gardens, particularly attractive from May to July. The garden was created, starting in 1956, by Mr. & Mrs. Neil Macdonald as a memorial to their elder son Angus. Now run by younger son Sam Macdonald, Barguillean features daffodils, azaleas, rhododendrons, flowering shrubs and heathers.

Barnaline Walks
Dalavich, on unclassified road along W shore of Loch Awe. Jan-Dec. Daily. Free. Parking available.
Three walks starting from Barnaline Car Park and Picnic Site, taking in Dalavich Oakwood Forest Nature Reserve (an interpretative trail with old stable information point), Avich Falls and Loch Avich. Panoramic views of Loch Awe.

Ben Nevis
Near Fort William. Parking available.
Britain's highest mountain (4,406 ft/1,344 m) and most popular mountain for both rock-climber and hillwalker. It is best seen from the north approach to Fort William, or from the Gairlochy Road, across the Caledonian Canal.

Ben Nevis Distillery Visitor Centre
Lochy Bridge, 2 miles N of Fort William on A82. Jan-Dec exc 2 weeks at Xmas. Mon-Fri 09.00-17.00 (July & Aug 19.30), also Sat, Apr-Sept. Last tour one hour before closing. Free.

Parking available. Gift shop. Tearoom. Tel: (01397) 700200.
Small exhibition, audio-visual display, guided tours for groups up to 15, whisky tasting. Guided tours are not suitable for disabled visitors due to the large number of steps in the distillery.

Bonawe Iron Furnace
At Bonawe, 12m E of Oban, off A85. Opening standard, Apr-Sep only. Parking available. (HS). Tel: 0131-244 3101.
The restored remains of a charcoal furnace for iron-smelting, established in 1753, which worked until 1876. The furnace and ancillary buildings are in a more complete state of preservation than any other comparable site.

Bridge of Carr
Carrbridge. All times.
High and narrow single-arch bridge. Built by John Niccelsone, mason, in summer 1717, for Sir James Grant.

Cairngorm Chairlift
A951 from A9 at Aviemore, then by Loch Morlich to car park at 2,000 feet. All year, daily 09.00-16.30, depending on weather. Tel: (0147 986) 1261.
At the car park is a large Day Lodge containing restaurant, bar, shop and snack bar. At the top of the chairlift is the Ptarmigan snack bar, the highest observation building in Great Britain at 3,600 feet with magnificent views to west and north-east. Also alpine garden.

The Cairngorm Reindeer Centre
Reindeer House, Glenmore. A951 from Aviemore. All year, daily 10.00-17.00. Herd visits, 11.00 departure. Extra afternoon trips at peak times. Parking available. Tel: (01479) 861 228.
Visitors may accompany the guide to see the reindeer herd free-ranging in their natural surroundings. Also visit the Reindeer Centre at Reindeer House. Disabled visitors welcome, prior notice would be helpful.

Caledonian Canal
Canal Office, Seaport Marina, Muirtown Wharf, Inverness. Tel: (01463) 233140.
Designed by Thomas Telford and completed in 1822, the Caledonian Canal links the lochs of the Great Glen (Loch Lochy, Loch Oich and Loch Ness). It provides coast to coast shortcut between Corpach near Fort William and Clachnaharry at Inverness. The Canal has been described as the most beautiful in Europe - the spectacular Highland scenery of lochs, mountains and glens is unusual for a canal. A

wide variety of craft on the canal throughout the year and can usually be seen at close quarters as they pass through locks and bridges. There are a number of pleasure cruises available on the canal and small boats are available.

Carnasserie Castle
Off A816, 9m N of Lochgilphead. All reasonable times. Free. (HS). Tel: 0131-244 3101.
The house of John Carswell, first Protestant Bishop of the Isles, who translated Knox's *Liturgy* into Gaelic, and published it in 1567, the first book printed in that language. The castle was captured and partly blown up during Argyll's rebellion in 1685.

Castle Stalker
On a tiny island offshore in Loch Linnhe, 25m NNE from Oban on A828. Apr-Aug, open by appointment. Entrance charge includes boat trip. Car parking only. Tel: (0163 173) 234.
This picturesque ancient home, c. 1500, of the Stewarts of Appin, and associated with James V, has recently been restored.

Clachan Bridge
B844 off A816, 12m SW of Oban. All times. Free.
This picturesque single-arched bridge, built in 1792, which links the mainland with the island of Seil, is often claimed to be the only bridge to 'span the Atlantic' (though there are others similar). The waters are actually those of the narrow Seil Sound, which joins the Firth of Lorne to Outer Loch Melfort, but they can with some justification claim to be an arm of the Atlantic.

Clan Cameron Museum
Achnacarry, Spean Bridge. Turn off A82 before Commando Monument, turn right after crossing canal. Easter-Oct, 14.00-17.00. Parking available. Tel: (01397) 772473.
A reconstructed 17th-century croft house. Memorabilia of Bonnie Prince Charlie, the Commandos, the Camerons and Queen's Own Cameron Highlanders.

Clan MacPherson Museum
In Newtonmore on A9/A86, 15m S of Aviemore. May-Sep, Mon-Sat 10.00-17.30, Sun 14.30-17.30. Free. Parking available. Tel: (01540) 673332.
Relics and memorials of Clan Chiefs and other MacPherson families. Exhibits include a letter to Prince Charles Edward Stuart from his father, a massive silver epergne depicting an

incident in the life of Cluny of the '45 after the Battle of Culloden, green banner of the clan, Victorian royal warrants, crests, James MacPherson's fiddle and other historical relics.

Clava Cairns
Near Culloden, off B9006, 6m E of Inverness. All reasonable times. Free. (HS). Tel: 0131-244 3101.
Late Neolithic or Early Bronze Age chambered cairns with standing stone circles.

Cobb Memorial
Between Invermoriston and Drumnadrochit by A82. All times. Free.
A cairn commemorates John Cobb, the racing driver, who lost his life near here in 1952 when attempting to beat the water speed record, with his jet speedboat, on Loch Ness.

Combined Operations Museum
Cherry Park, in grounds of Inveraray Castle, Inveraray. First Sat in Apr-second Sun in Oct. Mon-Sat, 10.00-18.00, Sun 13.00-18.00, closed Fri except in Jul-Aug. Last admissions: 17.30. Entrance charge. Parking available. Tel: (01499) 2203.
The museum sets out to show by means of photographs, models, posters and displays, the work of the Combined Training Centre at Inveraray during World War II.

Commando Memorial
Off A82, 11m NE of Fort William. Parking available.
An impressive sculpture by Scott Sutherland, erected in 1952 to commemorate the Commandos of World War II who trained in this area. Fine views of Ben Nevis and Lochaber.

Corrimony Cairn
At Glen Urquhart, 8.5 miles W of Drumnadrochit, Loch Ness. All times. Free. (HS). Tel: 0131-244 3101.
This neolithic chambered cairn is surrounded by a slab kerb, outside which is a circle of standing stones.

Craggan Fishery
1 mile S of Grantown-on-Spey on A95. Apr-Oct, daily. Oct-Mar, Wed-Sun, weather permitting 10.00-18.00, also Thur 18.00-22.00. Entrance charge. Car parking only. Snack bar. Tel: (01479) 2120.
Two trout fishing lochs. Main loch, fly only, brown and rainbow trout. Small loch has bait fishing for under-15s. Rod hire, permits sold on site.

Crinan Canal

Crinan to Ardrishaig, by Lochgilphead. Tel: (01546) 603210/603797.

Constructed between 1793 and 1801 to carry ships from Loch Fyne to the Atlantic without rounding Kintyre. The 9-mile stretch of water with 15 locks is now almost entirely used by pleasure craft. The towing path provides a very pleasant, easy walk with the interest of canal activity. There are magnificent views to the Western Isles from Crinan; where the Crinan basin, coffee shop, boatyard and hotel make a visit well worthwhile.

Cruachan Pumped Storage Power Station

Off A85, 18m E of Oban. Easter-Oct, daily 09.00-16.30. Parking available. Tel: (0186 62) 673.

In a vast cavern inside Ben Cruachan is Scottish Power's 400,000 kilowatt pumped storage power station which utilises water pumped from Loch Awe to a reservoir 1,200 feet up the mountain. New Visitors' Centre, guided minibus tour, picnic area and snack bar. Car park.

Culloden Moor

B9006, 5m E of Inverness. Site open all year. Visitor Centre: all year exc 25/26 Dec and all Jan. Early Feb-Mar, Nov-Dec, 10.00-16.00; Apr-mid May, mid Sept-Oct, 09.00-17.00; late May-mid Sept, 09.30-18.00. Entrance charge. (NTS). Tel: (01463) 790607.

Here Prince Charles Edward's cause was finally crushed at the battle on 16 April 1746. The battle lasted only 40 minutes: the Prince's army lost some 1,200 men, and the King's army 310. Features of interest include the Graves of the Clans, communal burial places with simple headstones bearing individual clan names alongside the main road; the great memorial cairn, erected in 1881; the Well of the Dead, a single stone with the inscription 'The English were buried here'; Old Leanach farmhouse, now restored as a battle museum; and the huge Cumberland Stone from which the victorious Duke of Cumberland is said to have viewed the scene. Information available on cassette programme for groups in French, German, Gaelic, Italian and Japanese. Study room, bookshop and self-service restaurant. Induction Loop.

Darnaway Farm Visitor Centre

Off A96, 3m W of Forres. May-mid Sept, daily 10.00-17.00. Entrance charge. Also available: estate tours including Darnaway Castle - Jul, Aug, Wed, Thurs and Sun 13.00 and 15.00 with estate ranger. Tearoom. Tel: (01309) 4469.

At the Visitor Centre, an exhibition of the farms and forest of Moray Estates, with audio-visual programme. Viewing platform to watch cows being milked. Nature trails and woodland walks, picnic areas, tearoom and play area.

Dochfour Gardens

Approx. 6m SW of Inverness on the A82 Inverness-Fort William road. The entrance is near the south end of Loch Dochfour. Apr-Oct, Mon-Fri 10.00-17.00, Sat & Sun 14.00-17.00. Honesty box. Parking available. Plants and fruit for sale. Tel: (0146 386) 218.

Fifteen acres of terraced gardens are set against the background of Loch Dochfour in the famous Great Glen. Special features are the magnificent specimen trees, naturalised daffodils, rhododendrons, water garden and extensive yew topiary. The large kitchen garden has soft fruit in season.

Eden Court Theatre

Bishops Road, Inverness. Restaurant and bar. Parking available. Tel: (01463) 221718.

An 800-seat, multi-purpose Theatre, Conference Centre and Art Gallery, completed in 1976 and situated on the banks of the River Ness. Part of the complex is the 19th-century house built by Robert Eden which houses the new luxury cinema - The Riverside Screen. There is a wide variety of entertainment throughout the year including classical concerts, drama, variety shows, films, pantomime and art exhibitions. The Theatre Restaurant is open for morning coffees, lunch, afternoon teas, dinner and late suppers.

Eilean Donan Castle

Off A87, 9m E of Kyle of Lochalsh. Easter-Sep, daily 10.00-18.00. Entrance charge. Parking available. Tel: (01599) 85 202.

On an islet (now connected by a causeway) in Loch Duich, this picturesque castle dates back to 1220. It passed into the hands of the MacKenzies of Kintail who became Earls of Seaforth. In 1719 it was garrisoned by Spanish Jacobite troops and was blown up by an English man o'war. Now completely restored, it incorporates a war memorial to the Clan MacRae, who held it as hereditary Constables on behalf of the MacKenzies. Gift Shop.

European Sheep and Wool Centre

Drimsynie Estate, Lochgoilhead. A83 to top of Rest and Be Thankful, B828 to Lochgoilhead. Signposted. Mid Mar-late Oct. Daily, 09.00-23.00. Shows: Mon-Fri 11.00, 13.00, 15.00, Sat & Sun 13.00, 15.00. Entrance charge. Parking available. Gift shop. Restaurant, snacks. Tel: (0130 13) 247.

An all-weather indoor attraction in a scenic lochside setting. Forty-minute live show with 19 different breeds of sheep, dog obedience trials, sheep shearing. Sheep are penned indoors and can be seen around the custom-built theatre. Adjoining is Drimsynie Leisure Centre, with swimming pool, ice rink and indoor bowling.

Farigaig Forest Centre
Off B862 at Inverfarigaig, 17m S of Inverness. Easter-Oct. Daily, 08.00-18.00. Free. Parking available. (FE). Tel: (01463) 791 575.
A Forestry Commission interpretation centre in a converted stone stable, showing the development of the forest environment in the Great Glen. Forest walks.

Fort Augustus Abbey & Fort
S end of Loch Ness on A82. May-Sep, Mon-Sat 10.00-12.30, 13.30-17.00. Sun 13.30-17.00. Entrance charge. Parking available. Gift shop. Tel: (01320) 6232.
A development which interprets the history of the military fort and the monastery on this site, tells the story of monks in the Highlands since Celtic times. Historical link with Scottish monasteries in Germany from the 16th to 19th centuries.

Fort George
B9039, off A96 W of Nairn. Opening standard. Parking available. (HS). Tel: 0131-244 3101.
Begun in 1748 as a result of the Jacobite rebellion, this is one of the finest late artillery fortifications in Europe, which is still in use. There is also the Regimental Museum of the Queen's Own Highlanders.

Garvamore Bridge
6m W of Laggan Bridge, on unclassified road, 17m SW of Newtonmore. All times. Free.
This two-arched bridge at the south side of the Corrieyarick Pass was built by General Wade in 1735.

Glen Affric
A831 to Cannich and to head of Loch Benevean car park. Jan-Dec. Leaflets available from Forest Enterprise, Strathoich, Fort Augustus. (FE).
The area is a Forest Nature Reserve, with a great variety of wildlife at all points on walks and trails through native pinewoods and other beautiful woodland.

Glenan Bay
10 miles W of Tighnabruaich via B8000 and unclassified road from Millhouse to Portavadie. All reasonable times. Free. Car parking only. (FE).

Glenan Bay is a secluded bay on the shore of Loch Fyne, well away from traffic and disturbance. It lies on the edge of Glenan Oakwood Forest Nature Reserve. A path leads from the car park through the ancient semi-natural woodland and returning to the car park. Stout footwear is recommended.

Glenbarr Abbey Visitor Centre (Macalister Clan)
Glenbarr, on A83, 12 miles NW of Campbeltown. Easter-mid Oct. Daily exc. Tues, 10.00-18.00. Entrance charge. Parking available. Gift shop. Tearoom. Tel: (0158 32) 247.
18th/19th century Gothic style house gives glimpse of family living, with antique toys, Spode and Sevres china. Gloves worn by Mary, Queen of Scots are among the exhibits in the museum. A large collection of thimbles, owned by the present Mrs. Macalister, is on display. Lovely grounds, riverside and woodland walks. Tours conducted by the Laird and Lady Glenbarr (Mr. & Mrs. Macalister).

Glencoe and Dalness
A82, 3m E of Glencoe Cross, runs through the glen. (Visitor Centre) 1 Apr-25 May, 10 Sept-21 Oct, daily 10.00-17.30; 26 May-9 Sept, daily 09.30-18.30. (NTS). Tel: (0185 52) 307.
The finest and perhaps the most famous glen in Scotland through which a main road runs. Scene of the Massacre of Glencoe, 1692, and centre for some of the best mountaineering in the country (not to be attempted by the unskilled). Noted for wildlife which includes red deer, wildcat, golden eagle, ptarmigan. NTS owns 14,200 acres of Glencoe and Dalness. Ski centre, chairlift and ski tows (weekends and New Year and Easter holiday periods only, other times by charter arrangement) at White Corries. Visitor Centre gives general information, particularly on walks. Visitor Centre, special presentation, Ranger Service, walks and trails, shop, picnic area and tea bar.

Glencoe and North Lorn Folk Museum
In Glencoe Village, off A82, on S shore of Loch Leven. May-Sep, Mon-Sat 10.00-17.30.
Clan and Jacobite relics, also domestic implements, weapons, costumes, photographs, dolls' houses and dolls, agricultural tools, dairy and slate quarrying equipment are included in this museum housed in a number of thatched cottages.

Glencoe Chairlift
Off A82 by Kingshouse. Jan-Apr, Thurs to Mon

inclusive of Easter; June-Sept, daily 10.00-17.00. Tel: (018556) 226.

Chairlift to 2,100 feet offers magnificent views of the areas around Glencoe and Rannoch Moor. Summer: access chairlift, snack bar, car park, toilets. Winter: two chairlifts and three tows for ski-ing, car park, toilets and snack bars.

Glenelg Brochs

Unclassified road from Eilanreach, 12m W of Shiel Bridge. All times. Free. (HS). Tel: 0131-244 3101.

Two Iron Age brochs, Dun Telve and Dun Troddan, have walls still over 30 feet high.

Glenfeochan House Gardens

Kilmore, 5m S of Oban, A816. Daily, 1 Apr-31 Oct, 10.00-18.00. Parking available. Tel: (0163177) 273.

Glenfeochan House, built in 1875, is surrounded by six acres of mature gardens. Many of the trees were planted in the 1850's. A wide variety of rhododendron are on view, including a Loderi Collection. Walled garden with herbaceous borders, vegetables and large greenhouse (containing peaches, nectarines) and herb beds.

Glenfinnan Monument

A830, 18.5m W of Fort William. Apr-late May, early Sept-mid Oct, daily 10.00-13.00, 14.00-17.00. Late May-early Sept, daily 09.00-18.00. Entrance charge. Parking available. Gift shop. Snack bar. (NTS). Tel: (0139 783) 250.

The monument commemorates the raising of Prince Charles Edward Stuart's standard at Glenfinnan on 19 August 1745. It was erected by MacDonald of Glenaladale in 1815; a figure of a Highlander surmounts the tower. The Visitor Centre tells of the Prince's campaign from Glenfinnan to Derby and back to the final defeat at Culloden. Audio-visual programme, snack bar and viewpoint.

Glen Grant Distillery

Rothes. Late Apr-end Sep, Mon-Fri 10.00-16.00, also Sats, Jul and Aug. Free. Tel: (0134 03) 413 (during season) and (015422) 8924 (during winter).

Tours of the distillery, with Reception Centre and whisky sample. Children under 8 not admitted to production areas but welcome in Reception Centre.

Glenmore Forest Park

7m E of Aviemore, off B9152. Open all year (exc. 2 weeks in Nov). (FE). Tel: (01479) 861220.

Over 12,000 acres of pine and spruce woods

and mountainside on the north-west slopes of the Cairngorms, with Loch Morlich as its centre. This is probably the finest area in Britain for wildlife, including red deer, reindeer, wildcat, golden eagle, ptarmigan, capercailzie, etc. Remnants of old Caledonian pinewoods. Well-equipped caravan sites and hostels open all year, canoeing, sailing, fishing, swimming, forest trails and hillwalking, and an Information Centre. Campsite, forest walks, toilets, picnic area, shop, cafe and wayfaring trail.

Glen Nant Forest Nature Reserve

2 miles S of Taynuilt on B845. All reasonable times. Car parking only. (FE). Tel: (01631) 66155.

A site which combines historical interest with high nature conservation value. A 2.5 mile walk through the reserve gives an insight into the management of native woodland for charcoal and tannin production. Rich flora and fauna, especially lichens and ants. Disabled visitor trail.

Highbank Porcelain Pottery, Lochgilphead

On A816 on the W outskirts of Lochgilphead. Jan-Dec. Pottery tours, Mon-Fri 10.30 and 14.00. Shop open Mon-Fri 09.00-17.00, Sat 10.00-17.00, Sun 11.00-17.00. Charge for tour: children free. Parking available. Shop. Tel: (01546) 602044.

Pottery producing slip cases, hand-decorated porcelain model animals and vases.

Highland Folk Museum

A9 at Kingussie, 12m SW of Aviemore. All year, Apr-Oct, Mon-Sat 10.00-18.00, Sun 14.00-18.00; Nov-Mar, Mon-Fri 10.00-15.00; closed Xmas & New Year. Entrance charge. Parking available. Gift shop. Tel: (01540) 661 307.

The open air museum includes an 18th century shooting lodge, a 'Black House' from Lewis, a Clack Mill, a turf-walled house from the Central Highlands and exhibits of farming equipment. Indoors, the farming museum has fine displays of a barn, dairy, stable and an exhibition of Highland tinkers; and there are special features on weapons, costume, musical instruments and Highland furniture. Picnic garden. Special events Easter-September.

Highland Wildlife Park

Off A9 (B9152), 7m S of Aviemore. Open daily 10.00-16.00 (June-Aug, 17.00); closed winter season. Entrance charge. Shop. Restaurant. Tel: (01540) 651270.

This notable wildlife park features breeding groups of Highland animals and birds in a beautiful natural setting. Drive-through section has red deer herd, bison, Highland cattle, etc. Aviaries display capercailzie, eagles; also wolves, wildcats and nearly 60 other species. There is an exhibition on 'Man and Fauna in the Highlands', and a children's animal park. Also souvenir shop, cafeteria and picnic area.

Highland Wineries
Moniack Castle, Kirkhill, 7m W of Inverness off the A862. All year, 10.00-17.00; closed Sun. Free. Parking available. Tel: (01463 83) 283.
Winery making country wines and liqueurs. Tours of the winery show the processes involved in wine making. Free tasting, tours, shop and licensed restaurant.

Inchnacardoch Walks
Strathoich, 1 mile out of Fort Augustus on the Auchterawe/Jenkins Park road. Jan-Dec. All reasonable times. Free. Car parking only. (FE). Tel: (01320) 6322.
A variety of walks, mainly woodland, with riverside paths, picnic sites and parking at both ends. A leaflet is available at the Forest Office, Strathoich.

Inveraray Bell Tower
In Inveraray. Early May-late Sep, Mon-Sat 10.00-13.00, 14.00-17.00; Sun 14.00-17.00. Charge to ascend the tower. Exhibition free. Tel: (01499) 2259.
The 126-feet high granite tower houses Scotland's finest ring of bells and the world's third-heaviest ring of ten bells, which are rung regularly. Excellent views, pleasant grounds.

Inveraray Castle
0.5m N of Inveraray. Early Apr-Jun, Sep-mid Oct, Mon-Sat (not Fri) 10.00-12.00, 14.00-17.00, Sun 13.00-17.00; Jul-Aug, Mon-Sat 10.00-17.00, Sun 13.00-17.00. (Closing times indicate last admission). Entrance charges. Parking available. Tel: (01499) 2203.
Inveraray has been the seat of the chiefs of Clan Campbell, Dukes of Argyll, for centuries. The present castle was started in 1743 when the third Duke engaged Roger Morris to build it. Subsequently the Adam family, father and sons, were also involved. The magnificent interior decoration was commissioned by the fifth Duke from Robert Mylne. In addition to many historic relics, there are portraits by Gainsborough, Ramsay and Raeburn. Tearoom and craft shop. Gardens open on selected weekends.

Inveraray Jail
Church Square, Inveraray. Jan-Dec, exc Xmas and New Year, 09.30-18.00 (last admission 17.00). Entrance charge. Parking available. Gift shop. Tel: (01499) 2381.
The living 19th-century prison. Trained 'prisoners' and 'warders', lifelike figures, imaginative exhibitions, sounds, smells and trials in progress all bring the 1820 courtroom and former county prison back to life. Shop.

Inverawe Smokery
2 miles off A85 Oban-Glasgow road at Bridge of Awe, by Taynuilt. Daily, 09.00-18.00. Entrance charge. Car parking only. Gift shop. Tearoom. Tel: (018662) 446.
A detailed exhibition of how fish is cured & smoked in the old traditional fashion. Fisheries: 3 lochs stocked with trout for fishing. Good walks. Toilets, light refreshments, children's play area.

Inverness Museum & Art gallery
Castle Wynd, Inverness. Mon-Sat 09.00-17.00; Jul & Aug, Sun 14.00-17.00. Free. Museum shop. Coffee shop. Tel: (01463) 237114.
The museum interprets the social and natural history, archaeology and culture of the Highlands, with fine collections of Highland silver, bagpipes, and Jacobite relics. Special exhibitions, performances and talks. Coffee shop. Museum shop.

Jacobite Cruises
From Inverness centre on A82, 1.25m at roadside. Easter-mid Oct. Cruises at 10.00, 14.00 and 18.30. Parking available. Bar and refreshments available. Tel: (01463) 233999.
Cruises on the Caledonian Canal and Loch Ness. Bar and light refreshments available on board.

Kilchurn Castle
N tip of Loch Awe, 21m E of Oban. Access at all reasonable times. (HS). Tel: 0131-244 3101.
The keep was built in 1440 by Sir Colin Campbell of Glenorchy, founder of the Breadalbane family. The north and south sides of the building were erected in 1693 by Ian, Earl of Breadalbane, whose arms and those of his wife are over the gateway. Occupied by the Breadalbanes until 1740, in 1746 it was taken by Hanoverian troops. A gale in 1879 toppled one of it towers.

Kilmory Castle Gardens
Off A83 road to Inveraray, on outskirts of Lochgilphead. Parking available. Tel: (01546) 602127.
The garden was started in the 1770's and included around 100 varieties of rhododendron, supplied plants for Kew Garden and contained

a collection of hardy ferns and alpines. The gardens are being restored with woodland walks and a nature trail. There are also footpaths and a herbaceous border.

Kilravock Castle
2m from Croy, 6m W of Nairn off the B9091. End Apr-Sept, Castle: Wed 11.00-17.00. Garden and grounds: Mon-Sat 09.00-17.00. Entrance charge. Parking available. Sales point. Tearoom (Wed). Lunches by prior arrangement. Tel: (0166 78) 258.
The extensive grounds and garden of this 15th-century castle are noted for a large variety of beautiful trees, some centuries old and unique in this country. The tree garden, nature trails and river host an abundance of wildlife. A plan location of trees is available on request. Guided tours of the castle and afternoon tea are available on Wednesdays. Lunch is available by prior request daily except Sundays.

Kingfisher Cruises
Ardfern Yacht Centre, between Oban and Lochgilphead, take B8002 off A816. Jan-Dec. All times, weather permitting. Charge for cruises. Car parking only. Tel: (0185 25) 662.
Various cruises, from 1.5 hours viewing seals, seabirds and scenery in sheltered Loch Craignish, 45 minutes cruises visiting nearby islands such as Jura, Scarba, Luing and Shuna, to 5-8 hours visiting the McCormaig Islands or the Garvellachs. Walkers 'ferry' service to Jura.

Kinlochlaich House Gardens
Midway between Oban and Fort William on A828. Entry by police station. Parking available. Tel: (0163) 173 342.
Walled garden, incorporating West Highland's largest nursery garden centre. There are display beds of primulas, alpines, rhododendrons, heathers as well as fruiting and flowering shrubs and trees.

Kintail
N of A87 between Lochs Cluanie and Duich, 16m E of Kyle of Lochalsh. Jan-Dec. Countryside Centre at Morvich (unmanned) open May-late Sept, Mon-Sat 10.00-17.00, Sun 14.00-17.00. Entrance charge, honesty box. Car parking only. (NTS). Tel: (0159 981) 219.
Magnificent Highland scenery including the Five Sisters of Kintail (four of them over 3,000ft). Red deer and wild goats. Visitor Centre at Morvich gives best access to mountains. Site of Battle of Glen Shiel, 5 miles east of village beside road. Ranger-led walks in season.

Kyle House
0.5m from jetty at Kyleakin. Open May-Aug. All reasonable times. Free (charity donation box). Car parking only. Tel: (01599) 4517.
Situated by Loch Alsh the garden is protected in winter by the Gulf Stream. This allows many tender plants to attain quite large sizes. Most of the garden was planted around 30 years ago by the late Mr. Colin Mackenzie. It covers about 3 acres. Also a kitchen garden and a viewpoint from which can be seen the Cuillin Hills on the Isle of Skye, the Isle of Raasay and many other small islands.

Lady Rowena, Steam Launch
Sails from BR Station Pier at Lochawe Village on A85. May-Sept 10.30-16.00, 7 days a week, hourly from 10.00. Charge for cruises. Tel: 0141-334 2529 or (018382) 440/449.
Restored Edwardian launch with genuine steam engine and peat-fired boiler. Cushioned seating and enclosed cabin. Variety of cruises (50 mins. to 3 hrs.) to places of interest on Loch Awe. Comfortable Pullman Carriage Tearoom on the pier with superb views of Kilchurn Castle. Ferry to castle.

Landmark Visitor Centre
Carrbridge, 6m N of Aviemore on old A9. Jan-Dec. Apr-Jun, Sept-Oct, daily 09.30-18.00. Jul & Aug 09.30-20.00. Nov-Mar 09.30-17.00. Entrance charges. Parking available. Scottish craft and bookshop. Restaurant, bar, snack bar, picnic area. Tel: (0147 984) 613.
This 'Landmark' Visitor Centre was the first of its kind in Europe. Ten thousand years of Highland history are shown in the triple-screen audio-visual theatre and a dramatic exhibition interprets the history of Strathspey. Now has sculpture park, tree-top trail and woodland maze. Adventure playground with giant slides and aerial net walkways. Also new pine forest nature centre. Craft and bookshop, restaurant, bar, snack bar, picnic area and plant centre. Free parking.

Lochalsh Woodland Garden
Balmacara Estate, off A87, 3m E of Kyle of Lochalsh. Garden: Jan-Dec, daily 09.00-sunset. Information kiosk and Coach House: May-late Sept, Mon-Sat, 10.00-17.00, Sun 14.00-17.00. Entrance charge. Parking available. (NTS). Tel: (0159 986) 207.
Set in the 5,616 acre Balmacara Estate, Lochalsh Woodland Garden provides pleasant sheltered walks by the loch. A wide variety of native trees and shrubs and more exotic plants from Tasmania, New Zealand, the Himalayas, Chile, Japan and China grow in the grounds of

Lochalsh House (not open to the public). Information and coach house display, ranger-led walks in the summer.

Loch an Eilein Pottery
2.5 miles SW of Aviemore, just off B970 on road to Loch an Eilein. Jan-Dec. Daily, 10.00-18.00 in summer, mornings only in winter. Free. Car parking only. Pottery shop. Tel: (01479) 810837.

Small rural craft pottery workshop with display area of pots for sale. Pottery is red earthenware, domestic and functional, specialising in jugs of all sizes, and garden pots. Thursday is 'throw-your-own' day, when visitors can try their hand at making a pot which will be glazed, fired and posted on to them.

Loch-an-Eilein Visitor Centre
B970, 2.5m S of Aviemore. All year, exc. Xmas Day. Daily, 09.30-16.30. Charge for car park. Coaches by arrangement. Tel: (01479) 810 858.

This exhibition which is held in a cottage by the loch and a beautiful ruined castle, traces the history of the native Scots Pine forest from the Ice Age until today, its management and conservation. Good local interest for birdwatchers.

Loch Etive Cruises
Taynuilt, 12 miles E of Oban on A85, follow signs on reaching village. May-Sep, cruises Mon-Fri at 10.30 and 14.00, Sat & Sun 14.00. Easter-end Apr, Oct, cruises daily at 14.00 only. Duration 3 hours. Charge for cruise. Parking available. Free transport from Taynuilt village to vessel for foot passengers. Refreshments. Tel: (0186 62) 430.

Cruises on lovely Loch Etive, inaccessible except by boat, take in 20 miles of sheltered water from Connel Bridge to the mountains of Glencoe. Seals may be visible on the rocks, golden eagle on Ben Starav, deer on crags, the ancient home of Deirdre of the Sorrows, fine mountain scenery.

Loch Garten Nature Reserve
Off B970, 8m NE of Aviemore. If Ospreys present, daily mid Apr-Aug 10.00-20.00 along signposted track to Observation Post. Other access into bird sanctuary strictly forbidden Apr-Aug but elsewhere on the reserve access unrestricted throughout the year. (RSPB). Tel: (01479) 83694 or 0131-557 3136.

Ospreys, extinct in Scotland for many years, returned here to breed in 1959. Their treetop eyrie may be viewed through fixed binoculars from the Observation Hut. Other local specialities include crested tits, crossbills and

capercailzies. The surrounding area owned by the RSPB, includes extensive stretches of old Caledonian Pine forest with rich and varied wildlife.

Loch Morar
SE of Mallaig
Said to be the deepest loch in Scotland and the home of Morag, a monster with a strong resemblance to the Loch Ness Monster.

Loch Nan Uamh Cairn
Off A830, S of Arisaig.
The loch is famous for its association with Bonnie Prince Charlie. The memorial cairn on the shore marks the spot from which Prince Charles Edward Stuart sailed for France on 20 September, 1746 after having wandered round the Highlands as a fugitive with a price of £30,000 on his head.

Loch Ness
SW of Inverness
This striking 24-mile long loch in the Great Glen forms part of the Caledonian Canal which links Inverness with Fort William. For much of its length it is over 700 feet deep. The loch contains the largest volume of fresh water of any lake in the British Isles. Famous world wide for its mysterious inhabitant, the Loch Ness Monster. It is also ideal for cruising and sailing.

Loch Ness Lodge Visitor Centre
A82 S from Inverness to Drumnadrochit, turn onto A831 to Cannich 50 metres on right. All year 09.00-18.00, June-Sept 09.00-21.00. Parking available. (Loch Ness Lodge Hotel Co. Ltd.) Tel: (014562) 342.

Large screen cinema on Loch Ness, its history and myth. Pictorial display of local culture and items of interest. Gift shop. Coffee shop specialising in home baking. Loch Ness sonar scanning cruises.

Loch Ness Video Show
Kiltmaker, 4/9 Huntly Street, Inverness. Jun-mid Sept, Mon-Sat 09.00-21.00, Sun 09.00-17.00. Oct-May, Mon-Sat 09.00-16.00. Entrance charge. Parking available. Tel: (01463) 222781.

A thirty to forty minute video show on the art of kiltmaking and the Loch Ness Monster search and preview of the Loch Ness Monster Exhibition at Drumnadrochit.

McCaig's Tower
On a hill overlooking Oban. All times. Free.
McCaig was a local banker who tried to curb unemployment by using local craftsmen to build

this tower from 1897-1900 as a memorial to his family. Its walls are two feet thick and from 30-47 feet high. The courtyard within is landscaped and the tower is floodlit at night in summer. An observation platform on the seaward side was added in 1983.

Flora MacDonald's Monument
Inverness Castle. All times. Free.
Monument to Flora MacDonald (1722-1790) on the esplanade of the Victorian castle. Flora MacDonald is famed for the help she gave to the Young Pretender in June 1746, enabling him to escape from Benbecula to Portree.

Roderick Mackenzie Memorial
1m E of Ceannacroc on A887, 13m W of Invermoriston. All times. Free.
A cairn on the south of the road commemorates Roderick Mackenzie, who in 1746 pretended to be Prince Charles Edward Stuart and was killed by soldiers searching for the Prince after Culloden.

Mallaig Marine World
The Harbour, Mallaig, 45 miles N of Fort William on A830. June-Sept, daily, 09.00-21.00, Oct-May 09.00-17.00. Entrance charges. Parking available. Gift shop. Tel: (01687) 2292.
Marine aquarium and exhibition featuring local marine species. Fishing displays on the work of the Mallaig fishing fleet. Video illustrating boats at work at different fishings and in all weathers, including the work of the lifeboat. Pond garden, indoor and outdoor seating, marine scientist on hand.

Minard Castle
Off A83, 14m S of Inveraray. May-Oct, Mon-Fri 11.00-16.00. Viewing by appointment only. Tel: (01546) 86272.
The castle is originally 16th-century with subsequent extensions and contains paintings of the Franco-Scottish Royal House.

Monument Hill
2m SW of Dalmally, off the old road to Inveraray. All times. Free.
Monument to Duncan Ban Macintyre (1724-1812), the 'Burns of the Highlands', who was born near Inveroran.

Neptune's Staircase
3m NW of Fort William off A830 at Banavie.
A series of 8 locks, built between 1805 and 1822, which raises Telford's Caledonian Canal 64 feet.

Nevis Range
Torlundy. New access road signposted Aonach Mor, 6 miles N of Fort William on A82. Jan-Apr, daily 09.00-16.30. May-Oct, daily 10.00-17.00 (and evenings July & Aug). Charge for gondola trip. Parking available. Gift shop. Restaurant, bar, cafeteria. Tel: (01397) 705825.
Ski area and summer visitor attraction in the heart of the western Highlands on Aonach Mor (4,006 feet) beside Ben Nevis. A ride in one of eighty enclosed gondolas gives spectacular views. Restaurant and bar at 2,150 feet, shop and mountain walks at top gondola station. At base, cafe, forestry walks and mountain bike hire. In winter, extensive skiing with eight ski lifts, ski school and ski hire.

Oban Distillery
Stafford Street. Jan-Dec, exc. Xmas and New Year. Mon-Fri 09.30-17.00. Gift shop. Tel: (01631) 64262.
The distillery, founded in 1794, is famous for its Classic Malt Whisky. Reception centre exhibition tells the story of the Stevenson family who developed Oban from a fishing village into a resort with light industry. Tours, tastings.

Oban Experience
Heritage Wharf, Railway Pier. Jan-Dec, dawn-dusk. Free. Parking available. Gift shop. Tearoom. Tel: (01631) 66969.
Visitor centre depicting Oban in Victorian times with audio-visuals and exhibits.

Oban Glass
Heritage Wharf, Railway Pier. Free. Factory shop: May-Oct, Mon-Sat 09.00-21.00, Sun 11.00-17.00. Nov-Apr, Mon-Sat 09.00-17.30. Factory viewing: Mon-Fri 09.00-17.00 (all year). Parking available. Tel: (01631) 63386.
See paperweight making from the raw materials stage through all the processes to the finished article. Visit the factory shop with an extensive range of glassware. Ample car/coach parking.

Official Loch Ness Monster Exhibition
Drumnadrochit, 15 miles S of Inverness. Jan-Dec exc Xmas and Boxing Day. Peak opening: daily, 09.30-21.30. Mid-season: daily, 09.30-17.30. Winter: daily, 10.00-16.00. Entrance charges. Parking available. Shops. Restaurant, bar, coffee shop, hotel on site. Tel: (0145 62) 573 or 218.
40 minute audio-visual presentation and exhibition which displays much of the equipment used in the exploration of Loch Ness. The centre also houses a number of shops - woollen shop, glass blowers, jewellery with craft demonstration. Garden includes life-size 'Nessie' on an outdoor lochan.

Original Loch Ness Visitor Centre

Drumnadrochit, 14 miles W of Inverness on A82. June-Oct, daily 08.00-21.30. Oct-May, daily, 09.00-17.00. Entrance charges. Parking available. Woollen shop, bookshop, kitchen and whisky shop, Celtic craft shop, 2 gift shops. Licensed all day coffee house, ice cream kiosk, hotel on site. Tel: (0145 62) 342.

Visitor centre specialising in foreign language service, with simultaneous translations of its film, which focuses on the history, mystery and latest developments on Loch Ness. Boat cruises on loch with commentary by local skipper, and on-board sonar for monster-spotting. Eight acres of woodland to explore, garden with seating. Entertainment and all facilities at hotel.

Parallel Roads

Glen Roy, unclassified road off A86, 18m NE of Fort William

These 'parallel roads' are hillside terraces marking levels of lakes dammed by glaciers during the Ice Age.

James Pringle Weavers of Inverness

Holm Woollen Mills, Dores Road. Signposted (Holm Mills) on B862. Jan-Dec. Mill: Mon-Fri 09.00-17.00. Visitor facilities: summer, daily, 09.00-17.30; winter, Mon-Sat 09.30-17.00. Free. Parking available. Gift shop. Restaurant. Tel: (01463) 223311.

James Pringle Weavers of Inverness offers tours round a fully-operational weaving mill which dates back to 1790. Self-guided tours with information in six languages. Clan tartan centre where ancestral roots can be researched. Mill shop, weaving mill and restaurant have wide aisles and no steps for wheelchairs.

Puck's Glen

In Argyll Forest Park, 5 miles W of Dunoon on A815. All reasonable times. Free. Car parking only.

One of the most famous walks on the Cowal peninsula. The path runs through the narrow gorge of the Eas Mor, which is lined by magnificent Douglas firs, some of which are 120 feet high. This spectacular walk is not suitable for disabled visitors; however, a wheelchair access route following an abandoned public road gives views of the lower parts of the glen.

Queen's Own Highlanders Regimental Museum

Fort George, near Ardersier. Apr-Sept, Mon-Fri 10.00-18.00, Sun 14.00-18.00. Oct-Mar, Mon-Fri 10.00-16.00. Free. Parking available. Tel: (01463) 224380.

Regimental museum with collections of medals, uniforms and other items showing the history of the Queen's Own Highlanders, Seaforth Highlanders and The Queen's Own Cameron Highlanders and Lovat Scouts.

Rothiemurchus Estate Visitor Centre

1m from Aviemore. All year, 09.00-17.00. Parking available. Tel: (01479) 810858.

Highland cattle, red deer, Caledonian pine forest, Cairngorms National Nature Reserve, trout farm (feed the fish), fresh and smoked trout for sale. Designer knitwear and crafts, estate tours, tractor and trailer rides, Land Rover safaris, clay pigeon shooting range, loch and river fishing.

Ruthven Barracks

On B970, 0.5m S of Kingussie. All reasonable times. Free. (HS). Tel: 0131-244 3101.

Considerable ruins, on a site once occupied by a fortress of the Wolf of Badenoch, of barracks built 1716-18 to keep the Highlanders in check, and added to by General Wade in 1734. After the disaster of Culloden, 1746, Prince Charles' Highlanders assembled at Ruthven hoping he might take the field again. When they realised the cause was hopeless, they blew up the barracks.

St. Andrews Cathedral, Inverness

Ness Walk, Ardross Street, below Ness Bridge. Jan-Dec. Daily, 08.30-18.00. Later opening May-Sept. Donations requested. Parking available. Gift shop and tearoom (May-Sept). Tel: (01463) 233535.

Cathedral Church in Gothic style built, 1866-69, by local architect Alexander Ross. It was the first cathedral to be built in this style since the Reformation. Monolithic pillars of polished Peterhead granite, stained glass, sculpture, carved reredos. Angel font after Thorvaldsen (Copenhagen), Founder's Memorial, ikons presented by Tsar of Russia, ten bells. Fine choir sings at Sunday services.

St. Columba's Cave

1m N of Ellary on W shore of Loch Killisport (Caolisport), 10m SW of Ardrishaig. All times. Free.

Traditionally associated with St. Columba's arrival in Scotland, the cave contains a rock-shelf with an altar, above which are carved crosses. A large basin, perhaps a Stone Age mortar, may have been used as a font. The cave was occupied from the Middle Stone Age. In front are traces of houses and the ruins of a chapel (possibly 13th century) and another cave is nearby.

Sea Life Centre
Barcaldine, on A828, 10m N of Oban. Mid Feb-Nov, daily. 09.00-18.00. (19.00 in July & Aug). Dec-mid Feb, weekends only. Entrance charges. Parking available. Gift shop. Restaurant. Tel: (01631) 72386.

Centre houses a large and exciting display of native marine life. Visitors can experience the feeling of being on the sea-bed without getting wet and come face to face with octopus, catfish and seals. Both the aquarium and restaurant have a beautiful lochside setting.

Skipness Castle and Chapel
Skipness, B8001, 10m S of Tarbert, Loch Fyne. Closed to the public but may be viewed from outside. (HS). Tel: 0131-244 3101.

The remains of the ancient chapel and the large 13th-century castle overlook the bay.

Statesman Cruises
Kylesku Bridge, A894 over Loch a'Cairn Bhan. March-Oct. Daily, 11.00 & 14.00. Charge for cruise. Parking available. Tel: (0157 14) 446.

Boat cruises up Loch Glencoul to Eas Coul Aulin, Britain's highest waterfall, most of which can be seen from the boat. During the cruise, in sheltered waters, seals may be seen, also golden eagles, herons, ravens, guillemot, peregrine falcon, red and black throated divers, greylag geese, terns and shag.

Strathspey Steam Railway
Aviemore (Speyside) to Boat of Garten. Access at Aviemore: cars B970 then Dalfaber Road, pedestrians take underpass from Main Road at Bank of Scotland. Boat of Garten: Station beside Boat Hotel. Open daily, July & Aug, daily exc. Sat, June & Sept. Other dates: timetables available locally. Stations open 09.30-18.00. 1st and 3rd class single and return fares, children half fare, under 5 free. Parking available. Buffet car. Coffee service. Tel: (01479) 810725.

The line is part of the former Highland Railway (Aviemore-Forres section) closed in 1965 and reopened 1978 after restoration work begun in 1972. Passenger steam train service run entirely by volunteers. Station buildings at Aviemore (Speyside) were brought from Dalnaspidal and the footbridge from Longmorn. Timetables available. Museum of small relics and other static rolling stock on display at Boat of Garten.

Ann R Thomas Gallery
Harbour Street, Tarbert, Loch Fyne. Just off A83 Glasgow-Campbeltown, facing fish quay. Jan-Dec exc Xmas and New Year. Summer, *Mon-Sat 09.00-18.30. Winter, 10.00-17.30. Early closing Wed, open Sun for shorter period. Free. Gift shop. Tel: (01880) 820390.*

Art gallery featuring paintings and prints by Ann Thomas, book, crafts, gifts, stationery, art materials.

Tomatin Distillery
Off A9, 16m S of Inverness at Tomatin. Mar-Oct. Mon-Fri 09.00-16.30. Also Sat, Jun-Oct, 09.30-12.30. All other times by prior arrangement. Free. Parking available. Gift shop. Tel: (0180 82) 234.

Scotland's largest malt whisky distillery. Reception centre (opened 1992) with video, static displays and full product range. Guided tour (approx 45 mins) is followed by a taste of 'The Tomatin'.

Treasures of the Earth
Mallaig Road, Corpach, 4 miles outside Fort William on A830. Feb-Dec. Daily, 10.00-17.00 (20.00 in July & Aug). Entrance charge - free entry to gift shop. Parking available. Coach service from Fort William TIC. Gem and gift shop. Tel: (01397) 772283.

Award-winning attraction with superb collection of priceless gemstones, many weighing hundreds of pounds, beautiful crystals and exotic minerals from around the world. Display, covering 6,500 square feet, recreates the fascinating world beneath our feet with glistening rock cavities and caverns set among primeval scenes. Shop specialises in gemstone jewellery, ornaments from around the world and many local stone items.

The Tree Shop
Ardkinglas Estate Nurseries, Clachan Farm. At head of Loch Fyne near Cairndow on A83 Glasgow-Oban and Campbeltown. Apr-Sept, daily 09.30-19.00. Oct-Mar (exc Jan), daily 09.30-17.00. Free. Parking available. Gift shop. Plant sales. Tel: (0149 96) 263 or 261.

The Tree Shop at the head of Loch Fyne specialises in specimen trees, indigenous Highland trees, rhododenrons and azaleas, heathers and unusual shrubs. Much of the plant sales area is under cover, with a canopy designed to ensure the hardiness of the plants. Inside the Tree Shop, a range of quality woodwork, basketware and shepherd's crooks.

Urquhart Castle
2m SE of Drumnadrochit, on W shore of Loch Ness. Apr-Sept, daily 09.30-18.30. Oct-Mar, Mon-Sat 09.30-16.30, Sun 11.30-16.30. Entrance charge. Parking available. (HS). Tel: 0131-244 3101.

Once one of the largest castles in Scotland, the castle is situated on a promontory on the banks of Loch Ness, from where sitings of the 'monster' are most frequently reported. The extensive ruins are on the site of a vitrified fort, rebuilt with stone in the 14th century. The castle was gifted by James IV, in 1509, to John Grant of Freuchie, whose family built much of the existing fabric and held the site for four centuries. The castle was blown up in 1692 to prevent its being occupied by Jacobites.

Waltzing Waters
Balavil Brae, Newtonmore. All year exc mid Jan-late Feb. Daily, 10.00-17.00, shows on the hour, and at 20.30. Entrance charges. Craft shops. Refreshments. Tel: (01540) 673752.
Elaborate light, water and music spectacle, patterns of moving water synchronised with a wide variety of music. Spacious reception has craft area, children's play area and tourist information points. Wide-screen audio visual introduction to Scotland.

Waterfowl and Country Park
The Croft, Drumsmittal, North Kessock. Just N of Inverness over Kessock Bridge. Jan-Dec. Daily, 10.00-dusk. Entrance charge. Parking available. Tel: (0146 373) 656.
Ornamental waterfowl, ducks, geese, swans, rare breeds, cattle, sheep, pigs, goats, rabbits, chickens, bantams, pheasant. Children's corner in farmyard area has ponds, chicks hatching most days in summer. Chambered cairn on site.

Well of the Seven Heads
Off A82 on the W shore of Loch Oich. All times. Free. Parking available.
A curious monument inscribed in English, Gaelic, French and Latin and surmounted by seven men's heads, stands above a spring and recalls the grim story of the execution of seven brothers for the murder of the two sons of a 17th century chief of Keppoch.

West Highland Museum
Cameron Square, Fort William. All year, Mon-Sat 10.00-13.00, 14.00-17.00, Jul & Aug, Mon-Fri 09.30-18.00, Sun 14.00-17.00. Closed Mon, Nov-Mar. Entrance charge. Gift shop. Tel: (01397) 702169.
Historical, natural history and folk exhibits, local interest and a tartan section. Jacobite relics including a secret portrait of 'Bonnie Prince Charlie'.

A World in Miniature
North Pier, Oban. Easter-Oct, Mon-Sat 10.00-17.00, Sun 12.00-17.30. Entrance charges. Tel: (0185 26) 272 or (01631) 66300.
Exhibition of half scale miniature rooms, furniture, dioramas, etc.

CENTRAL AND SOUTH WEST SCOTLAND

Ailsa Craig
Island in Firth of Clyde, 10m W of Girvan. Visitors must obtain permission from the Marquis of Ailsa, the Factor, Cassillis Estates, Maybole Castle, 4 High Street, Maybole. Tel: (01655) 82103.
A granite island rock, 1,114 feet high with a circumference of 2 miles. The rock itself was used to make some of the finest curling stones and the island has a gannetry and colonies of guillemots and other seabirds.

Airdrie Observatory
Public Library, Wellwynd. Meetings of ASTRA every Friday exc public hols, in Airdrie Arts Centre, Anderson Street, with access to Observatory on clear nights. Visits at other times by arrangement. Entrance free to visitors, charge for ASTRA membership. Parking available. Shop. Refreshments at meetings. Tel: (01236) 763221.
Original observatory with 3-inch refractor, founded 1895. After the new Airdrie Library opened in 1920, a 6-inch Cook refractor was donated anonymously, and set up in 1936. A new dome was fitted after storm damage in 1987. The telescope was refurbished by members of the Association in Scotland to Research into Astronautics Ltd (ASTRA), and the society became curators of the observatory for the district council.

Aldessan Gallery
The Clachan, Campsie Glen, 3 miles east of Strathblane on A891, Jan-Dec exc. Xmas and New Year. Mon-Fri 11.00-17.30, Sat & Sun 11.00-20.00. Parking available. Shop. Coffee shop with light meals.
Gallery and batik studio in Grade B listed building shows monthly exhibitions of contemporary art. Craft area specialising in Scottish goods. Silk batik is produced in the studio, and workshop classes can be arranged. Campsie Glen has walks and waterfalls, historic graveyard. Conservation area. Adjoining craft workshops include stained glass, jewellery, violin and guitar-making, sculptor-in-residence.

Alloway Auld Kirk
In Alloway. 2.5m S of Ayr. All reasonable times. Free. Tel: (01292) 441252 (mornings).
Ancient church, a ruin in Burns' day, where his father William Burns is buried. Through its window, Tam saw the dancing witches and warlocks in the poem *Tam o'Shanter*. Adjacent to Burns Centre, Burns Monument Hotel and [1/] [2] mile from Burns Cottage/Tearoom.

Antartex Village
Loch Lomond, By Balloch, just off A82. Open daily 10.00-18.00 (closed Christmas & New Years Day). Free. Parking available. Public transport. Shops. Spinning Wheel coffee shop/restaurant. Tel: (01389) 52393.
Plenty of free parking. Seating capacity for over 150 within the Spinning Wheel Coffee Shop. Disabled facilities. Situated at the Southernmost tip of Loch Lomond, which enjoys the most dramatic scenery in the West of Scotland. It features a variety of craft workshops, where crafts-people work and sell their goods. Aspects of the famous Antartex Sheepskin processing and manufacturing make up an interesting factory tour, finally leading into the newly extended retail area, full of Antartex sheepskins and leathers. The full range of the Edinburgh Woollen Mill garments, knitwear, tartans and tourist lines plus something for the teenagers in the trading post.

Aquatec
1 Menteith Road, Motherwell. Jan-Dec, exc Xmas and New Year. Charges for activities. Parking available. Shop. Restaurant, refreshments. Tel: (01698) 276464.
Built in 1989, Aquatec has a well-designed leisure pool with flume tyre ride, water cannon, air beds, children's beach area, lagoon, wild water channel. Leisure Ice Rink has the only Ice Tunnel in Britain, and a log fire. Health suite, gym.

Arbigland Gardens
By Kirkbean, off A710, 12m S of Dumfries. May-Sept: Tue-Sun, Bank Hol Mondays, 14.00-18.00. House open afternoons Whit Week. Entrance charge. Parking available. Shop. Tearoom. Tel: (0138 788) 283.
These extensive woodlands, formal and water gardens are arranged round a sandy bay which is ideal for children. John Paul Jones' birthplace is nearby, and his father was the gardener at Arbigland. Tearoom.

Ardrossan Castle
Ardrossan, on a hill overlooking Ardrossan Bay. All year, all reasonable times. Free. Tel: (01294) 602617.
Mid 12th-century castle on a hill with fine views of Arran and Ailsa Craig. Castle was destroyed by Cromwell and only part of the north tower and two arched cellars remain. Car park.

Argyll's Lodging
Castle Wynd, Stirling. Seen from the outside.
This fine example of an old town residence was built c. 1632 by Sir William Alexander of Menstrie, later Earl of Stirling, who eleven years earlier helped to found Nova Scotia (New Scotland). It is now a youth hostel.

Argyll and Sutherland Highlanders' Museum
In Stirling Castle. Easter-end Sept, Mon-Sat 10.00-17.30, Sun 11.00-17.00. Oct-Easter, Mon-Fri 10.00-16.00. Free. Parking available. Tel: (01786) 75165.
Fine regimental museum, with a notable silver and medal collection.

Auld Kirk
Off High Street, Ayr. Open Tues & Thur in July and August between 19.30-20.30. Free. Tel: (01292) 262938.
A fine church, dating from 1654, with notable lofts inside. Robert Burns was baptised and sometimes attended church there.

Auld Kirk Museum
Take A803 through Springburn and Bishopbriggs to Kirkintilloch Cross. Jan-Dec. Tues, Wed, Fri, 10.00-12.00, 14.00-17.00. Thurs 10.00-17.00, Sat 10.00-13.00, 14.00-17.00. Free. Tel: 0141-775 1185.
The Auld Kirk Museum, formerly the parish church for Kirkintilloch dating back to 1644, houses changing temporary exhibitions featuring local history, art, craft and photography.

Ayr Gorge Woodlands
At Failford, S of A758 Ayr-Mauchline road. Jan-Dec. Free. Parking available. (SWT).
Gorge woodland, partly semi-natural, dominated by oak and some coniferous plantation. Situated by the River Ayr. Historic sandstone steps and viewing platform. Extensive network of well-maintained footpaths.

Bachelors' Club
Tarbolton, B744, 7.5m NE of Ayr off A758. Apr-Oct, daily 12.00-17.00. Entrance charge. Parking available. Tel: (01292) 541940.
A 17th-century house where in 1780 Robert Burns and his friends founded a literary and debating society, the Bachelors' Club. In 1779, Burns attended dancing lessions here, and in 1781 he was initiated as a Freemason. Period furnishings, with reminders of Burns' life at Lochlea Farm. Small coffee shop.

Baird Institute Museum
Centre of Cumnock, off the Square. All year, Fri 09.30-13.00, 13.30-16.00, Sat 11.00-13.00. Free. Parking available. Tel: (01290) 22111.
The Baird Institute dates back to 1891 when it was built from money bequeathed by a local draper named John Baird. Now a local history

museum with a varied programme of temporary exhibitions. Major collections include Cumnock pottery, Mauchline box ware, Ayrshire embroidery. James Keir Hardie Room is dedicated to the early Scottish Labour leader's links with Cumnock.

Balloch Castle Country Park
E of Balloch at S end of Loch Lomond. Easter-Sep weekend. Daily 10.00-18.00. Free. Parking available. Trains from Glasgow. Shop. Refreshments. Tel: (01389) 58216.
Balloch Castle sits in 200 acres of woodland, parkland and ornamental gardens on the shore of Loch Lomond. The Visitor Centre on the ground floor tells the story of the park and the surrounding region through slides and stained glass display panels. Loch Lomond Park Authority ranger service organises walks and events in the area. Picnic and barbecue sites, toilets for disabled people.

Bannockburn Heritage Centre
Off M80, 2m S of Stirling. 1 Apr–28 Oct, daily 10.00-18.00. Audio-visual presentation (last showing 17.30). (NTS). Tel: (01786) 812664.
The audio-visual presentation tells the story of the events leading up to the significant victory in Scottish history (1314). In June 1964 the Queen inaugurated the Rotunda and unveiled the equestrian statue of Robert the Bruce. Information available on cassette.

Bargany Gardens
4m from Girvan, 18m S of Ayr on B734. Mar-Oct, 09.00-19.00 or sunset. Parking available, coaches by advance contact. Tel: (0146 587) 249.
Woodland garden centred on a lily pond surrounded by azaleas and rhododendrons. Daffodils and snowdrops in spring. Fine trees, rock garden and extensive walled garden. Small picnic area near the car park.

Barnsoul Farm
1.5 miles from Shawhead village, off A75 from Dumfries. Apr-Oct. Free. Car parking only. Tel: (0138 773) 249.
Farm with wide variety of nature and bird life which visitors can watch.

Baron's Haugh
North Lodge Avenue. Adele Street, Motherwell. Jan-Dec. Daily. Donation cairn. Parking available. (RSPB). Tel: 0131-557 3136.
Nature reserve with floods, marshes, woodland. Of interest all year round, particularly winter.

Barony Chambers Museum
Take A803 through Springburn and Bishopbriggs to Kirkintilloch Cross. Jan-Dec, Tues, Thur, Fri 14.00-17.00; Sat 10.00-13.00 and 14.00-17.00. Free. Tel: 0141-775 1185.
Barony Chambers is a museum of local life. It looks at the domestic and working life of the people in the area.

Barsalloch Fort
Off A747, 7.5m WNW of Whithorn. All reasonable times. Free. (HS). Tel: 0131-244 3101.
Remains of an iron-age fort on the edge of a raised beach bluff. 60-70 feet above the shore, enclosed by a ditch 12 feet deep and 33 feet wide.

Bell Obelisk
Off A82 W of Bowling. All times. Free.
The obelisk at Douglas Point erected to commemorate Henry Bell, who launched the *Comet,* the first Clyde passenger steamer. Bowling is where the Forth and Clyde Canal enters the Clyde, and where the first practical steamboat, Symington's *Charlotte Dundas* was tried out in 1802 and 1812.

Blackshaw Farm Park
On the B781 between West Kilbride and Dalry. End Mar-mid Aug, daily. Mid Aug-end Sep, Sat, Sun, Mon only 10.30-17.00. Entrance charge. Parking available. Tel: (01563) 34257.
Working farm with seasonal demonstrations of clipping and shearing sheep, milking, cows, feeding calves, etc. Nature trails. Cup and ring stone of historic interest. Four-wheel all-terrain motorbikes, tractor and trailer rides, grass sledging, aerial cableway.

Blacksmith's Shop Visitor Centre
Gretna Green, just off A74 at Scottish/English border. Daily, all year. Tel: (01461) 38441 or 38224.
The old Blacksmith's Shop, famous for runaway marriages, has a museum with anvil marriage room and coach house. Gretna was once a haven for runaway couples seeking to take advantage of Scotland's then laxer marriage laws, when couples could be married by a declaration before witnesses; this was made illegal in 1940. Elopers can still, however, take advantage of Scots law permitting marriage without parental consent at 16. Among places where marriages took place were the Old Toll Bar (now bypassed) when the road opened in 1830, and the Smithy. Restaurant, bar and souvenir shop.

Blair Drummond Safari and Leisure Park
Exit 10 off M9 N of Stirling, 4 miles towards Callander. Apr-early Oct. Daily, 10.00-17.30

(last admission 16.30). Entrance charge. Discount for groups over 15, paid in advance, discount for handicapped visitors and helpers. Parking available. Bus from Stirling. Transport in park available for visitors without cars. Shops. Ranch Kitchen restaurant. Watering Hole Bar, kiosks, picnic and barbecue areas.

Park with drive-through wild animal reserves to see and photograph animals close at hand. Boat safari around Chimpanzee Island and Waterfowl Sanctuary, walks around Pets' Farm. Performing sea lions; giant slide and adventure playground; cable slide across lake; pedal boats and splash cats; face painting and amusements.

Blairquhan Castle
Straiton, Maybole. 14m S of Ayr on B7045. Mid July-mid Aug. Tues-Sun, 13.30-16.15. Entrance charge. Tearoom. Parking available. Tel: (0165 57) 239.

Blairquhan was a castle built in 1820-24 for Sir David Hunter Blair, 3rd Baronet, replacing an earlier one which dated from the 14th century, part of which is included in the new castle. It was designed by the well known Scottish architect, William Burn.

Blowplain Open Farm
Balmaclellan, Castle Douglas. 13m W of Castle Douglas on A713, turn off on A712 (Balmaclellan). Signposted 1 mile on right. Easter-end Oct, 14.00 every day except Sat. Other times by arrangement. Entrance charge. Parking available. Tel: (0164 42) 206.

Guided tour showing day-to-day life on a small hill-farm, and in particular the different types of animals and their uses. Winner of the 1987 Best Scottish Farm Tour Award; also Dumfries & Galloway Tourist Board Good Service Award.

Boswell Museum and Mausoleum
In Auchinleck. A76, 17m E of Ayr. Seen from outside at all times. For entry and guided tour, contact Mrs. Wilson, Chrissie's Shop, 86 Main Street, Auchinleck; prior notice appreciated. Free: donations welcome. Parking available. Tel: (01290) 20931.

The ancient Parish Church, formerly a Celtic well, was enlarged by Walter fitz Alan in 1145-65, and again by David Boswell in 1641-43. It is now a museum of the Boswell family, and also contains a memorial to William Murdoch (1745-1839), a pioneer of lighting and heating by gas. The Boswell Mausoleum, attached, built by Alexander Boswell (Lord Auchinleck) in 1754, is the burial place of five known generations, including James Boswell, Dr Johnson's famous biographer. (Tour 1.5 hrs). Small car park. 2 miles away at Lugar a walking tour on

Murdoch, including his birthplace at Belo Mill, opened in 1984.

Bothwell Castle
At Uddingston on A74, 7m SE of Glasgow. Opening standard, except Oct–Mar closed. Thu afternoon and Fri. (HS). Tel: 0131-244 3101.

Once the largest and finest stone castle in Scotland, dating from the 13th century and reconstructed by the Douglases in the 15th century. In a picturesque setting above the Clyde Valley.

Bruce's Stone
6m W of New Galloway by A712. All reasonable times. Free. (NTS).

This granite boulder on Moss Raploch records a victory by Robert the Bruce over the English in March 1307, during the fight for Scotland's independence.

Bruce's Stone
N side of Loch Trool, unclassified road off A714, 13m N of Newton Stewart. All times. Free.

A massive granite memorial to Robert the Bruce's first victory over the English leading to his subsequent success at Bannockburn. Fine views of Loch Trool and the hills of Galloway.

Buchlyvie Pottery Shop
15 miles W of Stirling on A811. Jan-Dec. Mon-Sat, 09.00-17.00, Sun 12.30-16.30. Car parking only. Tel: (0136 085) 405.

Fine porcelain pottery hand cast and hand painted on the premises, designed by Alison Borthwick. Some of the processes can be seen from the shop.

Robert Burns Centre
Mill Road, Dumfries. Apr-Sept, Mon-Sat 10.00-20.00, Sun 14.00-17.00. Oct-Mar, Tues-Sat 10.00-13.00, 14.00-17.00. Audio-visual theatre. Parking available. Tel: (01387) 64808.

The Robert Burns Centre is the major feature on the Scottish Tourist Board Burns Heritage Trail which runs through Dumfries and Galloway. The centre is housed in an attractive sand stone mill built on the banks of the River Nith in 1781. The mill now contains a 70 seat luxury theatre used for audio visual presentations, an exhibition on Burns life in Dumfries, a bookshop and a cafe. Also public film theatre in evenings. Induction loop.

Burns Cottage and Museum
B7024, at Alloway, 2m S of Ayr. All year. Jun-Aug 09.00-18.00, Sun 10.00-18.00, Apr, May, Sept, Oct 10.00-17.00 (Sun 14.00-17.00(; Nov-

Mar 10.00-16.00 (not Sun). Entrance charge. Tearoom. Shop. Museum and gardens. Parking available (includes Burns Monument). Tel: (01292) 441215.

In this thatched cottage built by his father, Robert Burns was born, 25 January 1759, and this was his home until 1766. Adjoining the cottage is a leading museum of Burnsiana. This is the start of the Burns Heritage Trail which can be followed to trace the places linked with Scotland's greatest poet. Tearoom, gift shop, museum and gardens. Information available on cassette.

Burns House, Dumfries

Burns Street. All year. Mon-Sat 10.00-13.00, 14.00-17.00, Sun 14.00-17.00. Closed Sun and Mon Oct-Mar. Entrance charge. Parking nearby. Tel: (01387) 55297.

In November 1791 Robert Burns moved to Dumfries as an Exciseman and rented a three-room flat (not open to public) in the Wee Vennel (now Bank Street). In May 1793 he moved to a better house in Mill Vennel (now Burns Street) and here he died on 21 July 1796, though his wife Jean Armour stayed in the house until her death in 1834. The house has been completely refurbished and many relics of the poet are on show.

Burns House Museum, Mauchline

Castle Street, Mauchline, 11m ENE of Ayr. Easter-30 Sept, Mon-Sat 11.00-12.30, 13.30-17.30, Sun 14.00-17.00 (or by arrangement). Tel: (01290) 50045.

On the upper floor is the room which Robert Burns took for Jean Armour in 1788. It has been kept intact and is furnished in the style of that period. The remainder of the museum contains Burnsiana and a collection of folk objects. There is a large collection of Mauchline boxware and an exhibition devoted to curling and curling stones which are made in the village. Nearby is Mauchline Kirkyard (scene of *the Holy Fair*) in which are buried four of Burns' daughters and a number of his friends and contemporaries. Other places of interest nearby are 15th-century Mauchline Castle and Poosie Nansie's Tavern.

Burns Mausoleum

St Michael's Churchyard, Dumfries. All reasonable times. Free. Tel: (01387) 53862.

Burns was buried in St Michael's Churchyard near to the house in Mill Vennel where he died in 1796. In 1819 his remains were moved into the present elaborate mausoleum.

Burns Monument, Alloway

B7024 at Alloway, 2m S of Ayr. Open all year. June-Aug 09.00-18.00; Apr, May, Sept, Oct

10.00-17.00 (Sun 14.00-17.00), Nov-Mar 10.00-16.00 (not Sun). Tel: (01292) 41321.

Grecian monument (1823) to the poet with relics dating back to the 1820's. Nearby is the attractive River Doon, spanned by the famous Brig o' Doon, a single arch (possibly 13th century), central to Burns' poem *Tam o' Shanter*. Museum, gift shop, gardens.

Burns Monument and Museum, Kilmarnock

Kay Park. Closed till further notice. View from outside only. Tel: (01563) 26401.

The Monument is a statue by W G Stevenson, offering fine views over the surrounding countryside. The Kay Park Museum houses displays on the life and works of Burns, and has an extensive Burns Library.

Caerlaverock Castle.

Off B725, 9m S of Dumfries. Opening standard. (HS). Tel: 0131—244 3101.

This seat of the Maxwell family dates back to 1270. In 1330, Edward I laid siege to it and in 1638 it capitulated to the Covenanters after a siege lasting 13 weeks. The castle is triangular with round towers. The heavy machicolation is 15th century and over the gateway between two splendid towers can be seen the Maxwell crest and motto. The interior was reconstructed in the 17th century as a Renaissance mansion, with fine carving.

Caerlaverock National Nature Reserve

B725, S of Dumfries by Caerlaverock Castle. All year. Free. (NCC). Tel: (0138 777) 275.

13,594 acres of salt marsh and intertidal mud and sand flats between the River Nith and the Lochar Water. A noted winter haunt of wildfowl, including barnacle geese. Access unrestricted, except in sanctuary area (600 acres), but intending visitors should contact the warden for advice on safety. Care must be taken relating to tides and quicksand.

Cairnsmore of Fleet Reserve

Buckshead, Gatehouse of Fleet. Take B796 from Gatehouse for 6 miles, turn right at junction for 1 mile, then gates to Dromore Farm Steading. All year. Free. Car parking, limited coach parking. Tel: (01557) 814435 or (01671) 3440.

Internationally important reserve of 2,370 hectares of mountain moorland rising to over 700 metres and home to a wide range of wildlife and upland plants. Traditional hill sheep farming is part of the site management centred around the reserve office which sits close to the scenic back-drop of the Clints of Dromore, the old "Paddy" line and the big Fleet viaduct and the river. On the open hill, no paths and difficult terrain. No restrictions on access-only climbing.

Calderglen Country Park
Strathaven Road, East Kilbride. Park: all times. Visitor Centre (summer): Mon-Fri 10.30-17.00, Sat & Sun, public hols. 11.30-18.30; (winter): 11.30-16.00. Free. Tel: (013552) 36644.
Park consists of over 300 acres of wooded gorge and parkland 5km in length. Extensive path system, nature trails, picnic sites, woodland and river with large waterfalls. Visitor Centre gives history of the landscape in the area and includes 'hidden worlds' natural history display. Ornamental garden, children's zoo and adventure playground. Ranger service.

Callendar House
Callendar Park, Falkirk. Jan-Dec. Mon-Sat 10.00-17.00, Sun (Apr-Sept) 14.00-17.00. Entrance charge. Shop. Tel: (01324) 614031.
Mansion set in beautiful parkland close to centre of Falkirk. Exhibition tells the 900 year history of the house, costumed interpreters describe early 19th century life in the restored kitchens. Temporary exhibition gallery in restored dining room.

Cambuskenneth Abbey
1m E of Stirling. Open all reasonable times. Free. (HS). Tel: 0131-244 3101.
Ruins of an abbey founded in 1147 as a house of Augustinian Canons. Scene of Bruce's Parliament, 1326.

Cameronians (Scottish Rifles) Regimental Museum
Mote Hill, off Muir Street, Hamilton. All year. Mon-Sat 10.00-13.00, 14.00-17.00, closed all day Thursday. Free. Tel: (01698) 428 688.
Display of uniforms, medals, banners, silver and documents, relating to the regiment and also to Covenanting times.

Cardoness Castle
On A75, 1m Sw of Gatehouse of Fleet. Opening standard. Apr-Sept, weekends only Oct-Mar. Entrance charge. Parking available. (HS). Tel: 0131-244 3101.
This 15th-century tower house was long the home of the McCullochs of Galloway. It is four storeys high, with a vaulted basement. Features include the original stairway, stone benches and elaborate fireplaces.

Carfin Grotto
Carfin Village, 2m N of Motherwell. Daily. Free. Parking available. Tel: (01698) 263308.
Grotto of Our Lady of Lourdes and a place of pilgrimage. Hall open for teas during the summer (Sunday only).

Carleton Castle
Off A77, 6m S of Girvan. All reasonable times. Free.
One in a link of Kennedy Watchtowers along the coast. Now a ruin, it was famed in ballad as the seat of a baron who got rid of seven wives by pushing them over the cliff, but was himself disposed of by May Culean, his eighth wife.

Carlyle's Birthplace
A74 at Ecclefechan, 5.5m SE of Lockerbie. 1 Apr-28 Oct, daily 12.00-17.00 (last tour 16.30). (NTS). Tel: (015763) 666.
Thomas Carlyle (1795-1881) was born in this little house built by his father and uncle, both master masons, and itself of considerable architectural interest.

Carlsuith Castle
A75, 7m W of Gatehouse of Fleet. Open all reasonable times. Free. Parking available. (HS). Tel: 0131-244 3101.
A roofless 16th-century tower house on the L-plan, built in the 1560s for the Browns.

Cartland Bridge
On A73 W of Lanark. All times. Free. Tel: (01555) 25444.
An impressive bridge built by Telford in 1822 over a gorge, carrying the Mouse Water. It is one of the highest road bridges in Scotland.

Castle Campbell
In Dollar Glen, 1m N of Dollar. Opening standard, except Oct-Mar closed Thurs afternoon and Fri. (HS). Tel: 0131-244 3101.
On a steep mound with extensive views to the plains of the Forth, this castle was built towards the end of the 15th century by the first Earl of Argyll, and it was at one time known as Castle Gloom. It was burned by Cromwell's troops in the 1650's. The courtyard, great hall, and the great barrel roof of the third floor are well worth seeing. The 60 acres of woodland of Dollar Glen (NTS) make an attractive walk to the castle. The glen has a variety of steep paths and bridges through spectacular woodland scenery.

Castle Kennedy Gardens
N of A75, 3m E of Stranraer. Apr-Sep, daily 10.00-17.00. Tel: (01776) 2024.
The Earl and Countess of Stair live at the adjoining Castle. These are nationally famous gardens particularly well known for their rhododendrons, azaleas, magnolias and

embothriums. The notable pinetum was the first in Scotland. Tearoom and plant centre.

Castle of Park
Off A75, by Glenluce, 9m ESE of Stranraer. Parking available. (HS). Tel: 0131-244 3101.
A tall, imposing castellated mansion, still entire, built by Thomas Hay of Park in 1590.

Castle of St. John
In Stranraer town centre, Castle Street. Mid Apr-mid Sept, Mon-Sat 10.00-13.00, 14.00-17.00. Entrance charge. Shop. Tel: (01776) 5088.
16th-century towerhouse later used as the town jail. Now open as a visitor centre with displays on Stranraer and Wigtown District. Shop. Information point.

Castle Semple Collegiate Church
At Castle Semple, 3m W of Howwood. Not open to public, may be viewed from outside. (HS). Tel: 0131-244 3101.
The church is a rectangular structure. A square tower projects from the west gable. The apse is three-sided, each side having three windows of debased Gothic form.

Castle Semple Country Park
Off Largs Road, Lochwinnoch, 9m SW of Paisley. Jan-Dec, 09.00-dusk in summer; 09.00-16.30 winter. Free, but charges for use of loch. Parking available. Snack trailer in summer. Picnic areas and information centre. Tel: (01505) 842882.
Country park based on Castle Semple Loch; about 200 acres. Bring your own boat or hire (no motor boats or keel boats). Bank angling. Next to RSPB visitor centre. Picnic areas and information centre.

Castle Sween
On E shore of Loch Sween, 15m SW of Lochgilphead. All reasonable times. Free. (HS). Tel: 0131-244 3101.
This is probably the oldest stone castle on the Scottish mainland, built in the mid-12th century. It was destroyed by Sir Alexander MacDonald in 1647.

Cathcartston Visitor Centre
Centre of Dalmellington. Jan-Dec, Mon-Fri, 10.00-17.00. Easter-Oct, also open Sat & Sun 14.00-17.00. Free. Tel: (01292) 550633.
Interpretation centre containing tableau of weaving period, exhibition area and audio visual presentation.

Chatelherault Country Park
At Ferniegair, 1m S of Hamilton off A72.

Visitor Centre: 1 Apr-30 Sept 10.30-18.00; 1 Oct-31 Mar 10.30-17.00 daily. Last admission 30 mins. before closing. House: All year, daily 11.00-16.00 (last admission 15.45) closed for functions - check. Parking available. House free. Visitor Centre, entrance charge. Gift shop. Tearoom. Tel: (01698) 426213.
Magnificent hunting lodge and kennels built in 1732 by William Adam for the Duke of Hamilton. The buildings have been restored and there are extensive country walks and a fascinating visitor centre giving a vivid portrayal of the 18th century characters who helped to build it.

Christian Heritage Museum
Benadictine Monastery, Mackerston Place, Largs. Apr-Sep, Mon-Sat 10.00-12.30, 14.00-17.00, Sun 14.00-17.00. Other times by appointment. Groups by prior arrangement. Free. Parking available. Gift shop. Tearoom.
Display boards tell the story of the spread of Christianity and monasticism. Illustrations depict monastic life - the Rule, the Community and the Crafts. There are examples of Church needlework and a collection of beautifully embroidered vestments, religious items on display and models of ancient monasteries in south-west Scotland. The Monastery Chapel is also open and visitors are welcome.

The Church of the Holy Rude
St. John's Street, Stirling. May-Sept, weekdays 10.00-17.00. Free. Sundays 11.00 (worship). Tel: (01786) 747154.
The only church in Scotland still in use which has witnessed a coronation, when in 1567, the infant James VI, aged 13 months, was crowned. John Knox preached the sermon. The church dates from 1414, and Mary, Queen of Scots worshipped there. Notable pipe-organ; extensive restoration currently in progress.

Cloch Lighthouse
A770, 3m SW of Gourock. Seen from the outside only.
This notable landmark stands at Cloch Point with fine views across the Upper Firth of Clyde estuary. The white-painted lighthouse was constructed in 1797.

Clock Mill Heritage Centre
Upper Mill Street, Tillicoultry. Apr-Oct. Daily, 10.00-17.00. Parking available. Free. Shop with crafts and woollens. Tel: (01259) 752176.
Housed in an impressive former mill building of 1824, at the foot of Mill Glen, the Clock Mill Heritage Centre introduces the long tradition of woollen mills and textile production in the "Wee County" of Clackmannan. Exhibition

looks at life in the mills during the Industrial Revolution and includes examples of old spinning and weaving machinery. Story boards, audio-visual. Starting point for the Mill Trail, linking several mills and factory shops in Clackmannan.

Clydebank District Museum
Old Town Hall, Dumbarton Road, Clydebank. 3 miles N of Glasgow on A814. Jan-Dec exc public holidays. Mon & Wed 14.00-16.30, Sat 10.00-16.30. Free. Parking available. Shop. Tel: 0141-941 1331, ext. 402.
Community-based local history museum located within Clydebank Town Hall and forming part of the district council's libraries and museums department. Collections reflect early prehistory and the Roman period, but the main emphasis is on the last two centuries of social, economic, political and industrial history. Famous Singer collection of sewing machines, shipbuilding and engineering material, and several items surviving from the Clydebank Blitz.

Coats Observatory
Coats Observatory, Oakshaw Street, Paisley. Mon, Tues & Thur 14.00-20.00, Wed, Fri and Sat 10.00-17.00. Free. Groups by prior arrangement. Tel: 0141-889 2013.
There has been a continuous tradition of astronomical observation and meteorological recording since the observatory was built in 1882. The recent updating of seismic equipment and the installation of a satellite weather picture receiver has made it one of the best equipped observatories in the country.

PS "Comet" Replica
Port Glasgow town centre, adjacent to A8. May be viewed from outside. Jan-Dec. Car parking available.
Replica of the first sea-going paddle steamer in Europe which was built in Port Glasgow in 1812, to carry freight and passengers between Greenock, Helensburgh and Glasgow.

Comlongon Castle
Situated in Clarencefield, midway between Dumfries and Annan on B725. Apr-Sep, by appointment only. Entrance charge. Gardens not open to public. Parking available. Tel: (0138787) 283.
Exceptionally well-preserved 15th century Border castle now being restored. It contains many original features including dungeons, kitchen, great hall, Heraldic devices, bed chambers with 'privies'. Picnic area, nature trail, woodland walks, peacocks etc. Bed and Breakfast available.

Craignethan Castle
2.5m W of A72 at Crossford, 5m NW of Lanark. Apr-Sept, opening standard. Closed Oct-Mar. Entrance charge. Parking available. (HS). Tel: 0131-244 3101.
This extensive and well-preserved ruin, chief stronghold of the Hamiltons who were supporters of Mary, Queen of Scots, was repeatedly assailed by the Protestant party and partly dismantled by them in 1579. The oldest, central portion is a large tower house of unusual and ornate design. Recent excavations have revealed possibly the earliest example in Britain of a caponier, a covered gun-looped passageway across a defensive ditch.

Crarae Glen Garden
A83, 10m SW of Inveraray. All year, daily 09.00-18.00 (dusk in winter). Entrance charge. Visitor Centre, crafts. Information area. Refreshment area. (Crarae Garden Charitable Trust). Tel: (01546) 86614.
Among the lovliest open to the public in Scotland, these gardens of Crarae Lodge, beside Loch Fyne and set in a Highland Glen, are note for rhododendrons, azaleas, conifers and ornamental shrubs.

Creebridge Mohair and Woollens
Creebridge Mill, Newton Stewart. Jan-Dec 09.00-17.00. Free. Parking available. Mill shop. Tel: (01671) 2868.
Mohair and woollen weavers with retail outlet. Processes include winding, warping, weaving, brushing.

Creetown Gem Rock Museum & Gallery
Approach by A75 to Creetown, turn up opposite clock tower. Apr-Oct, daily, 09.30-18.00. Nov-Dec, closed Thur-Fri. Closed Xmas-early Jan. Other times, weekends only, 10.00-16.00 or by appointment. Entrance charge. Parking available. Tearoom. Shop. Tel: (0167 182) 357.
A beautiful collection of gems and minerals from around the world. This large worldwide collection has taken over 50 years to gather together and is recognised as being one of the most comprehensive collection of its type, and shows the many fascinating mineral forms created by nature. Tearoom, gift shop and custom gemstone cutting workshop.

Crichton Royal Museum
Off B725 Glencaple road, 1m S of Dumfries centre in hospital grounds. Square building with clock face behind church. All year, Thurs, Fri 13.30-16.30, Easter-Oct Thurs, Fri, Sat 13.30-16.30. Outwith these times, open for parties by appointment. Free. Parking available. Tel: (01387) 55301, ext.2360.

Museum highlights, in a spacious setting, developments in one of Britain's leading hospitals. Special features include operating theatre, patients' art 1839-61; library and reading room. Beautiful grounds with splendid rock garden and arboretum; garden shop and tearoom.

Cross of Lorraine
Lyle Hill, Greenock. Access via Newton Street. Jan-Dec, all reasonable times. Free. Parking available.
Monument to the contribution made by the Free French Navy during World War II. The Cross of Lorraine is situated at a popular viewpoint overlooking the Clyde.

Crossraguel Abbey
A77, 2m SW of Maybole. Apr-Sept, opening standard. Closed Oct-Mar. Entrance charge. Parking available. (HS). Tel: 0131–244 3101.
A Cluniac monastery built in 1244 by the Earl of Carrick during the reign of Alexander II. The Abbey was inhabited by Benedictine monks from 1244 until the end of the 16th century, and the extensive remains are of high architectural distinction. The gatehouse and dovecot are specially illuminating.

Cruggleton Church
Cruggleton Farm, 3 miles S of Garlieston on B7004. Jan-Dec. Key available at farmhouse. Free.
Ancient church containing Norman arch, rebuilt end of 18th century.

Culzean Castle and Country Park
A719, 12m SSW of Ayr. Gardens, Country park: daily all year 09.00-sunset. Castle, Restaurant, Shops: Apr-Oct, daily 10.30-17.30. Entrance charges to castle. Parking available. Plant sales in walled garden. Inductive loop. Tel: (0165 56) 274.
The splendid castle, one of Robert Adam's most notable creations, although built around an ancient tower of the Kennedy's dates mainly from 1777. Special features are the Round Drawing Room, the fine plaster ceilings and magnificent oval staircase. The Eisenhower Presentation explains the General's associaion with Culzean.
In 1970 Culzean became the first country park in Scotland; in 1973 a Reception and Interpretation Centre with exhibition etc was opened in the farm buildings designed by Robert Adam. The 565-acre grounds include a walled garden established in 1783, aviary, swan pond, camelia house and orangery. Ranger naturalist service with guided walks, talks and films in summer. Licensed self-service restaurant.

Cumbernauld Theatre
Kildrum, Cumbernauld. Jan-Dec. 10.00-23.00. Charges vary according to event. Parking available. Restaurant and bars. Tel: (01236) 737235.
Based in a row of 18th century cottages, this theatre complex houses an arena-style auditorium seating 250, a studio theatre, restaurant and bars. Year-round programme mixes drama, music, comedy, children's theatre and dance.

Dalbeattie Museum
Southwick Road, centre of Dalbeattie. Open most days May-Oct. Free. Gift shop. Tel: (01556) 610437.
The story of Dalbeattie's industrial development, with displays of artefacts produced in the water-powered industries, such as granite memorials, bobbins, paper, brick and tiles, gloves and fertiliser. Over 10,000 photographs, displays of harbour. Gallery featuring work of local artists.

Dalgarven Mill - The Ayrshire Museum of Countryside and Costume
On A737, Dalry Road, Kilwinning. Mon-Sat 10.00-17.00, Sun 12.30-17.00. Tel: (01294) 52448.
The museum is within a restored working water mill. There are extensive displays of agricultural and rural life including machinery, hand tools, furnishings and photographs. The costume collection has been gathered locally and there are three display changes per year. The mill has been in the same family since 1883 and was in existence prior to 1602. There is a bakehouse which supplies wholemeal bread and rolls and home baking for the coffee room.

Barbara Davidson Pottery
Muirhall Farm, Larbert, near Stirling. Jan-Dec exc Xmas and New Year. Mon-Sat 09.00-17.30, Sun 14.00-17.30. Free. Car parking only. Pottery shop. Tel: (01324) 554430.
Living and working pottery in a picturesque converted 17th century farm steading has the workshop in the barn, shop in the cowshed, and a place for visitors to try making pots (small charge, July and August) in the cobbled stable.

Dean Castle and Country Park
Dean Road, off Glasgow Road, Kilmarnock. Daily 12.00-17.00. All year (Closed Dec. 25,26; Jan 1,2). Country park: all year, free. Parking available. Tel: (01563) 22702/26401.
14th-century fortified keep with dungeon and

battlements and 15th-century palace, the ancestral home of the Boyd family. It contains an outstanding collection of medieval arms, armour, tapestries and musical instruments. Display of Burns manuscripts. The country park has 200 acres of woodland with rivers, nature trail, children's corner, fawns, picnic areas. Tearoom and riding centre.

Denny Ship Model Experiment Tank
Building adjacent to Safeway supermarket, access by Castle Street 200yds E of Dumbarton town centre. Daily, Mon-Sat 10.00-16.00. Parking available. Tel: (01389) 63444
The world's oldest surviving ship model experiment tank. Visitors can witness the process of making wax hull forms, unchanged since 1883.

Dick Institute
Elmbank Avenue, off London Road, Kilmarnock. Jan-Dec. Mon, Tues, Thurs, Fri 10.00-20.00; Wed & Sat 10.00-17.00. Free. Parking available. Tel: (01563) 26401.
The museum has an important collection of geological specimens, local archaeology, Scottish broadswords, firearms and natural history. The Art Gallery has frequently changing exhibitions.

Doon Valley Heritage
Dunaskin Ironworks site, Waterside, 2 miles S of Patna on A713 Ayr-Castle Douglas road. May-Oct, daily 11.00-16.00. Entrance charge - allows entry to all sites belonging to Dalmellington & District Conservation Trust. Parking available. Gift shop. Tel: (01292) 531144.
The newest of Scotland's open-air industrial museums, Doon Valley Heritage is situated at the old Dalmellington Iron Company works, and has exhibits illustrating local and social history, countryside and architecture. Nearby, Chapel Row Ironworker's Cottage, a reconstructed dwelling of 1914, may be seen by arrangement with the Conservation Trust.

Doune Castle
Off A84 at Doune, 8m NW of Stirling. Opening standard except Oct-Mar closed Thur pm and all day Fri. Entrance charge. Parking available. (HS). Tel: 0131-244 3101.
Splendid ruins of one of the best preserved mediaeval castles in Scotland, built late 14th or early 15th century by the Regent Albany. After his execution in 1424 it came into the hands of the Stuarts of Doune, Earls of Moray, in the 16th century, and the 'Bonnie Earl of Moray' lived here before his murder in 1592. The

bridge in the village was built in 1535 by Robert Spittal, James IV's tailor, to spite the ferryman who had refused him a passage.

Doune Motor Museum
At Doune on A84, 8m NW of Stirling. Apr-Oct, daily 10.00-17.00. Tel: (01786) 841 203.
The Earl of Moray's collection of vintage and post-vintage cars, including examples of Hispano Suiza, Bentley, Jaguar, Aston Martin, Lagonda and the second oldest Rolls Royce in the world. Cafeteria.

Drumcoltran Tower
Off A711, 8m SW of Dumfries. Open all reasonable times, apply key-keeper. Free. (HS). Tel: 0131-244 3101.
Situated among farm buildings, this is a good example of a Scottish tower house of about the mid-16th century, simple and severe.

Drumlanrig Castle and Country Park
Off A76, 3m N of Thornhill, Dumfriesshire and 16m off A74 by A702. First Sat in May-late Aug Bank Hol. Castle: Mon-Sat 11.00-17.00, Sun 13.00-17.00 (closed Thurs). Grounds: Mon-Sat 11.00-18.00, Sun 12.00-18.00. Entrance charges for house and grounds. Shop. Tearoom. Tel: (01848) 30248.
Unique example of late 17th century Renaissance architecture in pink sandstone, built on the site of earlier Douglas strongholds. Set in parkland ringed by the wild Dumfriesshire hills. Louis XIV furniture, and paintings by Rembrandt, Holbein, Murillo, Ruysdael. Adventure woodland play area, nature trail, gift shop and tearoom. Guide dogs by prior arrangement. Lift available but unaccompanied.

Drumpellier Country Park
From Glasgow leave M8 at junction 8 to A89 to traffic lights, filter left to B8752 and proceed 1.25m to 'T' junction. Turn right and proceed for 700yds for entrance to park. Jan-Dec. Visitor Centre (closed Xmas and New Year) 10.30-19.30 (summer), 12.00-16.00 (winter). Butterfly House open summer only. Free. Parking available. Tearoom. Tel: (01236) 22257.
Modern pursuit centre, site of crannog plus walks round loch and Monkland Canal. Orienteering course with maps. Ranger-guided walks, play areas; exhibitions. Peace garden, butterfly house, glass house complex.

Drumtrodden
Off A714, 8m SSW of Wigtown. All times. Free. (HS). Tel: 0131-244 3101.
A group of cup-and-ring markings of Bronze Age date on a natural rock face. 400 yards south is an alignment of three adjacent stones.

Dumbarton Castle
Dumbarton, off A814 on Dumbarton Rock. Opening standard exc Oct-Mar closed Thur pm and all day Fri. Entrance charge. Parking available. (HS). Tel: 0131-244 3101.
Though mainly modern barracks, a dungeon, a 12th-century gateway and a sundial gifted by Mary, Queen of Scots are preserved. It was from Dumbarton that Queen Mary left for France in 1548, at the age of five.

Dumfries and Galloway Aviation Museum
Heathhall Industrial Estate, off A701, 3 miles N of Dumfries. Signposted. Easter-Oct, Sat & Sun 10.00-17.00, other times by arrangement. Entrance charge. Parking available. Gift shop. Tel: (01387) 51895 (Mr. R. Waugh).
Award-winning museum run by volunteers who have amassed an impressive collection of aeroplane relics and components including a Spitfire, currently under restoration, recovered from Loch Doon. Visitors can sit in the cockpit of Mystere IVa, one of six complete aircraft. "Firsts" include the first jet-powered aircraft and the first jet trainer to enter RAF service, and the first British-built helicopter. Aero-engines, Air Force uniforms and memorabilia.

Dumfries Ice Bowl
King Street, Dumfries. Open 11 months, daily 09.00-23.00. Entrance charges. Parking available. Refreshments. Tel: (01387) 51300.
Leisure facility with artificial indoor bowling green, ice rink open for skating and curling.

Dumfries Museum and Camera Obscura
The Observatory, Dumfries. All year, Mon-Sat 10.00-13.00, 14.00-17.00, Sun 14.00-17.00, closed Sun and Mon Oct-Mar. Camera Obscura closed Oct-Mar. Museum: free, charge for Camera Obscura. Parking available. Gift Shop. Tel: (01387) 53374.
This regional museum for the Solway area has recently been refurbished and contains a wide variety of interesting exhibits. It is based on an 18th century windmill and has a camera obscura.

Dunblane Cathedral
In Dunblane, A9, 6m N of Stirling. Open all reasonable times. Free. (HS). Tel: 0131-244 3101.
The existing building dates mainly from the 13th century but incorporates a 12th-century tower. The nave was unroofed after the Reformation but the whole building was restored in 1829-95.

Dundrennan Abbey
A711, 7m SE of Kirkcudbright. Apr-Sept, *opening standard, closed Oct-Mar. Entrance charge. Parking available. (HS). Tel: 0131-244 3101.*
A Cistercian house founded in 1142 whose ruins include much late Norman and transitional work. Here it is believed Mary, Queen of Scots spent her last night in Scotland, 15 May, 1568.

Dunmore Pineapple
N of Airth, 7m E of Stirling off A905, then B9124. Not open to public, viewed from the outside only. Parking nearby. (NTS, leased to the Landmark Trust). Tel: (01738) 31296.
This curious structure, built as a 'garden retreat' and shaped like a pineapple, stands in the grounds of Dunmore Park, and bears the date 1761. It is the focal point of the garden and is available for holiday and other short lets by phoning the Landmark Trust (01628) 825925.

Dunoon Ceramics
Hamilton Street, Dunoon. 0.5 miles north of town on A815. Jan-Dec exc Xmas and New Year. Mon-Fri, 09.00-12.30, 13.00-16.30. Free. Parking available. Gift shop. Tearoom (mornings only). Tel: (01369) 4360.
Factory site of the famous Dunoon mug. Production processes can be viewed from start to finish, including clay making and decorating. Visitors learn about design, manufacture and quality control.

Durisdeer Parish Church (Queensberry Aisle)
6 miles N of Thornhill, unclassified road off A702. All reasonable times. Free.
A post-Reformation 'T' church, a major monument in the Scottish Baroque style. The Queensberry Aisle, with its elaborate monument by Van Nost, commemorates the second Duke of Queensberry (d. 1711) and his Duchess (d. 1709).

Eglinton Country Park
2m N of Irvine. Park: Jan-Dec, daily, Dawn-dusk. Visitor Centre: Easter-Oct, daily 10.00-16.30. Free. Parking available. Gift shop. Tearoom. Tel: (01294) 51776.
This is a major country park built around the former Eglinton Montgomery Estate. Displays in the visitor centre explain the natural history and the history of the area, including material on the Eglinton tournament of 1839.

Electric Brae
A719 9m S of Ayr (also known as Croy Brae). All times. Free.
An optical illusion is created so that a car

appears to be going down the hill when it is in fact going up.

Ellisland Farm

Off A76, 6.5m NNW of Dumfries. All reasonable times, but intending visitors are advised to phone in advance. Free. (Ellisland Trust). Tel: (01387) 74 426.

Robert Burns took over this farm in June 1788, built the farmhouse, and tried to introduce new farming methods. Unsuccessful, he became an Exciseman in September 1789; in August 1791 the stock was auctioned, and he moved to Dumfries in November 1791. Some of the poet's most famous works were written at Ellisland, including *Tam o'Shanter and Auld Lang Syne*. The Granary houses a display showing Burns as a farmer. Farmhouse with museum room; granary building with Burns display; riverside walk.

Falkirk Museum

15 Orchard Street, Falkirk. All year. Mon-Fri, 10.00-12.30, 13.30-17.00. Free. Shop. Tel: (01324) 24911, ext 2202/2472.

Permanent displays on the archaeology of the district, Dunmore Pottery, 19th century foundry products and natural history. Museum shop.

Finlaystone

By A8 W of Langbank, 17m W of Glasgow. Gardens open daily 10.30-17.00. (House) Apr-Aug, Sun afternoon, or by arrangement. Tel: (0147 554) 285 (12.30-13.00 or evenings) or (0147 554) 505.

Country estate with woodland walks, nursery gardens, formal gardens, adventure playgrounds and pony trekking. Countryside Ranger Service. The house has some fine rooms, Victorian relics, flower prints and an international collection of dolls shown in the billiard room. Historical connections with John Knox and Robert Burns. Afternoon teas (Apr-Sep).

Forth and Clyde Canal

Between the Rivers Forth and Clyde. Tel: (01324) 612415 or 0141-332 6936.

Opened in 1790, the Canal linked the industrial towns of West Central Scotland with the east coast at Grangemouth. The surrounding scenery varies widely from the impressive industrial monuments near the centre of Glasgow to the remains of the Antonine Wall still visible in the more rural areas. Although closed to navigation in 1963, the Canal is beginning to enjoy a renaissance through recreation activity. The towing path provides delightful walks through town and country with plenty of interest for both nature and history enthusiasts. Excursions by Canal boat are available from the Stables Inn, Glasgow Road near Kirkintilloch and a restaurant boat also operates from this point. Canal Society boats from Auchinstarry, near Kilsyth. Fishing, canoeing etc. by permit. Countryside Ranger service. Guided Walks and Canal events during summer months.

Galloway Deer Museum

On A712, by Clatteringshaws Loch, 6m W of New Galloway. Apr-Sept, daily, 10.00-17.00. Free. Tearoom. Shop. Parking available (charge). (FE). Tel: (0164 42) 285/(01556) 3626.

The museum, in a converted farm steading, has a live trout exhibit as well as many features on deer and other aspects of Galloway wildlife, Geology and history. Bruce's Stone on Raploch Moss is a short walk away.

Galloway Footwear Co-op Ltd.

From Castle Douglas travel N on A713 (Ayr) for 13 miles, take right turn onto A712, Balmaclellan village 0.5m on left. Follow signs from bottom of village. Easter-Oct, Mon-Fri 09.00-17.00. Other times by appointment. Parking available. Shoes, leather goods for sale and to order. Tel: (0164 42) 465.

Visitors can watch footwear being made - 16 styles of boots, shoes, sandals and clogs - in the workshop. It is also the site of the school where Old Mortality's wife taught.

Galloway Forest Park

Off A714, 10m NW of Newton Stewart. Free. (FE). Tel: (01671) 2420.

250 square miles of magnificent countryside in Central Galloway, including Merrick (2,765 feet) the highest hill in southern Scotland. The land is owned by the Forestry Commission and there is a wide variety of leisure facilities including forest trails, fishing, a red deer range, a wild goat park, a forest drive and a deer museum. Murray's monument dominates a hillside off the A712. It was erected to commemorate the son of a local shepherd who became a professor at Edinburgh University.

Galloway House Gardens

At Garlieston, 8m S of Wigtown. Mar-Oct, daily 09.00-17.30. Admission by collection box. Tel: (0198 86) 680.

Galloway House was built in 1740 by Lord Garlies, eldest son of the 7th Earl of Galloway, and later enlarged by Burn, and the hall decorated by Lorimer. Not open to the public.

The grounds cover some 30 acres and go down to the sea and sandy beach. There are fine old trees, and as a speciality in May/June there is a well-grown handkerchief tree. In season there are many snowdrops, pretty old-fashioned daffodils and a good collection of rhododendrons and azaleas. Also a walled garden with greenhouses and a camellia house. Home-baked teas are available in Garlieston village.

Gartmorn Dam Country Park and Nature Reserve
By Sauchie, 2m NE of Alloa off A908. (Park) all year at all times. (Visitor centre) Apr-Sept, daily 08.30-19.30; Oct-Mar, Sat & Sun 14.00-16.00. Free. Tel: (01259) 214319.
The oldest dam in Scotland, with reservoir. The park is an important winter roost for migratory duck, there are pleasant walks and fishing is available. Visitor Centre has exhibits, information and slide shows. Talks and escorted walks can be arranged through the ranger service.

Gilnockie Tower
A7, 5m S of Langholm. All reasonable times. Free. Can only be viewed from outside. Tel: (013873) 80976.
Also known as Holehouse, the tower dates from the 16th century and has walls 6 feet thick. It was once the home of the 16th-century Border freebooter, Johny Armstrong.

MV 'Gipsy Princess'
B802, 1m S of Kilsyth. May-Oct. Guided cruises are advertised in local press. Charges on application. Parking available. Gift shop. Tel: (01236) 721856 or (01236) 822437.
The Gipsy Princess is a new (1990) custom-built, 36-seater passenger boat with open air and covered accommodation, designed and operated by the Forth & Clyde Canal Society. She follows the route of the former 'Gypsy Queen' which cruised in the early part of the century beneath the wooded slopes of Craigmarloch Hill through the historic Kelvin Valley.

Glenfinart Deer Farm
Barnacabber Farm, 0.5m N of Ardentinny. Easter-Oct, 11.00-17.00. Nov-Easter by appointment. Entrance charge. Parking available. Gift shop. Full refreshment facilities in adjacent Glenfinart Hotel. Tel: (0136 981) 331.
Deer visitor centre with audio-visual display and ranger-guided tours, set in scenic Glen Finart. The former farm has been converted into tearoom, restaurant and bar.

Glengoyne Distillery
On A81 Glasgow-Aberfoyle road, just S of junction with A875. Apr-Nov, conducted tours Mon-Fri, hourly from 10.00-16.00, Sat 11.00 and 15.00. July and Aug, also Tues and Thur, 19.00 and 20.00. Easter-Oct, nosing sessions at 19.30 (2hrs). Dec-Mar, by arrangement. Entrance charge for adults, children free. Parking

available. Gift shop and Heritage Room. Whisky Bar in reception room. Tel: (0136 050) 254.
Attractive, compact distillery, first licensed in 1833, nestles in Campsie Hills, and draws water from a 50-foot waterfall. Conducted tours in small groups show main processes of distilling a Highland malt whisky. Explanatory video. Heritage Room houses cooperage display, old artefacts and shop. Visitors taste a dram in reception room, overlooking dam, glen and waterfall.

Glenluce Abbey
Off A75, 2m N of Glenluce. Apr-Sept, opening standard. Oct-Mar, weekends only. Entrance charge. (HS). Tel: 0131-244 3101.
Founded in 1192 by Roland, Earl of Galloway, for the Cistercian order. A fine vaulted chapter house is of architectural interest.

Glenwhan Gardens
Signposted, 1 mile off A75 at Dunragit, between Glenluce and Stranraer. Apr-Sept. Daily exc Mon, 12.00-17.00. Other times by arrangement. Entrance charge. Parking available. Gift shop. Tearoom. Tel: (0158 14) 222.
This young garden was started in 1979, hewn from a hillside covered in bracken and gorse. Now rhododendrons and azaleas, shrubs and shrub roses and many unusual plants grow together around two small lochans which were made by damming up the boggy areas. A water garden creates a natural habitat for the bog-loving genera, and the rocky outcrops are home for alpines and scree plants, heathers and conifers. Extensive nursery and plant centre.

Globe Inn
Off High Street, Dumfries. Jan-Dec. Mon-Sat 11.00-23.00, Sun 12.30-23.00. Restaurant. Tel: (01387) 52335.
Burns' favourite howff (pub) where his chair, inscribed window pane and other relics can still be seen and enjoyed in a convivial atmosphere.

Gracefield Arts Centre
1 mile N of Dumfries town centre on A701. Jan-Dec. Closed Mon in Summer, Mon and Sun in winter. Please check details of opening times. Car parking only. Cafe/bar. Tel: (01387) 62084.
Gallery, studios and pottery situated in beautiful grounds overlooking the River Nith. Gracefield houses a collection of over 400 Scottish paintings, which are on show at regular intervals throughout the year, and shows regular exhibitions of contemporary art. Potter-in-residence at work, with products for sale. Studios, darkroom, printroom.

Grangemouth Museum

Victoria Library, Bo'ness Road, Grangemouth. All year Mon-Sat 14.00-17.00. Free. Parking available. Tel: (01324) 483291/24911, ext. 2472.

Display relating to growth of Grangemouth from sea-lock to a Victorian town. Exhibits on canals, shipping and shipbuilding. The world's first practical steamship, the Charlotte Dundas and local industries. Museum Shop.

Greenhill Covenanter's House

In Biggar on A702, 26m from Edinburgh, A74 (South) 12m. Easter-early Oct, daily 14.00-17.00. Entrance charge. Gift shop. Parking available. Tel: (01899) 21050.

Burn Braes Farmhouse, rescued in ruinous condition and rebuilt at Biggar, ten miles from the original site. Exhibits include relics of local Covenanters, Donald Cargill's bed (1681), 17th century furnishings, costume dolls rare breeds of animals and poultry. Reduced price for joint admission to Gladstone Court Street Museum. Audio-visual programme.

Greenock Arts Guild Theatre

Campbell Street, Greenock. Jan-Dec. Charges for performances vary. Car parking only. Tearoom. Inductive loop. Tel: (01475) 23038.

Greenock Arts Guild was formed in 1945 as a venue for music, drama and the visual arts. A varied programme is offered throughout the year embracing professional and amateur acts. Exhibitions in the gallery change monthly.

Greenock Custom House Museum

Customhouse Quay, Bremner Street, Greenock. Jan-Dec. Mon-Fri. 10.00-12.30, 13.30-16.00. Tel: (01475) 26331.

This fine building has been in continuous use as a Customs Office since it was completed in 1819. Now restored, it houses some excise departments as well as the museum, which gives an insight into the activities of Customs and Excisemen through the ages. Apart from features on Robert Burns and other well-known past members of the Department, there are items showing the modern technology used in the battle against illegal drugs. Other items include examples of endangered species which have been seized at importation, and a computer game, which tests the visitor's skill at 'rummaging' a ship.

Grogport Organic Tannery

Grogport Old Manse, 4 miles N of Carradale on E coast of Kintyre. Jan-Dec. All reasonable times. Free. Car parking only. Tannery shop. Tel: (0158 33) 255.

Small, unusual organic tannery. Sheepskins, deerskins and other skins can be seen in the process of being tanned by the ancient methods, using tree bark, which are centuries-old and said to produce the best leather.

Guildhall

St. John's Street, Stirling. By arrangement. Free. Tel: (01786) 462373/479000.

The Guildhall, or Cowane's Hospital, was built between 1634 and 1649 as an almshouse for elderly members of the Guild of Merchants. It contains portraits of former Deans of Guild, and weights and measures.

Hamilton District Museum

0.5m SW of M74 at A723 interchange. All year, Mon-Sat 10.00-17.00. Closed 12.00-13.00 on Wed and Sat. Parking available. Free. Tel: (01698) 283981.

Local history museum housed in a 17th-century coaching inn complete with original stable and 18th-century Assembly room. Displays include costume, art, archaeology, natural history, transport and a reconstructed Victorian kitchen. Also regular temporary exhibition programme. Museum shop with a wide range of publications and souvenirs.

Hamilton Old Parish Church

All year, weekdays 10.00-15.00; Sat 10.00-12.00; Sunday Worship 10.45 (tour 12.30). Free. Group visits by arrangement. Coffee bar, Sat am and Sun after worship. Parking available. Inductive loop. Tel: (01698) 420002.

Present building (1734) is the only church designed by William Adam, the leading Scottish architect of his day. It is the oldest building in Hamilton still used for its original purpose and contains a pre-Norman Netherton Cross and the Covenanters 'Heads' Memorial. Also embroideries by Hannah Frew Paterson.

Harbour Cottage Gallery

Kirkcudbright. Mar-Dec, Mon-Sat 10.30-12.30, 14.00-17.00, certain Suns 14.00-17.00. Entrance charge.

Exhibitions of paintings and sometimes crafts in a picturesque whitewashed building beside the River Dee.

Keir Hardie Statue

Cumnock town centre. All times. Free. Parking available.

Bust outside the Town Hall to commemorate James Keir Hardie (1856-1915), an early socialist leader, and founder of the Independent Labour Party in 1893.

Highland Mary's Monument

At Failford, on B743 3m W of Mauchline. All times. Free. Tel: (01292) 282109.

The monument commemorates the place where, it is said, Robert Burns parted from his 'Highland Mary', Mary Campbell. They exchanged vows, but she died the following autumn.

Highland Mary's Statue
Dunoon, near pier. All times. Free. Parking available.
The statue of Burns' Highland Mary at the foot of the Castle Hill. Mary Campbell was born on a farm in Dunoon, and consented to become Burns' wife before he married Jean Armour.

The Hill House
Upper Colquhoun Street, Helensburgh. Apr-late Dec. Daily 13.00-17.00. Entrance charges. Parking available. Gift shop. Tearoom. (NTS). Tel: (01436) 73900.
Overlooking the estuary of the River Clyde, this house is considered to be the finest example of the domestic architecture of Charles Rennie Mackintosh. Gardens are being restored. Special display about Mackintosh. Tearoom.

Holy Loch Farm Park and Highland Cattle Centre
Dalinlongart, Sandbank, 4 miles from Dunoon on A815. Apr-Oct. Daily 10.00-18.00. Entrance charge. Parking available. Craft shop. Tearoom. Tel: (01369) 6429.
Small working farm on the edge of the western Highlands, with a variety of domestic and rare breeds of animals - sheep, cattle, goats, pigs, poultry, ponies, donkeys, a Clydesdale horse. Children's pets' corner with rabbits, guinea pigs and lambs. Sheep and goats can be fed, lambs bottle-fed in spring and early summer. Highland cattle are particularly featured.

Holy Trinity Church
Keir Street, Bridge of Allan, close to Stirling University. Jun-Sep. Sat 10.00-16.00. Free. Parking available. Gift shop. Inductive loop. Tel: (01786) 832093.
An attractive small church with fine stained glass windows. An important feature is the chancel furnishings which were designed in 1904 by Charles Rennie Mackintosh, and include pulpit carvings, communion table, organ screen and chancel rail.

Hornel Art Gallery and Library
Broughton House, High Street, Kirkcudbright. Easter-Oct. Daily exc Tues 11.00-13.00, 14.00-17.00 (Sun 14.00-17.00 only). Entrance charges. Car parking only, coaches in town centre. Gift shop. Tel: (01557) 30437.
Home, studio and gallery of the artist E.A.

Hornel (1864-1933), one of the group of artists known as the 'Glasgow Boys'. House contains collection of paintings by Hornel and other associated artists, fine furniture and oogramme of temporary exhibitions operates throughout the year covering Fine Art, Sculpture, Photography and Crafts. The gallery shows many major Arts Council exhibitions. Rozelle House operates a programme of temporary exhibitions and also houses the Maclaurin Contemporary Art Collection and the District Collection's Henry Moore sculpture in the gallery courtyard. Rozelle House Pantry offers meals and refreshments throughout the day. Open during gallery hours.

Anne Hughes Pottery
Auchreoch, Balmaclellan, 2 miles E of New Galloway on A712. Easter-Sept. Daily 10.00-18.00. Free. Car parking only. Pottery shop. Tel: (0164 42) 205.
A wide range of pottery work which is unusual, colourful and varied, with pierced flower plates a speciality, all made on the premises.

Hunterston Power Station
By the A78, 5m S of Largs. Mar-Nov, daily 09.30-16.30. Dec-Feb, tours by arrangement only. Tours last 1hr for Visitor Centre, 1hr for Power Station. Free. Parking available. Freephone (0800) 838557.
Nuclear Power Station, video plus displays. This plant, operated by Scottish Nuclear Ltd., produces a quarter of all electricity consumed in Scotland.

John Paul Jones Birthplace Museum
Arbigland, Kirkbean, off A710 14 miles S of Dumfries. Apr-Sept. Mon-Sat 10.00-13.00, 14.00-17.00. Sun 14.00-17.00. Entrance charge. Parking available. Gift shop.
The Birthplace Museum is based around the cottage in which John Paul Jones, Father of the American Navy, spent the first thirteen years before taking up an apprenticeship in the merchant navy. The original building has been restored to the style of a gardener's cottage of the 1840s with period furnishings. Information on headsets, slide tape audio visual, a replica of the cabin on the *Bonhomme Richard*, and a room containing a model of John Paul Jones and one of the cannons he is known to have used. The cottage gardens have been laid out in period style. Interpretative display and shop are in a former kennels block.

Kelburn Country Centre
Off A78 between Largs and Fairlie. Easter-mid Oct, daily 10.00-18.00. Tel: (01475) 568685.
The historic estate of the Earls of Glasgow,

famous for rare trees and the Kelburn Glen. Also waterfalls, gardens, nature trails, exhibitions, adventure course, Marine Assault Course, children's stockade, pets' corner and pony-trekking. The central, 18th-century farm buildings have been converted to form a village square with craft shop, workshops, display rooms and licensed cafe. Ranger Service. Car park. Picnic tables and Commando Assault Course.

M.V. 'Kenilworth' Cruises
Car and coach park at pier in Helensburgh. May-Sept, Mon-Sat, cruises from 10.40. Parking available. Tel: (01475) 21281.
Attractive 1930's vintage well-maintained passenger vessel. Other sailings to Dunoon, Rothesay, Millport, etc. Light refreshments available.

Kilberry Sculptured Stones
Off B8024, 20m SSW of Lochgilphead. All reasonable times. Free. (HS). Tel: 0131-244 3101.
A fine collection of late mediaeval sculptured stones.

Kilmun Arboretum
By Forest Office on A880, 1m E of junction with A815. 5m N of Dunoon. All year. Daily, all day. Free. Parking available. (FE). Tel: (0136 984) 666.
A fascinating collection of tree species on a hillside to the northeast of Holy Loch within the Argyll Forest Park.

Kilwinning Abbey
Kilwinning, Ayrshire. All times. Free. Can be viewed from outside only. (HS). Tel: 0131-244 3101.
The ruins of a Tironensian-Benedictine Abbey. Most of the surviving buildings date from the 13th century.

Kirkmaiden Information Centre
Take A77 S from Stranraer, continue S on A716 (not turning off to Portpatrick). Late May-mid Sept, Mon-Sat 10.00-16.00, Sun 13.30-16.00. Free. Parking available.
Visitor and information centre about the parish, places to visit and surrounding area, history, genealogy. Exhibition area.

The Lady Margaret Restaurant Boat
Forth and Clyde Canal, near the Stables Bar on A803 Bishopbriggs/Kirkintilloch road. All year. Dinner cruises Thur, Fri, Sat. Sunday lunch cruises. Prices on application. Parking available. Tel: 0141-776 6996 or (01236) 723523.
Restaurant boat on the Forth and Clyde Canal, providing quality lunch and dinner cruises for groups and individuals. Member of Taste of

Scotland scheme. Floodlighting illuminates passing scenery at night.

Lagoon Leisure Complex
Paisley, off Mill Street. Jan-Dec. Mon-Fri 10.00-22.00. Sat, Sun, public hols, 09.30-17.00. Charges vary. Parking available. Restaurant and bar. Tel: 0141-889 4000.
Modern swimming pool complex with bar and cafeteria. Sauna, steam room and jacuzzi.

Land O'Burns Centre
Opposite Alloway Kirk, 2m S of Ayr. All year, daily, 10.00-17.00 (exc July & Aug 17.30). Admission free, small charge for audio-visual display. Parking available. Tel: (01292) 443700.
This visitor centre has an exhibition area and an audio-visual display on the life and times of Robert Burns. Landscaped gardens.

Largs Museum
Manse Court, Largs. June-Sept, Mon-Sat 14.00-17.00. Open at other times by arrangement. Donation box. Tel: (01475) 687081.
The museum holds a small collection of local bygones, with a library of local history books and numerous photographs.

Lauder Forest Walks
3 miles S of Strachur on A815, turn right, signposted Glenbranter. All reasonable times. Free. Parking available. (FE). Tel: (0136 984) 666.
Glenbranter Estate, formerly owned by Sir Harry Lauder, was leased to the Forestry Commission in 1921. The village was later built on the site of a former World War II prisoner-of-war camp. The forest walks go through a mixed coniferous and broadleaved woodland, with a rhododendron collection established in 1925, and dramatic waterfalls. Half a mile away on the Dunoon road are the Lauder memorials. Sir Harry Lauder erected an obelisk here in memory of his only son John, killed in World War I, and a Celtic cross to commemorate Lady Lauder who died in 1927. The forest car park is on the site of the former Glenbranter House.

Lillie Art Gallery
Milngavie, off A81, 8m N of Glasgow. All year, Mon-Fri 10.00-17.00, Sat & Sun 14.00-17.00. Free. Parking available. Tel: 0141-943 3247.
A modern purpose-built art gallery with a permanent collection of 20th-century Scottish paintings, sculpture and ceramics, and temporary exhibitions of contemporary art. Alternative entrance with ramp.

Lincluden Collegiate Church
Off A76, 1m N of Dumfries. All reasonable times. Key keeper. Entrance charge. (HS). Tel: 0131-244 3101.

A 15th-century Collegiate Church and Provost's House remarkable for heraldic adornment and for the tomb of Princess Margaret, daughter of Robert III. There is a motte in the grounds.

"Little Wheels"

Portpatrick. Easter & main holiday season. 11.00-16.00, extended as necessary during July and Aug. Phone for latest times (Ansaphone service). Entrance charge. Limited parking available. Gift and collectors' shop. Refreshments. Tel: (0177 681) 536.

Model Railway (over 100 metres of track), Toy and Transport Exhibition. Children can usually 'drive' some of the trains. Special new displays each year. Hot and cold drinks, collectors' items and gifts for sale.

David Livingstone Centre

At Blantyre, A724, 3m NW of Hamilton. All year, Mon-Sat 10.00-17.00, Sun 13.00-17.00 (Last entry). Entrance charge. Parking available. Shop. Tearoom. Tel: (01698) 823140.

Shuttle Row is an 18th century block of mill tenements where David Livingstone, the famous explorer/missionary, was born in 1813, went to school and worked while studying to become a doctor. The David Livingstone Centre, which illustrates his life and contains many interesting relics of the Industrial Revolution and of Africa, is in this building, now surrounded by parkland.

Loch Doon Castle

From A713, 10m S of Dalmellington, take road to Loch Doon. All reasonable times. Free. (HS). Tel: 0131—244 3101.

This early 14th-century castle was devised to fit the island on which it was originally built. When the waters of the loch were raised in connection with a hydro-electric scheme the castle was dismantled and re-erected on the shores of the loch. The walls of this massive building, once known as Castle Balliol, vary from 7-9 feet thick and stand about 26 feet high.

Loch Lomond

Cruises available from a number of operators, including: MacFarlane & Son, Balmaha. Tel: (0136 087) 214. Sweeney's Boatyard, Balloch. Tel: (01389) 52376. Loch Lomond Sailings, Balloch. Tel: (01389) 51481. Lomond Lady, Luss Tel: (0143 686) 257.

Loch Lomond, largest stretch of inland water in Britain, and framed by lovely mountain scenery, is a popular centre for all watersports. Cruises around the banks and attractive small islands are available.

Lochmaben Castle

Off B7020 on S shore of Castle Loch, by Lochmaben, 9 miles ENE of Dumfries. All reasonable times. Free. (HS). Tel: 0131-244 3101.

This castle was captured and recaptured twelve times and also withstood six attacks and sieges. James IV was a frequent visitor, and Mary, Queen of Scots was here in 1565. Now a ruin, this early 14th-century castle is on the site of a castle of the de Brus family, ancestors of Robert the Bruce who is said to have been born here.

Lochore Meadows Country Park

Between Lochgelly and Ballingry on B920. (Country Park) At all times. (Park Centre) Summer 09.00-21.00, winter 09.00-17.00. (Fishery) 15 Mar-6 Oct. (Country Park facilities: rates on application). Tel: (01592) 860086.

Green, pleasant countryside around large loch reclaimed from coal mining waste in the 1960s. Reclamation makes fascinating story told in slide show, displays and ranger guided walks. Plenty of scope for birdwatching, wildlife study, walks, picnics. Many ancient historical remains. Cafe and information in park centre. Activities include boat and bank fishing, sailing, windsurfing, canoeing, golf, horse riding, trim trail, wayfaring, self-guided trails, picnic areas and cafeteria. Wide range of provisions for visitors with special needs. Groups welcome.

Lochwinnoch Nature Reserve

Largs Road, Lochwinnoch, 9m SW of Paisley. All year, daily 10.00-17.15. School parties by arrangement. (RSPB). Tel: (01505) 842663/0131-557 3136.

Purpose built Nature Centre with observation tower, displays and shop. Two observation hides overlooking marsh reached by walk through woods. Third hide overlooking Barr Loch. Shop.

Logan Botanic Gardens

Off B7065, 14m S of Stranraer. Daily 15 Mar-31 Oct 10.00-18.00. Tel: (0177 686) 231.

Here a profusion of plants from the warm and temperate regions of the world flourish in some of the mildest conditions in Scotland. There are cabbage palms, tree ferns and many other Southern Hemisphere species. Salad bar, meals served all day.

Logan Fish Pond

Off B7065, 14m S of Stranraer. Easter-Sept, daily 12.00-20.00. Tel: (01292) 268181.

This tidal pool in the rocks, 30 feet deep and 53 feet round, was completed in 1800 as a fresh-fish larder for Logan House. Damaged by a mine in 1942, it was reopened in 1955. It holds some 30 fish, mainly cod, so tame that they come to be fed by hand.

Loudoun Hall

Boat Vennel, off Cross in Ayr town centre. Jul-end Aug, Mon-Sat 10.00-17.00 or by arrangement. Free, but donation box available. Group visits if booked can have guided walk of Ayr (approx 1 hour) with light refreshments. Parking available. Tel: (01292) 282109.

A late 15th-century/early 16th-century town house built for a rich merchant, one of the oldest surviving examples of burgh architecture to remain in Scotland. For a period it was the town house of the Campbells, Earls of Loudoun, and the Moore family; both families played prominent parts in the life of Ayr. Local history publications for sale.

MacLaurin Gallery & Rozelle House

1.5m S of Ayr, off road to Burns Cottage at Alloway. Free. Parking. Tel: (01292) 45447.

Set in extensive parkland, the gallery was formerly stables and servants' quarters attached to the mansion house. A programme of temporary exhibitions operates throughout the year covering Fine Art, Sculpture, Photography and Crafts. The gallery shows many major Arts Council exhibitions. Rozelle House operates a programme of temporary exhibitions and also houses the Maclaurin Contemporary Art Collection and the District Collection's Henry Moore sculpture in the gallery courtyard. Rozelle House Pantry offers meals and refreshments throughout the day. Open during gallery hours.

McLean Museum and Art Gallery

Greenock. All year, Mon-Sat 10.00-12.00, 13.00-17.00. Free. Tel: (01475) 23741.

A local museum with art collection, natural history, shipping exhibits, ethnographic material and items relating to James Watt, who was born in Greenock. Small shop. Wheelchair access at rear of building.

MacLellan's Castle

Off High Street, Kirkcudbright. Opening standard except Oct-Mar closed Mon-Fri. (HS). Tel: 0131-244 3101.

A handsome castellated mansion overlooking the harbour, dating from 1577. Elaborately planned with fine architectural details, it has been a ruin since 1752. In Kirkcudbright also see the 16th/17th-century Tolbooth, the Mercat Cross of 1610 and the Stewartry Museum.

MacRobert Arts Centre

University of Stirling. Parking available. Tel: (01786) 61081 or 73171, ext. 2543.

A five-hundred seat theatre, art gallery and studio, providing all year theatre, opera, dance, films, concerts, conferences and exhibitions. Theatre bar. For details of events, contact the box office. Induction loop system.

Mabie Recreation Area

Mabie Forest, Ae Village, 3.5 miles S of Dumfries on A710. All reasonable times. Charge for car park (disabled drivers free). Tel: (01387) 86247.

Woodland recreational area with a variety of walks, including two for less able walkers, four cycle routes, children's play area with forest play structures, picnic sites with toilets including some for disable visitors, forest nature reserve (birds and butterflies), barbecues.

Magnum Leisure Centre

From Glasgow take the A736 to Irvine and follow signs for Harbourside (Magnum). All year, daily 09.00-22.00. Parking available. Tel: (01294) 78381.

Leisure Centre attractions include new state-of-the art indoor water park, indoor bowling, sports hall, ice rink, theatre/cinema, soft play area, kiddies superbounce area, squash courts, sauna, fitness salon. Two licensed bars, fast food area and restaurant.

Mainsriddle Pottery

The Tenements, Mainsriddle, 15 miles SW of Dumfries on A710. Jan-Dec. Daily 10.00-18.00 (Showroom only). Car parking only. Tel: (0138 778) 633.

Small studio pottery, specialising in handmade stoneware and porcelain. Showroom displays a changing selection of colourful pots, all made on the premises.

Mariner Leisure Centre

On A803 1m W of Falkirk's High Street and 24m from Glasgow and Edinburgh. All year, daily. Parking available. Tel: (01324) 22083.

Lagoon-shaped pool with wave machine, games hall, squash courts, sauna and solarium, fitness room, creche or general purpose room. Cafeteria and licensed lounge bar offering hot and cold snacks overlooking the pool below.

Mar's Wark

At the top of Castle Wynd, Stirling. All times. Free. (HS). Tel: 0131—244 3101.

Mar's Wark is one of a number of fine old buildings on the approach to Stirling Castle. Built c 1570 by the first Earl of Mar, Regent of

Scotland, it was a residence of the Earls of Mar until the 6th Earl had to flee the country after leading the 1715 Jacobite Rebellion.

Martyrs' Monument
Near Wigtown, A714, 7m S of Newton Stewart. All reasonable times. Free. Tel: (01671) 2431.
A monument on the hill and a pillar on the shore of Wigtown Bay where in 1685 two women, aged 18 and 63, were tied to stakes and drowned for their religious beliefs during the persecution of the Covenanters in 'the Killing Times'. Their graves may be seen in the churchyard.

Maxwelton House
13m NW of Dumfries on B729, near Moniaive. House, Gardens, Chapel and Museum: Easter-Sept, daily, 10.30-17.30. Parking available. Gift shop, antiques and crafts. Tearoom. Tel: (0184 82) 385.
The house dates back to the 14th/15th centuries. Originally it was a stronghold of the Earls of Glencairn and later the birthplace of Annie Laurie, to whom William Douglas of Fingland wrote the famous poem. Museum of early kitchen, dairy and small farming implements.

Maybole Collegiate Church
In Maybole, S of A77. Not open to the public - can be viewed from outside. Free. (HS). Tel: 0131-244 3101.
The roofless ruin of a 15th-century church, built for a small college established in 1373 by the Kennedies of Dunure.

Meadowsweet Herb Garden
Soulseat Loch, Castle Kennedy, Stranraer. Turn off A75 at Inch Church. May-Aug. Daily exc Wed, 12.00-17.00. Entrance charge. Parking available. Gift shop. Tel: (01776) 82288.
On the site of Soulseat Abbey, of which only a few mounds remain, Meadowsweet Herb Gardens occupies a 'tongue' in Soulseat Loch. Galloway's original herb garden has over 120 herbs in individual display beds. Fresh and dried herbs are sold, and herb teas can be sampled.

Menstrie Castle
In Menstrie, A91, 5m E of Stirling. Exhibition Rooms: Opening by arrangement with NTS Perth office. Tel: (01738) 31296.
The 16th-century restored castle was the birthplace of Sir William Alexander, James VI's Lieutenant for the Plantation of Nova Scotia. A Nova Scotia Exhibition Room (NTS) displays the coat of arms of 109 Nova Scotia Baronetcies.

Mill on the Fleet
High Street, Gatehouse of Fleet. Mar-Oct (all year for booked parties). Daily, 10.00-17.30 (last admission to exhibition 16.30). Nov-late Dec, weekends only 11.30-16.00. Entrance charge. Disabled parking on site. Gift shop. Tearoom. Tel: (01557) 814099.
The Mill on the Fleet Heritage Centre, based in a restored 18th century cotton mill, recalls the industrial history of the town. Exhibition with sound, two audio-visual programmes illustrating Galloway landscape and history, plus further temporary and permanent exhibits. Special feature about water and water power. Tearoom gives access to riverside terrace.

Morton Castle
A702, 17m NNW of Dumfries. Closed to the public but may be viewed from the outside (HS). Tel: 0131-244 3101.
Beside a small loch, this castle was occupied by Randolph, first Earl of Moray, as Regent for David II. It afterwards passed to the Douglases and is now a well-preserved ruin.

Mossburn Animal Centre
Hightae, 6 miles W of Lockerbie on B7020. Jan-Dec exc Xmas. Daily, 10.30-16.00. Donations appreciated. Parking available. Tel: (01387) 811288.
Horse and pony rescue centre with other animals and reptiles which visitors may handle while learning about their habits and needs. Picnic area with barbecue, woodland walks.

Motte of Mark
Off A710, 5m S of Dalbeattie. All reasonable times. Free.
An ancient hill fort on the estuary of the River Urr at Rockliffe, overlooking Rough Island, an NTS bird sanctuary. This motte is one of the best preserved examples in Scotland. Good views of Cumbrian Hills.

Motte of Urr
Off B794, 5m NE of Castle Douglas. All reasonable times. Free.
The most extensive motte and bailey castle in Scotland, dating from the 12th century A.D., though the bailey may have been an earlier earthwork of hillfort type.

Mugdock Country Park
3 miles N of Milngavie, 3 miles S of Strathblane on A81. Jan-Dec. Daily. Visitor Centre: 13.00-16.30. Free. Car parking only. Gift shop. Tearoom. Tel: 0141-956 6100.
Woodlands, marshes, lochs, pastures and the remains of Mugdock and Craigend Castles.

Information and exhibition centre, picnic areas, barbecue site, adventure play areas, footpaths (most suitable for wheelchairs), viewpoints, bridleway and orienteering course. Programme of guided walks, talks and educational facilities.

Muirshiel Country Park
Off B786, N of Lochwinnoch, 9m SW of Paisley. Jan-Dec, daily 10.00-16.00 (winter), 10.00-18.00 (summer). Free. Parking available. Tel: (01505) 842803.
Attractive countryside featuring trails and walks in a high valley above moorland, with picnic sites and an information centre.

Museum of Scottish Lead Mining
Wanlockhead, 6 miles from M74 Abington, 6 miles from A76 Mennock. Early Mar-Nov, daily, 11.00-16.30 (last tour 16.00). Nov-Mar, by appointment only. Entrance charge. Parking available. Gift shop. Restaurant, tearoom. Tel: (0165 974) 387.
Indoor museum with mining and social relics. Visitor lead mine. Open air museum with beam engines, mines, smelt mill, but-and-ben cottages. Miners' Reading Society Library, founded 1756. Local gold, silver and minerals collection. Situated near Scotland's highest village.

The National Burns Memorial Tower
Lies on A76 Dumfries-Kilmarnock Road in Mauchline. Oct-Easter, Mon-Fri, 09.15-13.00, 14.00-17.00. Free. Roadside parking. Tel: (01290) 51916.
Opened in 1896 as a memorial to Robert Burns. Tourist Information Office on ground floor. There is an interpretation centre on the first and second floors and viewing area at the top of the tower.

National Wallace Monument
Abbey Craig, off A807 Hillfoots Road, 1.5 miles NNE of Stirling. Apr-Oct, daily 10.00-17.00 (18.00 in Jul & Aug). Entrance charges. Gift shop. Coffee house. Tel: (01786) 475019.
The National Wallace Monument takes visitors back in time almost 700 years, to the days of Scotland's first struggle for independence. The story of William Wallace, freedom fighter and national hero, is told along with the background and events that shaped this period of history. The tower, 220 feet high, gives superb views. Not suitable for wheelchair access.

New Abbey Corn Mill
New Abbey, 6m S of Dumfries on A710. Opening standard, exc Oct-Mar closed Thur pm and all day Fri. Entrance charge. (HS). Tel: 0131-244 3101.

A late 18th-century water powered corn mill, still in working order and demonstrated regularly to visitors.

Newark Castle, Port Glasgow
Off A8, through shipyard at E side of Port Glasgow. Opening standard, closed Oct-Mar. Parking available (HS). Tel: 0131-244 3101.
A large, fine-turreted mansion house of the Maxwells, overlooking the River Clyde, still almost entire and in a remarkably good state of preservation, with a 15th-century tower, a courtyard and hall, the latter dated 1597.

Newton Stewart Museum
York Road, Newton Stewart. Apr-Sept, Mon-Sat 14.00-17.00. Jul, Aug, Sept, also Sun 14.00-17.00. Jul, Aug, also Mon-Sat 10.00-12.30. Entrance charges. Parking available. Gift shop.
This former church, which is a listed building, has displays covering local history and Scottish life, both domestic and agricultural.

North Ayrshire Museum
Manse Street, Saltcoats. Jun-Sept, Mon-Sat, exc Wed, 10.00-13.00, 14.00-17.00; Oct-May, Tue-Sat, exc Wed 10.00-13.00 and 14.00-17.00. Free. Car parking only. Tel: (01294) 64174.
A fine museum in a classic mid-18th century Scottish church. Exhibits include local and national items and a varied programme of temporary exhibitions.

North Glen Gallery
Palnackie, 5m SE of Castle Douglas. Daily 10.00-18.00 by arrangement. Parking available. Tel: (0155 660) 200.
Studio demonstrating the blowing of glass, assembly of sculpture, welding and cutting of steel.

Old Bridge House
Mill Road, Dumfries at Devorgilla's Bridge. Apr-Sept, Mon-Sat 10.00-13.00, 14.00-17.00; Sun 14.00-17.00. Free. Parking available. Tel: (01387) 56904.
The house, built in 1660, now has rooms furnished in period style to illustrate life in Dumfries over the centuries. Devorgilla's Bridge was originally built in the mid-15th century by Lady Devorgilla Balliol, who endowed Baliol College, Oxford. The present stone bridge dates from 1431.

Orchardton Tower
Off A711, 6m SE of Castle Douglas. Opening standard. Free. Apply custodian at nearby cottage. (HS). Tel: 0131—244 3101.
An example, unique in Scotland, of a circular tower house, built by John Cairns about the middle of the 15th century.

Paisley Abbey

In Paisley, 7m W of Glasgow. Outwith the hours of divine worship, open all year, Mon-Sat 10.00-15.30. Free. Tel: 0141—889 7654.

A fine Cluniac Abbey Church founded in 1163. Almost completely destroyed by order of Edward I of England in 1307. Rebuilt and restored after Bannockburn and in the century following. In 1553 the tower collapsed, wrecking N-transept, crossing the choir; they lay open to the sky for 350 years while the nave alone was the parish church; but they were rebuilt and rejoined to the nave this century (1898-1907 and 1922-28). The choir contains a fine stone-vaulted roof, stained glass and the tombs of Princess Marjory Bruce and King Robert III. See the St. Mirin Chapel with St. Mirin carvings (1499). Note outside the Norman doorway, cloisters and Place of Paisley. The Barochan Cross, a weathered Celtic cross, 11 feet high and attributed to the 10th century, is also in the Abbey.

Paisley Museum & Art Gallery

High Street, Paisley. All year, Mon-Sat 10.00-17.00. Free. Closed public holidays. Tel: 0141-889 3151.

The late 19th-century museum and art galleries house the world-famous collection of Paisley shawls. Displays trace the history of the Paisley pattern; the development of weaving techniques is explained and the social aspects of what was a tight-knit weaving community are explored. There are also fine collections of local history, natural history, ceramics and Scottish painting.

Palacerigg Country Park

Unclassified road, 2.5m SE of Cumbernauld. All year. (Park) dawn to dusk. (Visitor Centre) winter 10.00-16.30, summer 10.00-18.00 (closed Tues). No dogs. Free. Tearoom. Parking available. Tel: (01236) 720047.

Wildlife includes roe deer, badger, fox and stoat. Bison, wolves, lynx and chamois in paddocks. Deer park, 18-hole golf course and pony-trekking. Children's farm and rare breeds. Coffee shop from 11.00 daily in season (except Tues) and weekends in winter. Picnic sites and barbecues; ranger service.

Palgowan Open Farm

By Glentrool, Newton Stewart. From 14.00 each day. Parties any time by arrangement. Easter week, then mid-May, June, Sept, Oct, Tues, Wed & Thurs. Jul-Aug Mon-Fri. Tel: (01671) 84 227.

Highland and Galloway cattle, sheep, sheep dogs. Demonstrations in stane dyking, stick making, skin curing. Special career opportunity demonstrations and talk for schools. Picnic areas. Information on cassette.

Raiders Road

From A712 near Clatteringshaws Dam, or A762 at Bennan near Mossdale. Apr-Sept. Daily, 09.00-18.00 (21.00 in summer). Charge for drive. Cars only. (FE). Tel: (01556) 3626.

A 10-mile forest drive through the fine scenery of the Galloway Forest Park.

Rainbow Slides Leisure Centre

Goosecroft Road, central Stirling. Opening times vary with activities. Swimming: Mon, Wed, Fri 09.00-21.00. Tues 09.00-17.00. Thurs 09.00-18.00, Sat 09.00-16.00, Sun 08.30-16.00. Parking available. Restaurant. Tel: (01786) 62521.

Exciting water fun centre, with two swimming pools, three water slides, fully-equipped gymnasium, professional sports injury clinic, sauna suite. Holiday play sessions with inflatables for children.

Allan Ramsay Library

On B797 at Leadhills. Wed, Sat, Sun 14.00-16.00 or by arrangement. Entrance charge. Tel: (01659) 74326/74216.

Lead miners' subscription library, founded in 1741, with rare books, detailed 18th century mining documents and local records.

Red Deer Range

8 miles W of New Galloway on A712, car park signposted. Late June-early Sept, Tues, Thurs 11.00 and 14.00, Sun 15.00. Charge for tour of range. (FE).

Native Galloway red deer are seen close at hand in their natural habitat on a guided tour through the deer range, mingling with stags, hinds and calves. Tour last 1.5 hours, guided by forest ranger. Stout footwear advisable and, if possible, a camera.

Rob Roy's Grave

Balquhidder Churchyard, off A84, 14m NNW of Callander. All reasonable times. Free.

Three flat gravestones enclosed by railings are the graves of Rob Roy, his wife and two of his sons. The church itself contains St Angus' Stone (8th century), a 17th century bell from the old church and old Gaelic Bibles.

Rob Roy and Trossachs Visitor Centre

In Ancaster Square in Callander town centre. Mar-May and Oct-Dec, daily 10.00-17.00; June & Sept, daily 09.30-18.00; July & Aug, daily 09.00-22.00 (last admission 30 mins before closing). Entrance charge. Parking available. The-

med souvenir shop, bookshop. Tel: (01877) 30342.

Exciting new visitor attraction using modern technology to take the visitor back three centuries to rediscover the daring adventures of Scotland's most colourful folk hero, Rob Roy Macgregor, in the heart of his wildly beautiful homelands - the Trossachs. Themed souvenir shop. Full-scale tourist information centre. Refreshments nearby.

Roman Bath House
Roman Road, Bearsden, 5m NW of Glasgow. All times. Free. (HS). Tel: 0131-244 3101.
A Roman bath house built in the 140s AD for the use of the soldiers stationed in the adjacent Antonine Wall fort. The best surviving visible Roman building in Scotland.

Rough Castle
Off B816, 6m W of Falkirk. All reasonable times. Free. (HS). Tel: 0131-244 3101.
The best preserved of the forts of the Antonine Wall, with ramparts and ditches easily seen.

Rutherglen Museum
King Street. Mon-Sat 10.00-17.00; Sun 11.00-17.00. Small shop. Tel: 0141-647 0837.
A museum of the history of the former royal burgh of Rutherglen, with regularly changing displays and temporary exhibitions.

St. Bride's Church
Douglas, 12m SSW of Lanark. Open all reasonable times. Free. Apply keykeeper. (HS). Tel: 0131-244 3101.
The restored chancel of this ancient church contains the tomb of the 'Bell the Cat' Earl of Angus (died 1514). The nearby tower (1618) has a clock of 1565 said to have been gifted by Mary, Queen of Scots.

St. Ninian's Chapel, Isle of Whithorn
At Isle of Whithorn, 3m SE of Whithorn. All reasonable times. Free. (HS). Tel: 0131-244 3101.
Ruins of a 13th century chapel on a site traditionally associated with St. Ninian. On the shore by Kidsdale, 2m W, is St. Ninian's Cave, with early Christian crosses carved on the rock.

Sanquhar Post Office
Main Street, Sanquhar. Parking available. Free access during business hours. Tel: (01659) 50201.
Britain's oldest post office, functioning in 1763, 20 years before the introduction of the mail coach service, and still in use today.

Savings Banks Museum
In Ruthwell, 6.5m W of Annan. All year (except Sun and Mon in Winter) 10.00-13.00, 14.00-17.00. Free. Tel: (0138 787) 640.
The first Savings Bank, founded by Rev. Dr. Henry Duncan in 1810. This room is a mine of information on the early days of the Savings Bank movement and the restoration of the Ruthwell Cross.

Scots Dyke
Off A7, 7m S of Langholm. All reasonable times. Access is not easily identified. Free.
The remains of a wall made of clods of earth and stones, which marked part of the border between England and Scotland.

Scottish Industrial Railway Centre
At Minnivey Colliery, Dalmellington, take the A713 S from Ayr, turn left to Burnton just before Dalmellington Village, left again at 'T' junction, follow road right up to the Centre. June-Sept, every Sat. Also Steam Days, check dates. Entrance charge. Parking available. Gift shop. Tearoom. Tel: (01292) 313579 or 531144.
8 steam locomotives (including one fireless), 12 diesels and a large collection of rolling stock. Museum, loco shed, brake van rides. Tearoom seating 24.

Scottish Maritime Museum
Harbourside, Irvine. Apr-Oct. Tel: (01294) 78283.
Boatshed Special Exhibition. Historic vessels at pontoon moorings. Vessels include a Scottish puffer, lifeboat and tug. Wharf and harbour. Ferry. Restored Edwardian shipyard worker's flat. Shop and exhibition. Boatshed suitable for disabled.

Shambellie House Museum of Costume
New Abbey, 6m S of Dumfries on A710. May-Sep, Thur-Sat, Mon & Tues 11.00-17.00, Sun 12.00-17.00. Entrance charge. Tel: 0131-225 7534.
A mid-Victorian small country house designed by David Bryce. Each year there is a new display of material from the National Costume Collection.

SS "Sir Walter Scott"
From Trossachs Pier, E end of Loch Katrine, 9m W of Callander. Apr-Sept, Sun-Fri 11.00, 13.45 and 15.15; Sat 14.00, 15.30. Fares vary with sailings. Charter available. Parking available. Shop. Cafeteria. Tel: 0141-355 5333.
Regular sailings in summer from the pier to Stronachlachar in this fine old steamer. Winner of Steam Heritage's Premium Prize for 1989. Views include Ben Lomond. Cafeteria, shop, Visitor Centre.

Skelmorlie Aisle

Bellman's Close, off main street, Largs. Opening standard, closed in winter. (HS). Tel: 0131—244 3101.

A splendid mausoleum of 1636, with painted roof, interesting tombs and monuments.

Sma' Shot Cottages

11/17 George Place, Paisley. Apr-Sept, Wed & Sat 13.00-17.00, or parties by arrangement. Free. Tearoom. Tel: 0141-889 1708 or 0141-889 0530.

19th-century millworkers' two-storey houses. Traditionally Scottish, with back of house iron staircase. Two exhibition rooms with displays of linen, lace, Paisley shawls. There is also an 18th-century weaver's cottage which has recently been restored. Garden.

Smith Art Gallery and Museum

Dumbarton Road, Stirling. Open all year. Free. Cafe. Tel: (01786) 71917 for programme details and opening hours. Parking available.

A lively award-winning museum and art gallery near the King's Park, below the dramatic skyline of Stirling Castle and old town. There is a wide-ranging programme of exhibitions and events offering opportunities for seeing, joining in and finding out about art, history, craft and design. Small shop stocks local interest books, postcards and souvenirs.

Smollett Monument

On A82 N of Dumbarton at Renton. All times. Free.

A monument to Tobias Smollett (1721-1771), novelist and surgeon. Dr. Johnson wrote the Latin Epitaph to him in 1773.

Sorn Castle

3 miles E of Mauchline on B743. Grounds open Apr-Oct. House, 2 weeks in July and 2 weeks in Aug, daily 14.00-17.00. Entrance charge. Parking available. Tel: (01290) 51555.

The Castle stands on a cliff overlooking the River Ayr. It dates from 1380, with the main building from 1764. Essentially, a family home, it contains many fine paintings, mainly by Scottish artists. The grounds are laid out along the river bank, with fine trees and shrubs.

Souter Johnnie's Cottage

At Kirkoswald, on A77, 4m W of Maybole. April-Oct, daily 12.00-17.00, or by arrangement. (NTS). Tel: (0165 56) 274.

This thatched cottage was the home of the village cobbler (Souter) John Davidson at the end of the 18th century. Davidson and his friend Douglas Graham of Shanter Farm, known to Robert Burns in his youth in Kirkos-

wald, were later immortalised in Tam o' Shanter. The cottage contains Burnsiana and contemporary tools of the cobbler's craft.

Stained Glass Studio

Dalton, 5 miles S of Lochmaben. Signposted on A75 from Dumfries. Jan-Dec. Mon 12.00-17.00, Tues-Sat 11.00-17.00. Free. Shop. Coffee room. Tel: (0138 784) 688.

Small studio of character - a former Victorian soup kitchen - in picturesque setting. Displays of stained glassware, painting demonstrated in the studio. Small groups welcome.

Stewartry Museum

St. Mary Street, Kirkcudbright. Mar-Oct, Mon-Sat 11.00-16.00; later openings and Suns in summer. Nov-Easter, Sat only. Entrance charge. Parking available. Gift shop. Tel: (01557) 31643.

A museum depicting the life of the area with prehistoric articles, relics of domestic life and crafts of earlier days. Works of local artists are featured, especially Jessie M. King (1875-1949). John Paul Jones, a founder of the American Navy who was born in the Stewartry and had varied associations with Kirkcudbright, is also the subject of a special display.

Stirling Bridge

By A9 off Stirling town centre. All times. Free. (HS).

The Old Bridge built c 1400, was for centuries of great strategic importance as the 'gateway to the north' and the lowest bridging point of the River Forth.

Stirling Castle

In central Stirling. Apr-Sep, daily 09.30-17.15 (last entry). Oct-Mar, daily 09.30-16.15 (last entry). Castle closes 45 mins after last entry. Entrance charge. Parking available. (HS). Tel: 0131-244 3101.

Stirling Castle on its 250-feet great rock has dominated much of Scotland's vivid history. Wallace recaptured it from the English in 1297; Edward I retook it in 1304, until Bruce won at nearby Bannockburn in 1314. Later it was a favourite Royal residence: James II was born here in 1430 and Mary, Queen of Scots and James VI both spent some years here. Long used as a barracks, and frequently rebuilt, the old towers built by James IV remain, as do the fine 16th-century hall, the splendid Renaissance palace of James V, the Chapel Royal of 1594 and other buildings. On castle hill there is a visitor centre (same hours as castle; NTS) which has an audio-visual display as an introduction to the castle.

Stranraer Museum

Old Town Hall, George Street, Stranraer. All year, Mon-Sat 10.00-17.00. Free. Tel: (01776) 5088.

A local history museum with changing exhibitions. Free town trail leaflets available. Shop. Information on town trail which can be followed by wheelchair users. Exhibitions on the Town Hall, archaeology, farming and polar explorers. Shop, information point.

Strathclyde Country Park

On both sides of M74 between Hamilton and Bothwell interchanges (A723 and A725). All year. Tours start: Easter-Sept, daily at 15.00, also Sat & Sun at 19.00 during July & Aug; winter Sat & Sun at 14.00. Tel: (01698) 66155. Free (charges for facilities).

A countryside park with man-made loch, nature reserve (permit only), sandy beach and a wide variety of sporting facilities. Within the park is Hamilton Mausoleum, created in the 1840's by the 10th Duke of Hamilton, which has a remarkable echo and huge bronze doors. Tours start: Summer daily at 15.00, also Sat and Sun at 19.00; winter Sat and Sun at 14.00 (groups by arrangement, tel: Motherwell (0698) 66155).

Strathaven Castle

Kirk Street/Stonehouse Road, Strathaven, 14m W of Lanark. All reasonable times. View from outside only.

Also known as Avondale Castle, this ruin dates from the 15th century.

Summerlee Heritage Trust

West Canal Street, Coatbridge. All year, exc Xmas & New Year. Daily 10.00-17.00. Free. Parking available. Tel: (01236) 431261.

Museum of industrial and social history featuring machine exhibition hall with working historic machinery, reconstructed historic buildings, award winning archaeological excavations of 1835 ironworks, working electric tramway and restored canal. Shop, tearoom and picnic area.

Sweetheart Abbey

At New Abbey, A710, 7.5m S of Dumfries. Opening standard except Oct-Mar, closed Thurs pm and all day Fri. Entrance charge. (HS). Tel: 0131-244 3101.

Founded in 1273 by Devorgilla in memory of her husband, John Balliol (she also founded Balliol College, Oxford), this beautiful ruin has a precinct wall built of enormous boulders.

Thistle Bagpipe Works

Luss, Loch Lomond, 8 miles N of Balloch on A82. Jan-Dec. Daily, 09.00-17.00 (open later, May-Sept). Free. Car parking only. Gift shop. Tel: (0143 686) 250.

Bagpipe making, complete Highland dress outfitters, kiltmaker. Exhibition of antiques.

Threave Castle

N of A75, 3m W of Castle Douglas. Apr-Sept, opening standard. Oct-Mar, closed. Parking available. (HS). Tel: 0131—244 3101.

Early stronghold of the Black Douglases, on an island in the Dee. The four-storeyed tower was bult between 1639 and 1690 by Archibald the Grim, Lord of Galloway. In 1455 it was the last Douglas stronghold to surrender to James II.

Threave Garden

S of A75, 1m W of Castle Douglas. Gardens: all year, daily 09.00-sunset. Visitor Centre: Apr-Oct. Daily 09.00-17.00. Entrance charge. Parking available. Trust shop. Plant sales. Restaurant. (NTS). Tel: (01556) 2575.

The gardens of this Victorian mansion display acres of naturalised daffodils in April and May. There are peat, rock and water gardens and a visitor centre. The garden is of 60 acres and is at its best in June to August with good autumn colours in November. Threave Wildfowl refuge nearby is a roosting and feeding place for many species of wild geese and ducks on and near the River Dee, access during November to March, to selected points only to avoid disturbance. Tearoom.

The Time Capsule, Monklands

Just off the M8, 9m from Glasgow. Open daily 10.00-22.00. Tel: (01236) 449572.

The Time Capsule Monklands is a unique combination of ice, water, one million years of Scottish heritage. Skate, splash, slide, paddle, rubber ring, glide and soak under the watchful eyes of prehistoric monsters. Journey through the past, present and future from dinosaur infested primeval swamps to the swirling river of life to erupting volcanoes and river rapids, or cool down with a skate through gentle snowdrifts across the frozen loch with a giant woolly mammoth. Licensed Serpent Bar, Ice Cream and Soda Bar, Waterfall Cafe and Gift Shop. Disabled facilities in most areas.

Tongland Tour

By A711, 2m N of Kirkcudbright. Early May-end Aug. Guided tours, Mon-Sat 10.00, 11.30, 14.00, 15.30. Free. Free transport from Kirkcudbright. To book Tel: (01557) 30114 or (01294) 822311.

Hydro-electric power station and dam. Video plus displays.

Torhouse Stone Circle

Off B733, 4m W of Wigtown. All reasonable times. Free. (HS). Tel: 0131—244 3101.
A circle of 19 boulders standing on the edge of a low mound. Probably Bronze Age.

Turnberry Castle

Off A719, 6m N of Girvan. All reasonable times. Free.
The scant remains of the castle where Robert the Bruce was probably born in 1274.

Vale of Leven Swimming Pool

North Main Street, Alexandria, Dunbartonshire. Jan-Dec. Mon-Fri 09.00-21.00, Sat & Sun 09.00-16.00. Entrance charge. Parking available. Tearoom. Tel: (01389) 56931.
25-metre main swimming pool and children's splash pool. Sauna facilities, lounge suite with television and refreshments, tanning sunbeds, fitness room with computerised equipment.

Village Glass

Queen's Lane, Bridge of Allan, 4 miles N of Stirling. Jan-Dec. Mon-Thur 09.00-17.00, Fri 09.00-16.00, Sat 09.00-12.00. Free. Parking available. Gift shop. Tel: (01786) 832137.
Craftsmen at work, creating miniature bottles, fruit and flowers, glass ships in bottles, decorative glassware. Showroom and sales of items designed by Tom Young, collector's pieces, special commissions.

John Walker & Sons

Hill Street, Kilmarnock, Ayrshire. Tours: Mon-Thur 09.45 and 13.45, Fri 09.45 only. Each tour last approximately two hours. Minimum age 5. Entrance charge. Parking available. Shop. Tel: (01563) 23401 (Visitor Centre).
Whisky blending and bottling plant with guided tours.

Wanlockhead Beam Engine

Wanlockhead Village, Dumfries and Galloway. At all times. Free. Tel: (01659) 74387.
An early 19th-century wooden water-balance pump for lead mining with the track of a horse engine beside it. Nearby is the Museum of Scottish Lead Mines.

P.S. 'Waverley'

Rates and full details of departure points and times from Waverley Excursions Ltd., Anderston Quay, Glasgow G3 8HA. Parking available. Tel: 0141-221 8152.
Historically one of the most interesting vessels still in operation in the British Isles, the Waverley is the last paddle steamer to be built for service on the Clyde, and now the last seagoing paddle steamer in the world. A variety of cruises from Glasgow and Ayr along the Clyde Coast, with meals, bar and light refreshments available.

The Weather Centre

Lauriston, 6 miles NW of Castle Douglas. Apr-Oct, Tue-Fri, Sun. Tours at 10.00, 12.00, 14.30. Nov-Mar by arrangement. Entrance charge. Limited parking. Salespoint. Tel: (0164 45) 264.
Fully functioning weather centre, where visitors can see how weather forecasts are prepared, using instruments and satellite equipment.

Weaver's Cottage

At Kilbarchan, off A737, 5m W of Paisley. Apr-May, Sept-Oct, Tue, Thu, Sat and Sun 13.00-17.00; Jun-Aug, daily 13.00-17.00. Entrance charge. (NTS). Tel: (0150 57) 5588.
In the 18th century Kilbarchan was a thriving centre of handloom weaving. The cottage is preserved as a typical weaver's home of the period, with looms, weaving equipment and domestic utensils. Attractive cottage garden.

Westquarter Dovecot

In Westquarter, 2m E of Falkirk, off A9. May be viewed from outside only. (HS). Tel: 0131-244 3101.
A rectangular dovecot of considerable architectural merit. Over the entrance doorway there is a heraldic panel dated 1647 containing the arms of Sir William Livingstone of Westquarter.

The Whithorn Dig

45-47 George Street, Whithorn. Easter to end-Oct, daily 10.30-17.00. Tel: (019885) 508.
See the archaeologist at work at the site of Scotland's first recorded Christian community. Visitors can view work on medieval burials, the remains of a Norse settlement and early Christian buildings dating as far back as the 5th century AD. Explore the new Visitor Centre and exhibitions. See "The Light Shineth in the Darkness" - a new picture show, telling of St. Ninian, Dark Age settlers and medieval pilgrims. Go on an informal guided tour of the dig; see a re-created Hiberno-Norse building, the ruins of Whithorn Priory and the superb early Christian crosses in the Priory Museum. Other attractions include a herb garden, outdoor picnic area and craft shop.

Whithorn Priory and Museum

Main Street, Whithorn, 10m S of Wigtown. Opening standard except Oct-Mar closed, Mon-Fri. (HS). Tel: 0131—244 3101.
Here St Ninian founded the first Christian Church in Scotland in 397. The present priory ruins date from the 12th century. Early Christ-

ian crosses, some carved in the rock, others now displayed in the museum attached to the priory are notable.

Wigtown Museum
County Buildings, Wigtown. Summer months, Mon-Fri 14.00-16.00. Free. Tel: (01776) 5088.
Town Museum telling the story of Wigtown martyrs. New signposts to points of interest in Wigtown. Shop. Information on town trail which can be followed by wheelchair users.

Alexandra Wolffe Studio Gallery
The Toll House, High Street, Gatehouse of Fleet. Easter-Oct. Mon-Fri 10.00-12.00, or by request at house next door. Free. Parking available. Paintings and ceramics for sale. Tel: (01557) 814300.
Small gallery and ceramic workshop, where visitors are welcome to watch the artist making one-off ceramic models, such as portrait models of favourite pets, champion stock, etc. Models and paintings displayed and sold.

Wood of Cree Nature Reserve
On minor road from Minigaff, 4m NW of Newton Stewart. Can be viewed at any time from road or paths through the wood. Car park. (RSPB). Tel: (01671) 2861.
One of the finest areas of remaining native oak and birch woodland in Scotland with woodland birds and flowers.

Woodside Studio Gallery
William Street, Dalbeattie. All year, daily, 09.30-19.00. Free. Parking available. Tel: (01556) 610517.
Exhibition of large selection of original paintings of subjects including Galloway landscapes, for sale. Also framing.

Younger Botanic Garden, Benmore
A815, 7m NNW of Dunoon. 15 Mar-31 Oct, daily 10.00-18.00. Parking available. Tel: (01369) 6261.
Extensive woodland gardens featuring conifers, rhododendrons, azaleas, many other shrubs and a magnificent avenue of Sierra redwoods. Part of the Royal Botanic Garden, Edinburgh. Tearoom.

GLASGOW

Art Gallery and Museum
In Kelvingrove Park. Jan-Dec exc. Xmas and New Year. Mon-Sat 10.00-17.00, Sun 11.00-17.00. Free. Parking available. Gift shop. Restaurant. Tel: 0141-357 3929.
This fine municipal art collection has outstanding Flemish, Dutch and Italian canvases, including magnificent works by Giorgione and Rembrandt, as well as a wide range of French Impressionist and British pictures. Other areas include sculpture, furniture designed by Charles Rennie Mackintosh and his contemporaries, silver, pottery, glass and porcelain, an important collection of European arms and armour and displays of archaeological, historical and ethnographic material.
The natural history displays illustrate geology, with minerals, dinosaurs and other fossils. There is a comprehensive collection of British birds. The natural history of Scotland is treated in depth in a developing new gallery. Alternative entrance for wheelchairs.

The Barras
0.25m E of Glasgow Cross. All year, Sat and Sun 09.00-17.00. Free. Tel: 0141—552 7258 (Wed-Sun 10.00-16.00).
Glasgow's world famous weekend market, with an amazing variety of stalls and shops. Founded one hundred years ago, the Barras is now home to over 800 traders each weekend. Look out for the Barras archways, children's creche and buskers. Numerous licensed premises and cafes. All markets are covered.

Botanic Gardens
Entrance from Great Western Road (A82). Gardens 07.00-dusk; Kibble Palace 10.00-16.45; Main Range 13.00 (Sun 12.00)-16.45. Closes 16.15 Oct-Mar. Free. Tel: 0141—334 2422.
The glasshouses contain a wide range of tropical plants including an internationally recognised collection of orchids and the 'National Collection' of begonias. The Kibble Palace, an outstanding Victorian glasshouse, has a unique collection of tree ferns and other plants from temperate areas of the world. Outside features include a Systematic Garden, a Herb Garden and a Chronological Border.

The Burrell Collection
Pollok Country Park. Jan-Dec exc. Xmas and New Year. Mon-Sat 10.00-17.00, Sun 11.00-17.00. Free. Parking available. Gift shop. Restaurant and bar. Tel: 0141-649 7151.
Housed in a building opened in 1983, a world famous collection of textiles, furniture, ceramics, stained glass, art objects and pictures (especially 19th century French) gifted to Glasgow by Sir William and Lady Burrell. Restaurant and bar, parking and facilities for handicapped.

Cathcart Castle
In Linn Park. All reasonable times. Free. Tel: 0141-637 1147.
Sparse ruins of a 15th century castle now in a city park. Nearby is the Court Knowe, associated with Mary, Queen of Scots.

Glasgow Cathedral

At E end of Cathedral Street. Opening standard. Free. (HS). Tel: 0131—244 3101.

The Cathedral, dedicated to St. Mungo, is the most complete survivor of the great Gothic churches of south Scotland. A fragment dates from the late 12th century, though several periods (mainly 13th century) are represented in its architecture. The splendid crypt of the mid-13th century is the chief glory of the cathedral, which is now the Parish Church of Glasgow.

Citizens' Theatre

Gorbals. Sept-Jul. Box Office: Mon-Sat 10.00-18.00 (21.00 on performance nights). Sun 17.00-21.00, performance nights only. Charge for performances. Parking available. Bars, confectionary stalls, coffee. Inductive loop. Sign language performance. Tel: 0141-429 0022 (10.00-20.00, box office), 0141-429 5561 (admin).

Opened in 1878 originally as a Music Hall and now a listed building. Stalls, upper and dress circle bars, confectionary and coffee available during performances. Alternative wheelchair entrance.

City Chambers

George Square, Mon-Fri, guided tours at 10.30 and 14.30 or by arrangement. Sometimes restricted owing to Council functions. Free. Tel: 0141-221 9600.

Built in Italian Renaissance style, and opened in 1888 by Queen Victoria. The interiors, particularly the function suites and the staircases, reflect all the opulence of Victorian Glasgow.

Collins Gallery

University of Strathclyde, Richmond Street, off George Street. Open during exhibitions, Mon-Fri 10.00-17.00, Sat 12.00-16.00. Free. Sales Desk. Refreshments. Tel: 0141-552 4400, ext. 4145.

Modern Gallery which presents a lively programme of contemporary exhibitions throughout the year, ranging from contemporary painting and sculpture, crafts and photography to local history and architecture. Most exhibitions include demonstrations, talks, workshops or films with special events for children.

Compass Gallery

178 West Regent Street. Jan-Dec exc public hols. Mon-Sat 10.00-17.30. Free. Tel: 0141-221 6370.

Long established contemporary gallery with changing exhibitions of contemporary Scottish and international art. Paintings, original prints, sculpture and ceramics.

Crookston Castle

4m SW of city centre. Open all reasonable times. Keykeeper. Free. (HS) Tel: 0131-244 3101.

On the site of a castle built by Robert Croc in the mid-12th century, the present tower house dates from the early 15th century. Darnley and Mary, Queen of Scots stayed here after their marriage in 1565.

Custom House Quay

N shore of the Clyde, between Glasgow Bridge and Victoria Bridge.

The Quay is part of the Clyde Walkway, an ambitious project to give new life to the riverside. By Victoria Bridge is moored the *Carrick* (1864) and there is a fine view of Carlton Place on the opposite bank.

George Square

Glasgow city centre.

The heart of Glasgow with the City Chambers and statues of Sir Walter Scott, Queen Victoria, Prince Albert, Robert Burns, Sir John Moore, Lord Clyde, Thomas Campbell, Dr Thomas Graham, James Oswald, James Watt, William Gladstone and Sir Robert Peel.

Greenbank Garden

Flenders Road, Clarkston, Glasgow (6m S of city centre), off Mearns Road (B761) off A726. All year, daily 09.30-sunset. No access to house. (NTS) Tel: 0141-639 3281.

Two and a half acres of walled garden and 13 acres of policies surround an elegant Georgian house (not open to the public). Dogs on leash. Disabled visitors' facilities including special garden, greenhouse and also regular walks and events programme available on request. Shop and refreshments in season.

Haggs Castle

100 St. Andrew's Drive. All year, Mon-Sat 10.00-17.00, Sun 12.00-18.00. Free. Tel: 0141-427 2725.

Built in 1585 by John Maxwell of Pollok, the castle was acquired by the city in 1972, and, after restoration, was developed as a museum of history for children. As well as the exhibitions, there are workshops where every Saturday, there are museum-based activities for children. The gardens have been landscaped and include herb and vegetable plots and a knot garden. Shop and workshop.

Heatherbank Museum of Social Work

163 Mugdock Road, Milngavie. Jan-Dec exc public hols. Sun-Fri 14.00-17.00. Donations welcome. Car parking only. Gift shop. Refreshments. Sales area. Tel: 0141-956 2687.

A 'hands-on' exhibition on juvenile justice and attitudes towards physical disability. Activities for children, videos, audio-visual, recordings including 'rap' songs about crime, library, picture library, educational resource material.

Hunterian Art Gallery
Glasgow University, Hillhead Street, 2m NW of city centre. All year (closed Glasgow Public Holidays) Mon-Sat 09.30-17.00. Mackintosh House closed 12.30-13.30. Free. Tel: 0141—330 5431.
Unrivalled collections of work by Charles Rennie Mackintosh, including reconstructed interiors of the architect's house, and by J M Whistler. Works by Rembrandt, Chardin, Stubbs, Reynolds, Pissarro, Sisley, Rodin, plus Scottish painting from the 18th century to the present. Sculpture Courtyard. Varied programme of temporary exhibitions from 16th century to present. Sales point, university refectory nearby. Alternative wheelchair entrance.

Hunterian Museum
Glasgow University, 2m NW of city centre. All year, Mon-Sat 09.30-17.00. Free. Parking available (Sat only). Tel: 0141—330 4221.
Glasgow's oldest museum, opened in 1807. Exhibits include geological, archaeological and ethnological material; new coin gallery and exhibition on history of Glasgow University. Scottish Museum of the Year Award 1983 and 1984. Temporary exhibitions of scientific instruments are exhibited in the Natural Philosophy Building. The anatomical and zoological collections, and manuscripts and early printed books, can be seen on application. Bookstall and small coffee house in 18th-century style. Alternative wheelchair entrance (via lift), please telephone.

Hutchesons' Hall
158 Ingram Street, near SE corner of George Square. All year, Mon-Fri 09.00-17.00, Sat 10.00-16.00. Subject to functions in hall. Shop. Free. (NTS). Tel: 0141-552 8391.
Described as one of the most elegant buildings in Glasgow's city centre, Hutchesons' Hall was built in 1802-5 to a design by David Hamilton and includes a handsome meeting hall introduced by James Baird II in 1876. It incorporates on its frontage the statues of the founders, George and Thomas Hutcheson, from an earlier building. It is now used as a visitor centre, gift shop and the Trust's regional offices.

King's Theatre
Bath Street, Glasgow. Tel: 0141-227 5511.
This 1,785 seat theatre dates back to 1904 and preserves the style and elegance of the Edwar-dian period. Now carefully modernised, it has become one of the best equipped civic theatres in Scotland.

Barclay Lennie Fine Art
Semi-basement, 203 Bath Street. Jan-Dec exc public hols. Mon-Fri 10.00-17.00, Sat 10.00-13.00. Free. Tel: 0141-226 5413.
19th and 20th century Scottish art. Paintings, drawings, sculpture, decorative art. Usually four shows by contemporary artists per year.

McLellan Galleries
Sauchiehall Street. Mon-Sat 10.00-17.00, Sun 11.00-17.00. Admission: details of charges on request. Closed between exhibitions. Tel: 0141-331 1854.
The purpose-built 1854 exhibition galleries, completely refurbished in time for Glasgow's celebrations as Cultural Capital of Europe, now provide Glasgow Museums with a major exhibition venue for large exhibitions.

Merchants' House
W side of George Square. Open by appointment, please telephone. Free. Tel: 0141—221 8272.
This handsome building occupies one of the best sites in the city. Built in 1874 by John Burnet, it contains the Glasgow Chamber of Commerce, the oldest in Britain, the fine Merchants' Hall with ancient relics and good stained-glass windows, and the House's own offices. Tour and commentary on history of Merchants' House.

The Mitchell Library
North Street. Jan-Dec, exc public hols. Mon-Fri 09.30-21.00, Sat 09.30-17.00. Free. Tel: 0141—221 7030.
Founded in 1874, this is the largest public reference library in Scotland, with stock of over one million volumes. Its many collections include probably the largest on Robert Burns in the world. Coffee room (10.30-16.30).

Ewan Mundy Fine Art
48 West George Street, above Buchanan Street subway station entrance. Jan-Dec exc public hols. Mon-Sat 09.30-17.30. Free. Tel: 0141-331 2406.
A fine art gallery specialising in paintings, drawings and engravings by Scottish, English and French 20th-century artists.

Museum of Transport
Kelvin Hall, 1 Bunhouse Road. Free. Jan-Dec, Mon-Sat 10.00-17.00, Sun 11.00-17.00. Cafe. Tel: 0141—357 3929.

Opened Spring 1988. A new and considerably enlarged museum of the history of transport, including a reproduction of a typical 1938 Glasgow street. Other new features are a larger display of the ship models and a walk-in Motor Car Showroom with cars from the 1930s up to modern times. Other displays include Glasgow trams and buses, Scottish-built cars, fire engines, horse-drawn vehicles, commercial vehicles, cycles and motorcycles, railway locomotives and a Glasgow Subway station. Restaurant, fast food and bar facilities will be shared with the adjacent indoor Sports Centre Shop.

Necropolis
Behind Glasgow Cathedral. Access restricted: contact Cemeteries & Cremations, Port Dundas Place, Glasgow. Tel: 0141-333 0800.
Remarkable and extensive burial ground laid out in 1833, with numerous elaborate tombs of 19th-century illustrious Glaswegians and others; see particularly the Menteith Mausoleum of 1842.

People's Palace
In Glasgow Green. All year, Mon-Sat 10.00-17.00; Sun 11.00-17.00. Free. Tel: 0141—554 0223.
Opened in 1898, contains important collections relating to the tobacco and other industries, Glasgow stained glass, ceramics, and political and social movements including temperance, co-operation, women's suffrage and socialism. Wholefood snack bar/tearoom in Winter Gardens and shop. Alternative wheelchair entrance at west door (Winter Gardens).

Pollok House
2060 Pollokshaws Road (A736). All year, exc public hols. Mon-Sat 10.00-17.00. Sun 11.00-17.00. Free. Parking available. Tearoom, gardens, shop. Tel: 0141—632 0274.
Built c 1750, with additions 1890-1908 designed by Sir Robert Rowand Anderson. It houses the Stirling Maxwell collection of Spanish and other European paintings. Also displays of furniture, ceramics, glass and silver (mostly 18th century). Tearoom, gardens and shop. Alternative wheelchair entrance to tearoom.

Provan Hall
At Auchinlea Road (B806), Easterhouse, off M8, 4m E of city centre. Parking available. Garden. (NTS). Tel: 0141-552 8391.
Built in the 16th century, this is probably the most perfect example of a pre-Reformation house in Scotland. Now part of Auchinlea Park. The property is leased to the City of Glasgow District Council and while the old hall is closed at present, visitors may view surrounding garden and parkland. Situated in Auchinlea Park, Easterhouse.

Provand's Lordship
Castle Street, opposite the Cathedral. Jan-Dec. Mon-Sat 10.00-17.00, Sun 11.00-17.00. Free. Shop. Tel: 0141-552 8819.
The only surviving medieval building in Glasgow apart from the Cathedral. Built 1471 as the manse for the chaplain of the Hospital of St. Nicholas by Bishop Andrew Muirhead. Period house displays, 15.00-19.00. Shop.

Queen's Cross Church
870 Garscube Road, 0.5 mile W of City centre. Jan-Dec. Tue, Thur, Fri 12.00-17.30. Sun 14.30-17.00. Free. Parking available. Gift shop. Refreshments Tel: 0141-946 6600.
The only church (1897-1899) designed by Charles Rennie Mackintosh, architect, artist and designer who grew up and spent most of his professional life practising in Glasgow. Restored by The Charles Rennie Mackintosh society as its headquarters, the church has a small exhibition area, reference library and specialised shop.

Regimental Headquarters of the Royal Highland Fusiliers
518 Sauchiehall Street, Glasgow. Mon-Thu 09.00-16.30, Fri 09.00-16.00. Parking available. Free. Tel: 0141-332 0961.
The exhibits in this regimental museum include medals, badges, uniforms and records which illustrate the histories of The Royal Scots Fusiliers, The Highland Light Infantry and the Royal Highland Fusiliers, Princess Margaret's Own Glasgow and Ayrshire Regiment.

Rouken Glen
Thornliebank. All reasonable times. Free.
One of Glasgow's most attractive parks with lovely shaded walks and a waterfall.

Glasgow Royal Concert Hall
2 Sauchiehall Street. From M8 westbound exit at Junction 16; eastbound, Junction 17. Follows signs. Jan-Dec. Box office, daily, 10.00-18.00 (21.00 on show nights). Shop, daily, 10.00-17.30 (and on selected show nights). Public tours Mon-Fri 14.00. Other times by arrangement. Charge for tours and performances. Parking available. Gift shop. Restaurant/tearoom/refreshments. Induction loop. Tel: 0141-332 6633.
The Glasgow Royal Concert Hall, opened in 1990, provides a lasting tribute to Glasgow's reign as Cultural Capital of Europe in that

year. This world-class multi-purpose venue with excellent acoustics replaces the St. Andrew Hall which was destroyed by fire in 1964. The Hall has hosted performances by many major artistes and orchestras.

St. David's 'Ramshorn' Church
Ingram Street. All reasonable times. Access can be arranged with Director of Drama, University of Strathclyde. Free. Tel: 0141-552 3489.
Impressive church built in 1824 with a graveyard containing the graves of many notable citizens including David Dale, creator of New Lanark. Now University drama centre.

St. Mungo's Museum
Next to Cathedral, 1 mile NE of city centre. Jan-Dec. Mon-Sat 10.00-17.00, Sun 11.00-17.00. Free. Gift Shop. Restaurant. Tel: 0141-553 2557.
Opened in April 1993, this museum explores the universal themes of life, death and the hereafter, through evocative art objects associated with different religious faiths. Three galleries focus on art, religion and world religions. Japanese Zen garden.

St. Vincent Street Free Church
265 St. Vincent Street. Service times, or by arrangement with Church Officer. Free. Induction loop. Tel: 0141-221 1937.
Church by Alexander 'Greek' Thomson of varied styles high on a plinth. There is an open air theatre feature on the south side.

School of Art
167 Renfrew Street. Jan-Dec. Mon-Fri 09.30-17.00, Sat 10.00-12.00. Entrance to exhibitions free. Tours of building Mon-Fri 11.00, 14.00, Sat 10.00. Additional tours in summer. Charge for tours. Mackintosh shop. Refectory nearby. Tel: 0141-332 9797.
A fine example of the work by Charles Rennie Mackintosh, designed in 1896, and built between 1897 and 1909. Escorted tours of the building will operate throughout the summer. Further details from the School of Art.

Scotland Street School Museum of Education
225 Scotland Street, Glasgow. Take first exit (East Kilbride) off Kingston Bridge on S side. Jan-Dec exc public hols. Mon-Sat 10.00-13.00, 14.00-17.00. Free. Parking available. Gift shop. Cafe. Tel: 0141-429 1202.
Designed by Charles Rennie Mackintosh and opened in 1906. It served as an elementary and then as a primary school until 1979. It is now run by Glasgow's Museum Education Service and houses a Museum of Education with 2 reconstructed classrooms.

Springburn Museum
Ayr Street, off A803 to City Centre. All year, Mon-Fri 10.30-17.00, Sat 10.00-16.30, Sun & Bank Holidays 14.00-17.00. Tel: 0141-557 1405.
The museum preserves the heritage of this typical Glaswegian community by recording the memories of the local people at work and at home. Springburn was once the largest centre of steam locomotive manufacture in the world. Winner of the British Museum of the Year award for Social and Industrial History 1989.

Stirling's Library
111 Queen Street. Jan-Dec exc public hols. Mon, Tues, Thurs 09.00-20.00. Wed, Fri, Sat 09.00-17.00. Free. Tel: 0141-221 1876.
Formerly known as the Royal Exchange, and before that the Cunningham Mansion, the present building, used as a library, was designed in 1827 and has a particularly rich interior.

The International Stock Exchange
7 Nelson Mandela Place, St. George's Place. All year, Mon-Fri 09.00-16.30. Free. Tel: 0141-221 7060.
A 'French Venetian' building of 1877, with visitors gallery.

Former Templeton's Carpet Factory
Off Glasgow Green. View from outside only. Free.
Victorian factory built to copy the design of the Doge's Palace in Venice with ornate decoration of coloured glazed brick, battlements, arches and pointed windows.

The Tenement House
145 Buccleuch Street, Garnethill, N of Charing Cross. Apr-Oct, daily 14.00-17.00; early Nov-Mar, Sat/Sun 14.00-16.00. Weekday morning visits arranged for educational and other groups by appointment only. Entrance charge. (NTS). Tel: 0141-333 0183 (10.00-12.30 and 14.00-17.00).
A first-floor Victorian flat in a red sandstone tenement, with the furniture, furnishings and ephemera of the family who lived there for more than 50 years. Of great social significance, reflecting the inherent character of the City of Glasgow. A second flat on the ground floor, has been purchased to provide premises for reception, interpretative and educational facilities.

Theatre Royal
Hope Street. Booking office Mon-Sat 10.00 to end of first interval (18.00 on non-performance days). Groups rates for parties of 10 or more. Tel: 0141-332 9000.

A fine Victorian theatre, elegantly restored as the home of Scottish Opera. Performances also by Scottish Ballet, national visiting companies and major concert artists. Licensed bars, entertaining facilities. Induction loop.

Tron Theatre
63 Trongate, Glasgow G1 5HB. Tel: 0141-552 4257 (box office).
The 200 year old Adam kirk in the heart of Glasgow's Merchant City, provides the setting for the Tron. Boasting a unique and informal atmosphere, the Tron welcomes visitors to the city, as well as being a focus for the local community. The intimate auditorium (in the actual church itself) guarantees an entertaining and memorable night out!

University of Glasgow Visitor Centre
From Great Western Road (A82) turn into Byres Road at Botanic Gardens/Queen Margaret Drive junction. Go left at next lights into University Avenue. University on right at top of hill. Oct-Apr, Mon-Sat 09.30-17.00; May-Sept, Mon-Sat 09.30-17.00, Sun 14.00-17.00. Free. Tearoom. Tel: 0141-330 5511.
Visitor centre has exhibits of the university at work, interactive slide/computer and video displays plus a 'hands-on' information system. Conducted tours of mid-Victorian Gilbert Scott Building and Campus available at a small charge. Grounds open; Visitor centre has a coffee lounge seating about 25.

Victoria Park and Fossil Grove
Victoria Park Drive North, facing Airthrey Avenue. Mon-Sat 08.00-dusk; Sun 10.00-dusk. Fossil Grove open by arrangement. Free. Tel: 0141-959 9087.
Cornish elms, lime trees, formal flower garden and arboretum. Within the park is the famous Fossil Grove, with fossil stumps and roots of trees which grew here 230 million years ago.

Willow Tearoom
217 Sauchiehall Street, in precinct area above Henderson the Jeweller. Jan-Dec exc public hols. Mon-Sat 09.30-16.30. Tel: 0141-332 0521.
The Willow Tearoom is an original Charles Rennie Mackintosh building, designed for Miss Cranston 1904-1928. Re-opened in 1983, the tearoom still has original glass and mirror work and doors, and functions as a restaurant serving light meals, teas and coffees.

Zoo
6m SE of city centre on M74 (Glasgow/Carlisle). All year, daily 10.00-18.00 (17.00 winter). Entrance charge. Parking available. Shop. Cafeteria. Tel: 0141—771 1185.

A medium sized but developing open plan collection, taking in 25 hectares, with another 25 more being developed. Many rare animals, most of them breeding. Speciality cats, reptiles; also education department. Long walks, picnic areas, children's showground and car park.

Parks
Glasgow is rightly proud of its public parks - over 70, open from dawn till dusk. The oldest, **Glasgow Green,** is the home of the People's Palace Museum. The business centre nearby, a Victorian reproduction of the Doge's Palace in Venice, has battlements, arches and pointed windows. A herd of Highland cattle graze in **Pollok Park,** which extends over 361 acres. Here are the Burrell Collection, Pollok House, the Countryside Rangers' Service, the Demonstration Garden, Old Stables Courtyard and Sawmill.

At **Queen's Park,** known for its floral displays, a monument commemorates the Battle of Langside where Mary, Queen of Scots was defeated in 1568. **Linn Park** lying on the banks of the White Cart Water with a nature trail and children's zoo.

SCOTLAND'S ISLANDS
ARRAN
Arran & Argyll Transport Museum
Anchor Hotel Park, Corrie Road, Brodick. Apr-Oct, 4 days per week. Entrance charge. Parking available. Sales stall. Refreshments. Tel: (01770) 2150.
Independent museum run by enthusiasts, with displays of public transport in Arran and Argyll, from luxurious paddlesteamers to mailcarts and early motor buses. One section is housed in a converted bus, ex-Guernsey Railway Albion No. 70. Photographs, uniforms, advertisements, fittings and equipment from early transport of all kinds.

Arran Visitor Centre
Home Farm, Brodick. 1 mile from Brodick Pier on road N to Lochranza. Easter-Oct. Daily, 09.30-17.15. Free. Parking available. Shop. Tel: (01770) 2831.
Cheese factory and set of specialist shops stocking locally made foodstuffs, natural body care products, books, clothing, toys, jewellery on an environmental theme.

Brodick Castle Garden and Country Park
2m N of Brodick pier. Garden and Country Park: Jan-Dec daily 09.30-sunset. Castle: Easter holidays, May-Sept, daily 13.00-17.00. Also open between Easter and May, early-mid Oct,

Mon, Wed, Sat 13.00-17.00. Shop, restaurant, dates as castle, also open mornings. Please check exact dates and times. Entrance charge. Parking available. Tel: (01770) 2202.

This ancient seat of the Dukes of Hamilton dates in part from the 13th century, with extensions of 1652 and 1844. The contents include silver, porcelain and fine paintings, sporting pictures and trophies. There are two gardens: the woodland garden (1923) is now one of the finest rhododendron gardens in Britain; the formal garden dates from 1710. In 1980 the gardens became a country park, supported by the Countryside Commission for Scotland, with a ranger service. Nature trail specially designed for wheelchair users. Tearoom, shop, nature trail and adventure playground.

Glenashdale Falls and Giants' Graves
Whiting Bay, 9 miles S of Brodick on A841. Jan-Dec. All reasonable times. Free. Parking available. Tearoom close to start of walk, summer season. (FE). Tel: (01770) 2218.
Forest trail commencing at Whiting Bay, following the Glenashdale Burn and providing splendid viewpoints overlooking the falls, a magnificent sight when the burn is in full spate. On the south side of the glen, a signposted path to the Giants' Graves gives views over Whiting Bay and Holy Island. The cairns are 'horned gallery graves' dating from the Neolithic period. North of the falls are the remains of an Iron Age fort. Glenashdale Falls walk, 2 hours. Giants' Graves a steep 1.5 hours.

Goatfell
3.5m NNW of Brodick.
At 2,866 feet this is the highest peak on Arran. NTS property includes Glen Rosa and Cir Mhor, with grand walking and climbing. The golden eagle may occasionally be seen, along with hawks, harriers, etc.

Isle of Arran Heritage Museum
Rosaburn, Brodick. Early May to end Sep, Mon-Sat 10.00-13.00 and 14.00-17.00. Tel: (01770) 2636.
A group of old buildings which were originally an 18th-century croft farm on the edge of the village. Smithy, cottage furnished in late 19th-century style, stable block with displays of local history, archaeology and geology. Demonstrations of spinning and other hand crafts arranged periodically. Picnic area and tearoom.

Kilmory Cairns
At S end of Arran, off A841. All times. Free.
Cairn Baan, 3.5m NE of Kilmory village, is a notable Neolithic long cairn. 0.5m SW of A841 at the Lagg Hotel is Torrylin Cairn, a Neolithic chambered cairn. There are many other cairns in this area.

King's Cave
On shore; 2m N of Blackwaterfoot on the west coast of Arran. All times. Free.
A two-mile walk along the shore from the golf course at Blackwaterfoot leads to a series of caves, the largest being the King's Cave. Said to have been occupied by Finn MacCoul and later by Robert the Bruce, this is one of the possible settings for the 'Bruce and the spider' legend. Carvings of figures are on the walls.

Lochranza Castle
On N coast of Isle of Arran. Opening standard. Free. Apply custodian. (HS). Tel: 0131-244 3101.
A picturesque ruin of a castle erected in the 13th-14th centuries and enlarged in the 16th. Robert the Bruce is said to have landed here on his return in 1307 from Rathlin in Ireland at the start of his campaign for Scottish Independence.

Machrie Moor Standing Stones
1.5m E of A841, along Moss Farm Road, S of Machrie on W coast of Arran. All reasonable times. Free. (HS). Tel: 0131-244 3101.
These 15-feet high standing stones are the impressive remains of six Bronze Age stone circles. Some have now fallen.

BARRA

Cille Bharra
At Eolaigearraidh (Eoligarry), at N end of Isle of Barra. All times. Free.
The ruined church of St. Barr, who gave his name to the island, and the restored chapel of St. Mary formed part of the medieval monastery. Among the gravestones preserved there was a unique stone carved with a Celtic cross on one side and Norse runes on the other. A replica of this stone now stands in Cille Bharra.

Kisimul Castle
On a tiny island in the bay by Castlebay. May-Sept, Wed and Sat afternoons only. Charge for boatman and admission to the castle. Tel: (018714) 336.
For many generations Kisimul was the home and stronghold of the Macneils of Barra, widely noted for their lawlessness and piracy, and led by chiefs like Ruari the Turbulent, 35th chief, who did not fear to seize ships of subjects of Queen Elizabeth I of England. The main tower

dates from about 1120. Restoration was commenced in 1938 by the 45th clan chief, an American architect, and completed in 1970.

IONA

Iona

Off the SW tip of Mull; take A849 to Fionnphort, then ferry. (NTS). Tel: 0141-552 8391.

In 563 St Columba with 12 followers came to this little island to found a monastery from which his monks travelled over much of Scotland preaching Christianity to the Picts. The monastery, often attacked up to the 9th century by Norse raiders, was replaced in 1203 but, along with the cathedral, fell into decay. Restoration started early this century. The monastery is the home of the Iona Community, founded by Dr George MacLeod in 1938, who have done much restoration of the Cathedral, which has a beautiful interior and interesting carvings. For centuries Iona was the burial place of Scottish kings and chiefs. The oldest surviving building is St Oran's Chapel, c 1080 (restored). The remains of the 13th century nunnery can be seen and outside the Cathedral is 10th-century St Martin's Cross, 14 feet high and elaborately carved. Abbey gift and bookshop open 10.00-16.30 daily. Abbey coffee house open 10.00-16.30 daily except Sundays.

LEWIS

Museum Nan Eilean

Francis Street, Stornoway. Jun-Aug, Tues-Sat 10.00-12.30, 14.00-17.30, Sept-May, Tues-Sat 14.00-17.00. Free. Tel: (01851) 3773.

The museum contains displays illustrating aspects of the history of Lewis and the daily life and work of its people with sections on archaeology, agriculture and working life, domestic life, and fishing and the sea. A further gallery is devoted to a changing programme of temporary and travelling exhibitions.

Ness Historical Society
(Comunn Eachdraidh Nis)

Old School, Lionel, Ness. Open all summer. Tel: (01851) 81 576.

A permanent display of photographs and documents relating to local history with artefacts from domestic life, croft work and fishing. Videos and slides can be viewed on request.

Shawbost School Museum

A858, 19m NW of Stornoway. Apr-Nov, Mon-Sat, 10.00-18.00. Donation box. Tel: (01851) 71 213.

Created under the Highland Village

Competition 1970, the museum illustrates the old way of life in Lewis.

MULL

Carsaig Arches

On shore 3m W of Carsaig. All times. Free.

A 3-mile walk from Carsaig leads to these remarkable tunnels formed by the sea in the basaltic rock. Reached only at low tide. On the way is the Nun's Cave, with curious carvings; it is said that nuns driven out of Iona at the time of the Reformation sheltered here. Tearoom facilities available at Bunessan.

Duart Castle

Off A849, on E point of Mull. May-Sept, daily 10.30-18.00. Tel: (0168 02) 309.

The keep, dominating the Sound of Mull, was built in the 13th century. A royal charter of 1390 confirmed the lands, including Duart, to the Macleans. The clans supported the Stuarts and the castle, extended in 1633, was taken and ruined by the Duke of Argyll in 1691. During the 1745 Rising, Sir Hector Maclean of Duart was imprisoned in the Tower of London and his estate forfeited, not to be recovered until 1911 when Sir Fitzroy Maclean restored it. Tearoom.

Mull Museum

Tobermory. Easter-mid Oct, Mon-Fri 10.30-16.30, Sat 10.30-13.30. Entrance charge.

Local history museum situated on Main Street.

Mull Little Theatre

Dervaig. Open Spring-Autumn. Tel: (016884) 250/(01688) 2062.

Officially the smallest professional theatre in the country, according to the Guinness Book of Records, providing a variety of performances in summer.

Mull Railway

Old Pier Station, Craignure. Easter-mid Oct. Mon-Sat. Sunday operates only when Caledonian MacBrayne are running a Sunday service. Single/return fares. Family tickets. Souvenirs. Tearoom at Torosay Castle. Trains can be chartered by prior arrangement and group booking and charters must be made direct with the company. (Mull & West Highland Narrow Gauge Railway Co Ltd, Smiddy House, Aros Isle of Mull). Tel: (016802) 494 (out of season) or (01680) 300 389.

Narrow gauge railway operating a scheduled service to Torosay Castle and Gardens from Craignure (Old Pier) Station. Steam and diesel-hauled trains, superb sea and mountain panorama and woodland journey. Distance 1.25 miles, journey time 20 minutes. Souvenir shop at booking office at Craignure. Tearoom at Torosay Castle. Disabled must be able to get in and out of wheelchairs.

The Old Byre
Dervaig. 1m along Torloisk road. Easter-Oct, daily, 10.30-18.30. Tel: (016884) 229.
An audio-visual museum and visitor centre with displays of the bird and animal life of Mull, supported by audio-visual shows at half-hourly intervals. Licensed tearoom and craft/gift shop.

Torosay Castle and Gardens
A849, 1.5m SSE of Craignure. Mid Apr-mid Oct, daily 10.30-17.30. Gardens open 09.00-19.00 in summer, daylight hours in winter. Entrance charges. Parking available. Gift shop. Tel: (016802) 421.
The gardens and much of the house are open to the public. The Victorian castle is of Scottish Baronial architecture in a magnificent setting; its features include reception rooms and a variety of exhibition rooms. The 11 acres of Italian terraced gardens by Lorimer contain a statue walk and water garden. Served by a narrow inch gauge steam railway from Craignure Old Pier. Tearoom.

NORTH UIST
Balranald Nature Reserve
3m NW of Bayhead, turn off main road. Reception cottage at Goular near Hougharry. Apr-Sept, daily. Parking available. (RSPB). Tel: 0131-557 3136.
Hebridean marsh, machair and shore. Important for plants and nesting birds.

ORKNEY
Click Mill
At Dounby. All reasonable times. Free. (HS). Tel: 0131-244 3101.
The only working example of the traditional horizontal water mill of Orkney.

Cubbie Row's Castle
On the island of Wyre. Opening standard. Free. (HS). Tel: 0131-244 3101.
Probably the earliest stone castle authenticated in Scotland. The Orkneying Saga tells how (c. 1145) Kolbein Hruga built a fine stone castle in Wyre. It consists of a small rectangular tower, enclosed in a circular ditch. In a graveyard near the castle is St. Mary's Chapel, a ruin of the late 12th century. It is a small rectangular structure of nave and chancel. The walls are built of local whinstone.

Dwarfie Stane
On island of Hoy. All times. Free. (HS). Tel: 0131-244 3101.
A huge block of sandstone in which a burial

chamber has been quarried. No other tomb of this type is known in the British Isles. Probably third millenium BC.

Earl Patrick's Palace and Bishop's Palace
Kirkwall. (Both). Opening standard, except Oct-Mar closed. Parking available. (HS). Tel: 0131-244 3101.
Earl Patrick's Palace has been described as the most mature and accomplished piece of Renaissance architecture left in Scotland; it was built in 1607. The Bishop's Palace nearby dates back to the 13th century, with a 16th century round tower.

Earl's Palace, Birsay
At Birsay, N end of Mainland, 11m N of Stromness. All times. (HS). Tel: 0131-244 3101.
The impressive remains of the palace built in the 16th century by the Earls of Orkney.

Highland Park Distillery
Kirkwall. From the Cathedral, up Palace Road onto Dundas Crescent, turn onto Holm Road. Highland Park Distillery is on the A961, 0.25m on left-hand side. Easter-Oct, Mon-Fri 10.00-16.00. Tours every 30 mins. Also Sat, Jun-Aug, Nov-Easter, Mon-Fri, tour at 14.30. Free. Parking available. Gift shop. Tel: (01856) 4619 or 3107.
Famous Orkney distillery which produces malt whisky with a particular 'peaty' taste. Audio-visual display.

Knap of Howar
W side of island of Papa Westray, 800 metres W of Holland House. All reasonable times. Free. (HS). Tel: 0131-244 3101.
Only recently recognised as one of the oldest sites in Europe, these two 5000-year-old dwellings have also yielded many unusual artefacts - whalebone mallets and a spatula and unique stone borers and grinders.

Maes Howe Chambered Cairn
Off A965, 9m W of Kirkwall. Opening standard. (HS). Tel: 0131–244 3101.
An enormous burial mound, 115 feet in diameter, dating back to c 2500 BC, and containing a burial chamber which is unsurpassed in Western Europe. In the 12th century Viking marauders broke into it in search of treasures and Norse crusaders sheltered from a storm in the Howe. They engraved a rich collection of Runic inscriptions upon the walls.

Martello Tower
Hackness, Island of Hoy. All times. Can be viewed from the outside only. (HS). Tel: 0131-244 3101.

An impressive tower built during the Napoleonic and American wars at the beginning of the 19th century. The tower was renovated in 1866 and used again in the First World War.

Marwick Head Nature Reserve
Access along path N from Marwick Bay. Any time. Free. Parking available. (RSPB). Tel: (01856) 850176/0131-557 3136.
Seabird cliffs with huge and spectacular colonies of seabirds. Best time April-July.

North Hoy Nature Reserve
Reached by boat from Stromness. Access at all times. Free. (RSPB). Tel: (0185679) 298/0131-557 3136.
Extensive area of mountain and moorland with huge seacliffs including Old Man of Hoy. Moorland birds and large number of seabirds.

Old Man of Hoy
NW coast of Isle of Hoy.
A 450-feet-high isolated stack (pillar) standing off the magnificent cliffs of NW Hoy. It can also be well seen from the Scrabster-Stromness ferry. A challenge to experienced climbers.

Orkney Farm Park
Take the A986 out of Finstown and follows the signs. 14 May-end Sept, daily 10.00-18.00. Parking available. Tel: (0185 676) 243.
A collection of farm animals, many of which are rare breeds. Small gift shop.

Orkney Wireless Museum
St. Margaret's Hope, South Ronaldsay Island, 11m S of Kirkwall. 1 Apr-30 Sept, daily 10.00-19.00. Parking available.
Museum of wartime communications at Scapa Flow, with many of the instruments used by the thousands of service men and women posted here to protect the Home Fleet, shown in their proper context. Also many handsome wireless sets of the 1930s.

Pier Arts Centre
Victoria Street, Stromness. All year, Tues-Sat 10.30-12.30 and 13.30-17.00. Free. Parking available. Tel: (01856) 850 209.
Former merchant's house (c. 1800) adjoining buildings (Pier Gallery) former coal store and fishermen's sheds which have been converted into a gallery, housing permanent collection of 20th-century paintings and sculpture.

Pierowall Church
At Pierowall, Island of Westray. All reasonable times. Free. (HS). Parking available. Tel: 0131-244 3101.

A ruin consisting of nave and chancel, the latter canted out of alignment. There are some finely lettered tombstones.

Rennibister Earth House
About 4.5m WNW of Kirkwall on the Finstown road (A965). All reasonable times. Free. (HS). Tel: 0131-244 3101.
An excellent example of the Orkney type of Iron Age souterrain or earth-house, consisting of a passage and underground chamber with supporting roof-pillars.

Ring of Brogar
Between Loch of Harray and Loch of Stenness, 5m NE of Stromness, Mainland, Orkney. All times. Free. (HS). Tel: 0131-224 3101.
Magnificent stone circle of 36 stones (originally 60) surrounded by a deep ditch cut into solid bedrock. Nearby are large mounds and other standing stones, notably the Comet Stone.

St. Magnus Cathedral
Kirkwall, Orkney. May-Aug Mon-Sat 0900-1700. Sept-Apr, Mon-Sat 0900-1300, 1400-1700. Graveyard open all reasonable times. Closed Sun (except for services). Free. Inductive loop. Tel: (01856) 874894.
Founded by Jarl Rognvald in 1137 and dedicated to his uncle St. Magnus. The remains of both men are in the massive central piers. The original building dates from 1137 to 1200 but additional work went on for a further 300 years. It is still in regular use as a church, and contains some of the finest examples of Norman architecture in Scotland, with small additions in transitional styles and very early Gothic.

St. Magnus Church
Isle of Egilsay, Orkney. All reasonable times. Free. (HS). Tel: 0131-244 3101.
An impressive church, probably 12th-century, with a remarkable round tower of the Irish type, which still stands to a height of nearly 50 feet.

Scapa Flow
Sea area, enclosed by the mainland of Orkney and the islands of Burray, South Ronaldsay, Flotta and Hoy.
Major naval anchorage in both wars and the scene of the surrender of the German "High Seas" Fleet in 1919. Today a centre of marine activity as Flotta is a pipeline landfall and tanker terminal for North Sea Oil. Interpretation Centre at Lyness, Hoy in old pumphouse, used to feed fuel to ships. Scapa Flow is considered one of the best dive sites in Europe.

Skara Brae
19m NW of Kirkwall, Mainland, Orkney. Opening standard. (HS). Tel: 0131-244 3101.
A Neolithic village occupied from about 3000 BC to perhaps 2700 BC. The main period of settlement included eight or so houses joined by covered passages. Stone beds, fire places, cupboards and dressers survive. The inhabitants were farmers and herds who burned their dead in tombs like Quoyness. The amazing preservation of the village is due to its inundation by sand which buried it for 4500 years until it was revealed by a storm in 1850.

Standing Stones of Stenness
Between Loch of Harray and Loch of Stenness, 5m NE of Stromness, Mainland, Orkney. All times. Free. (HS). Tel: 0131-244 3101.
Four large upright stones are the dramatic remains of a stone circle, c 3000 BC, encircled by a ditch and bank. The area around Stenness is particularly rich in such remains.

Tankerness House
Broad Street, Kirkwall, Orkney. All year, Mon-Sat 1030-1230, 1330-1700; also May-Sep Sun 1400-1700. Entrance charge. Oct-Mar, free. Tel: (01856) 873191.
Dating from 1574, this is a fine example of an Orkney merchant-laird's mansion, with courtyard and gardens. Now a museum of life in Orkney through 5,000 years, with additional special exhibitions. A fine garden with lawns, flowerbeds and shrubbery, gravel paths.

RAASAY

Brochel Castle
The castle is now very ruinous and is usually dated somewhere in the 15th century and commands the normal sea route from Kyle of Lochalsh to Lewis. The last MacLeod chief to live in the castle was Iain Garbh, who died in 1671.

Kilmoluag - St. Moluag's Chapel
St. Moluag, like St. Columba, came as a missionary from Ireland in the sixth century. The old parish church, built in the 13th century, is dedicated to him. It is the largest of the three structures in the old burial ground behind Raasay House.

Raasay House
The home of the MacLeods of Raasay until 1834. The house was remodelled early in the 19th century and, in 1846, passed into the hands of various owners. It is now occupied by the Scottish Adventure School, a charitable trust which provides opportunities for boys

and girls to enjoy a variety of challenging outdoor activities.

The Symbol Stones
There are two of these Pictish symbolic designs, one cut in the natural rock at the Battery, and the other on the face of a free-standing cut monolith just inside the iron gate into the forestry plantation near the north gate of Raasay House. The stones date from between the late 7th century and the beginning of the 11th century.

RHUM

Kinloch Castle
Isle of Rhum, access by boat from Mallaig. Mar–Oct, as a hotel and hostel. Tours by arrangement with The Castle staff. Reserve and trail guides available from the Warden, White House, Kinloch, Rhum. Tel: (01687) 2026.
Extraordinary and magnificent residence built at the turn of the century for Sir George Bullough, still containing many of its sumptuous fittings. The island itself is a mountainous nature reserve where the Nature Conservancy Council have for some years conducted experiments in deer and forestry management.

SHETLAND

Fort Charlotte
Lerwick. Opening standard. Free. (HS). Tel: 0131-244 3101.
A fort roughly pentagonal in shape with high walls containing gun ports pointing seawards. Designed by John Mylne and begun in 1665 to protect the Sound of Bressay, it was burned in 1673 with the town of Lerwick by the Dutch, but repaired in 1781.

Jarlshof
Sumburgh Head, Approx. 22m S of Lerwick. Opening standard. Closed Oct-Mar afternoons in winter. Entrance charge. Parking available. (HS). Tel: 0131-244 3101.
One of the most remarkable archaeological sites in Europe with the remains of three extensive village settlements occupied from Bronze Age to Viking times, together with a mediaeval farmstead and the 16th-century house of the Earls Robert and Patrick Stewart.

Mousa Broch
On the island of Mousa, accessible by boat from Sandwick. Daily bus service between Lerwick and Sandwick. Boat for hire; May-Sep afternoons; also Sat and Sun mornings, and some evenings. Opening standard. Free. (HS). Tel: 0131-244 3101.
The best preserved example of the remarkable

Iron Age broch towers peculiar to Scotland. The tower stands over 40 feet high. Its outer and inner walls contain a rough staircase which can be climbed to the parapet.

Muness Castle
SE corner of Isle of Unst. Opening standard. Free. Apply key-keeper. (HS). Tel: 0131–244 3101.
The most northerly castle in Britain. A late 16th century tower house, rubble-built with circular towers at diagonally opposite corners. Fine architectural detail.

Ness of Burgi
On the coast at the tip of Scatness, about 1m SW of Jarlshof, S end of mainland Shetland. All reasonable times. Free. (HS). Tel: 0131-244 3101.
A defensive stone-built structure of Iron Age date, which is related in certain features to the brochs.

Old Haa Museum
Burravoe, Yell. Open Apr-Sept Tues, Wed, Thur, Sat, Sun 10.00-16.00. Groups and other times by arrangement. Free. Parking available. Tel: (0195 782) 339/(01957) 2127.
The Old Haa of Burravoe is the oldest building on Yell. It has been recently renovated and now includes a tearoom and exhibition areas for the display of local flora and fauna, arts and craft as well as themes of local historic interest; photographic collection, video and tape recordings of local musicians and storytellers; genealogical information may be available for inspection by arrangement. Craft shop and art gallery. Recording studio facilities available.

St. Ninian's Isle
By B9122 off W coast of Mainland. All times. Free.
Holy Well, foundations of chapel c. 12th century and pre-Norse church where a hoard of Celtic silver was discovered (now in the Royal Museum of Scotland, Queen Street, Edinburgh).

Scalloway Castle
6m W of Lerwick. Opening standard. Free. (HS). Tel: 0131-244 3101.
Built in 1600 by Earl Patrick Stewart, in' mediaeval style. When the Earl, a notoriously cruel character, was executed in 1615, the castle fell into disuse.

Scalloway Museum
Main Street, Scalloway. May-Oct, Tues, Wed & Thurs, 14.00-17.00. Sat 09.00-13.00, 14.00-17.00; Sun 14.00-17.00. Tel: (0159 588) 256/675.
The museum is located in a converted shop in Main Street. It is run by volunteers of the Scalloway History Group and contains displays of local artefacts. A new display is being set up recalling some of the exploits of the Norwegian Resistance fighters who created the legendary "Shetland Bus" of the last war. There is also an extensive display of photographs of old Scalloway. Car park opposite.

Shetland Croft House Museum
Voe, Dunrossness, on unclassified road E of A970, 25m S of Lerwick. May-Sept, daily 10.00-13.00, 14.00-17.00. Entrance charge. Parking available. Tel: (01595) 5057.
Typical mid-19th century thatched Shetland croft house, complete with all outbuildings and working water mill. Furnished in period style, c. 1860. Attendant in charge at all times.

Shetland Museum
Lower Hillhead, Lerwick. All year, Mon, Wed & Fri 10.00-19.00, Tues, Thurs & Sat 10.00-17.00. Free. Tel: (01595) 5057.
The collection in this museum is entirely local in character but international in interest. The theme is the history of man in Shetland from pre-history to the present day. Four continuous galleries are devoted to archaeology, art and textiles, folk life and shipping.

Tingwall Agricultural Museum
At Veensgarth off A971, 5m NW of Lerwick. Jul & Aug, daily, 14.00-17.00. Other times by arrangement. Entrance charge. Parking available. Tel: (0159 584) 344.
A private collection of tools and equipment used by the Shetland crofter, housed in a mid 18th-century granary, stables, bothy and smithy. Blacksmith's, wheelwright's, cooper's tools. Toilet facilities and parking.

SKYE

Clan Donald Centre and Armadale Gardens
At Armadale on A851, 0.5m N of Armadale Pier. Apr-Oct, every day 09.30-17.30. Entrance charge. Licensed restaurant and tearoom. Tel: (0147 14) 305.
Skye's Award-winning Visitor Centre, located in a rebuilt section of Armadale Castle, once home of Lord Macdonald. The Museum of the Isles has an audio-visual display telling the history of the great Gaelic Kingdom of the Lords of the Isles. The Stables houses a licensed Restaurant serving fresh local produce, particularly fish and home-baking. Shop well stocked with gifts and books. There are 46 acres of Sheltered Woodland Gardens and

several miles of Nature Trails. A Countryside Ranger Service offers guided walks and talks. Also a Children's Skyelark Scheme and evening Theatre and Music events. Quality self-catering cottages available. Toilets. Car-park, suitable for disabled. Contact the Visitor Services Manager.

Colbost Folk Museum
3m W of Dunvegan. Daily 10.00-18.00. Entrance charge. Parking available. Tel: (0147 022) 296.
Thatched traditional 'black house', typical of living conditions in the 19th century.

Dunvegan Castle and Gardens
Dunvegan. Mar-end Oct 10.00-17.30. Castle closed Sunday morning. Entrance charge. Tel: (0147 022) 206.
Historic stronghold of the Clan MacLeod, set on the sea loch of Dunvegan, still the home after 700 years of the chiefs of MacLeod. Possessions on view, books, pictures, arms and treasured relics, trace the history of the family and clan from the days of their Norse ancestry through thirty generations to the present day. Boat trips from the castle jetty to the seal colony. Restaurant and shops.

Kilt Rock
Off A855, 17m N of Portree. Seen from the road. Care should be taken not to go too near the edge of the cliff.
The top rock is composed of columnar basalt, the lower portion of horizontal beds, giving the impression of the pleats in a kilt. There is also a waterfall nearby.

Old Skye Crofter's House
Luib, 7m NW of Broadford. Daily 09.00-18.00. Entrance charge. Parking available. Tel: (0147 022) 296.
Thatched traditional dwelling house furnished in keeping with the early 20th century, including agricultural implements.

The Piping Centre, Borreraig
Dunvegan. Easter-mid Oct. Admission charge. Parking available. Tel: (0147 081) 369.
Old school and schoolhouse now museum of the Highland Bagpipe and the family MacCrimmon, pipers to the chiefs of the clan MacLeod from circa 1500 to 1800. Famous pipers, teachers and composers of piobaireachd.

Quirang
Off A855 at Digg, 19m N of Portree. Limited car parking.
An extraordinary mass of towers and pinnacles into which cattle were driven during forays. A rough track zigzags up to The Needle, an imposing obelisk 120 feet high, beyond which, in a large amphitheatre, stands The Table, a huge grass-covered rock-mass. Impressive views.

Skye Museum of Island Life
Off A855, 20m NNW of Portree. Apr-Oct, Mon-Sat 09.00-17.30. Entrance charge. Tel: (0147 052) 279.
Seven thatched cottages. Exhibits include a wall bed, farming and domestic implements, hand loom and a collection of old photographs and historical papers.

SOUTH UIST

Loch Druidibeg National Nature Reserve
In the N part of South Uist, Outer Hebrides. All year, daily. Please call at Wardens Office for full details of access. Free. Tel: (0187 05) 206.
One of the two remaining native populations of greylag geese in Britain breeds here, in a typical example of the Outer Hebrides environment, machair, fresh and brackish lochs.

STAFFA

W of Mull, Argyll, 6m NE of Iona. Access by local boats, including Gordon Grant Marine (Staffa Ferries), Isle of Iona. Tel: (0168 17) 338. (Apr-Oct); David R Kirkpatrick, Isle of Iona. Tel: (0168 17) 373; Iain Morrison, Penmore Mill, Dervaig. Tel: (0168 84) 242.
This romantic uninhabited small island is famous for its basaltic formations and remarkable caves, the best known of which is Fingal's Cave. Immortalised by Mendelssohn in his celebrated 'Hebrides' overture, its cluster columns and man-made looking symmetry gives the cave a cathedral-like majesty. Other famous visitors to the cave have included Queen Victoria and Prince Albert, the artist J M W Turner, and poets and writers Keats, Wordsworth, Tennyson and Sir Walter Scott. Improved landing stage with handrail.

SCOTLAND FOR THE MOTORIST
A Pastime Publication

I/We have seen your advertisement and wish to know if you have the following vacancy:

Name...

Address ....

....

Dates from pm...

Please give date and day of week in each case ....

To am ....

Number in Party ....

Details of Children ....

(Please remember to include a stamped addressed envelope with your enquiry.)

SCOTLAND FOR THE MOTORIST
A Pastime Publication

I/We have seen your advertisement and wish to know if you have the following vacancy:

Name...

Address ....

....

Dates from pm...

Please give date and day of week in each case ....

To am ....

Number in Party ....

Details of Children ....

(Please remember to include a stamped addressed envelope with your enquiry.)

PASTIME GUIDES FOR 1995

Pastime Publications Ltd is one of the leading Holiday Guide Publishers for U.K. Bed & Breakfast, Self Catering and Farm & Country Holidays as well as Activity and Motoring Holidays in Scotland.

The following publications are useful guides and make wonderful gifts throughout the year.

Whilst our guides are available in leading bookshops and Tourist Board Centres for your convenience we will be happy to post a copy to you or send books as a gift for you. We will post overseas but have to charge separately for post or freight.

The inclusive cost of posting and packing your selection of guides to you and your friends in the U.K. is as follows:

❏ **Farm & Country Holidays**
This guide gives details of over 300 farms, many of them working with livestock, as well as activity holidays. **£4.50**

❏ **Scotland for Fishing**
Permits, fishing rights, boat hire, season/dates, rods, fly fishing and spinning . . . it's all here. **£4.50**

❏ **Bed & Breakfast Holidays**
A comprehensive guide to over 300 hotels, guesthouses, farms and inns throughout Britain. **£4.50**

❏ **Scotland Home of Golf**
Over 400 golf clubs featured. Also places to stay. Editorial by well-known celebrities. **£4.50**

❏ **Self Catering Holidays**
Includes details of hundreds of houses, chalets, boats, caravans, cottages, farms and flats throughout Britain. **£4.50**

❏ **Scotland for the Motorist**
Over 1,000 places of interest plus road maps and where to stay. **£4.50**

❏ **Scotland Activity Holidays**
The finest walks and trails as well as hill walking, cycling, skiing, yachting, canoeing and trekking.
£4.50

Tick your choice and send your order and payment to:
Pastime Publications Ltd., 6 York Place, Edinburgh EH1 3EP.
Telephone: 0131-557 8092.
Deduct 10% for 2 or 3 titles and 20% for 4 or more titles.

Send to: **NAME** . . . .

  ADDRESS . . . .

  . . . .**POST CODE** . . . .

I enclose Cheque/Postal Order for £ . . . .

SIGNATURE . . . .**DATE** . . . .